Best of
German
Cooking

Edda Meyer-Berkhout

HPBooks®

Flavor of Germany

German cooking has been much maligned by those who know little or nothing about it. This has helped spread the myth that most German meals consist of large quantities of sausage and sauerkraut washed down by even larger volumes of beer. This is like saying that Americans are nourished exclusively on a diet of steaks and French-fried potatoes. Or, that the British eat only roast beef and Yorkshire pudding. This book dispells such fallacies. It offers a representative selection of German recipes revealing a rich and varied repertoire for the enterprising cook.

The 300 recipes given here are very straightforward and the ingredients are available. Recipes can be adapted according to the author's suggestions or varied to allow for individual taste and preference. Few involve a great deal of time spent in the kitchen or involve any but the simplest cooking techniques. For a minimum of effort, a wide selection of new dishes and menus can be tried and enjoyed without tying you to the stove for hours on end. Those which do take a little longer can usually be left for a time to complete one stage or another of their preparation. This may include steps such as marinating, proofing yeast dough or long, slow cooking. Many of these dishes are simple but introduce interesting blends of ingredients and exciting combinations of taste. They are a great discovery for those trying German cooking for the first time.

EDDA MEYER-BERKHOUT

Edda Meyer-Berkhout grew up in Germany and the Netherlands. She has since worked throughout Europe getting to know each country and learning about its cooking. She has also travelled abroad, making many visits to the Middle East. These experiences have enabled her to appreciate the ways in which various factors determine the development of each nation's cuisine and eating habits. They also have given her a new perspective on the cooking of her own country, its strengths and unique contribution to living well.

Ms. Meyer-Berkhout's interest in cooking was stimulated and encouraged by her family. After studying hotel management and catering, she continued her studies in the fields of nutrition and cooking at the universities of Frankfurt and Hamburg. After teaching home economics for many years, she was appointed to the post of Principal of the International College of Home Economics in Munich.

Since 1969, Edda Meyer-Berkhout has written 25 cookbooks. They have proven extremely popular and many have been translated into other languages.

Ms. Meyer-Berkhout was also responsible for photographing the dishes for this book, except as noted.

ANOTHER BEST-SELLING VOLUME FROM HPBOOKS®

Executive Editor: Rick Bailey
Editor: Retha M. Davis
Art Director: Don Burton
Layout: Leslie Sinclair
Typography: Cindy Coatsworth, Michelle Claridge

Published by HPBooks®
P.O. Box 5367, Tucson, AZ 85703
602/888-2150
ISBN 0-89586-279-4
Library of Congress Catalog Card Number 83-82399
©1984 Fisher Publishing, Inc. Printed in Italy

Cover photo: Ham en Croûte, page 48

First published under the title
Cucina Alla Tedesca
©1982 Arnoldo Mondadori Editore S.p.A., Milano

Photo credits: Centrale Marketinggesellschaft der deutschen Agrarwirtschaft m.b.; Fischwirtschaftliches Marketing Institute; Knorr Kochzentrum; Maggi Kochstudio; Ulla Mayer-Raichle; Edda Meyer-Berkhout; Pfanni-Werk Otto Eckard; Romertopf, Bay Company; Christian Teubner

Contents

Introduction

A traditional German breakfast consists of a large mug of steaming hot coffee with thick cream and sugar; a small basket of crusty, freshly baked rolls sprinkled with poppy seeds, sesame seeds or caraway seeds; fresh butter and several different kinds of jam and honey. In addition, you would probably be offered a soft-cooked egg, sausages and an assortment of cheeses. Unlike the inhabitants of the Mediterranean and some other countries, who tend to start the day by hastily downing a small cup of strong, black coffee, the Germans really enjoy their breakfast. It is usually a substantial meal, almost a small banquet, which is eaten at a leisurely pace and particularly enjoyed on Sundays and holidays at home with the family.

After this excellent, sustaining start to the day comes a long gap. The so-called "second breakfast" which used to be so popular at mid-morning is dying out and has already dwindled to a quick snack of a small roll or slice of bread and a refreshing drink. This is usually eaten in a hurry before people get back to their work.

A good hot lunch is an important part of the day. Until only a few years ago it was usual to start the meal with an appetizer or soup, but nowadays people usually restrict the meal to a main course of meat, vegetables or salad and potatoes, noodles or rice.

The consumption of potatoes in Germany has declined, possibly due to the time they take to prepare. They have also been replaced, to an ever-increasing extent, by pasta products and rice. Increased travel abroad also accounts for this trend. Lunch usually ends with a dessert such as a sweet pudding or simply fresh fruit.

In other countries where English or American influences are felt, tea or coffee may be drunk with the midday meal. This custom has not caught on with the Germans, who prefer beer or wine with their lunch. They prefer to drink large cups of delicious coffee, often in large family parties, at about 4 o'clock in the afternoon. The coffee plays a purely supporting role to the delicious, creamy gâteaux and many different kinds of cakes and pastries. Foreign visitors to Germany are always amazed at the enormous quantity and infinite variety of cakes, cookies and pastries available. These are loved by the Germans and consumed in large quantities.

Dinner or supper is usually a cold meal. Bread, often several kinds, and butter are served with pickled, smoked or dressed fish, sliced sausages and cured pork or ham, together with a choice of cheeses and often eggs. Sometimes supper or dinner is completed with a fresh salad or a light, hot snack.

Beer is unquestionably the Germans' favorite drink. German brewers take great pride in the knowledge and expertise they have acquired during hundreds of years of brewing. A visit to a Bavarian beer garden on a warm summer evening is an experience not to be missed. You will be entertained by the sight of vast quantities of foaming beer being drunk and abundant amounts of sausages being eaten with great relish.

The noblest and finest German drink is certainly wine. Vines are cultivated on the sunny slopes of river valleys and lakesides. They produce the earthy, sometimes flinty wines with plenty of fragrance or "bouquet."

In the high-quality food stores and delicatessens throughout Germany, customers find everything they could desire. Shelves are full of delicacies such as kirsch cherry brandy; raspberry liqueur; pure, clear fruit spirits or schnapps; spicy, highly seasoned smoked pork and ham and varieties of sausages of every conceivable size, shape and flavor. Also displayed are sweet breads, gingerbread and spiced breads, marzipan and other tempting goods to delight the eye and stimulate the appetite.

Starters & Snacks

Nowadays people seldom bother with tempting hors d'oeuvres for everyday meals. Usually a main course is enough, sometimes followed by dessert. But it's a very different matter when a family celebrates an important event or when eating out in a restaurant or entertaining special guests at home. On such occasions most of us would find it difficult to resist choosing something from the wide choice of appetizing starters. When friends drop in after dinner in Germany, they are usually offered a snack: either soup, or frequently, a well-filled toasted sandwich. Many of the recipes in this chapter can also be served as a welcome change from the usual fare of cold meats, sausages and cheeses which appear at suppertime in Germany. Salads are ideal for cold buffets, especially when there are a great many guests. On such occasions, basic dishes of hard-cooked eggs and attractively arranged cheeses are joined by two or three tasty fish, ham, chicken or mixed salads. Several types of bread, butter and a selection of desserts and fruit complete the buffet. Dishes that can be prepared in advance mean the cook does not have to work hard getting the food ready right up to the moment when the guests arrive.

Smoked Spur-Dog Salad
Schillerlockensalat

Smoked Salmon
Geräucherter Lachs

2 to 3 smoked spur-dog (about 1 lb.)
1 red bell pepper
1 green bell pepper
1 celeriac or 3 to 4 celery stalks
2 pickled cucumbers or gherkins
1/3 cup vegetable oil
1 tablespoon vinegar
Salt and pepper
1/2 teaspoon prepared mustard

Cut spur-dog into 1-inch-thick pieces. Cut peppers in rings. Dice or shred celeriac or celery. Slice pickles or gherkins. In a medium bowl, combine spur-dog, pepper rings, celeriac or celery and pickles or gherkins. In a small bowl, combine oil, vinegar, salt, pepper and mustard. Pour oil mixture over spur-dog mixture. Marinate until desired flavor is developed. Makes 4 to 6 servings.

Note: Smoked mackerel or smoked trout fillet can be used if spur-dog cannot be found. Spur-dog fish is sometimes known as *pickled dog fish* or *picky dog.*

1-1/4 lbs. smoked salmon
Bunch of fresh dill
Horseradish Cream, page 94

Slice salmon in small even-size pieces immediately before serving. Arrange salmon slices on a serving platter. Garnish with small sprigs of dill. Serve with Horseradish Cream, toast, fresh white bread or rolls, butter and sparkling white wine or champagne. Serve on a buffet or for special occasions. Makes 6 to 8 servings.

Bismarck Herring
Bismarckheringe

Helgoland Shrimp Salad
Helgoländer Krabbensalat

4 fresh herring
1 cup water
1 teaspoon mustard seeds
1 bay leaf
1 cup white-wine vinegar
1 large onion, cut in thin rings
1 mild onion, chopped
1/2 apple, thinly sliced
1 tablespoon lemon juice
1 tablespoon finely chopped chives

Remove herring heads and tails. Fillet and wash each herring. In a small saucepan, make a *court bouillon* by combining water, mustard seeds and bay leaf. Bring to a boil. Remove from heat; cool slightly. Add vinegar and onion rings. In a jar or earthenware pot, alternately layer herring and court bouillon. Cover and let stand 24 hours or more. Herring are best if marinated 1 week, but they should be kept covered in a cool place or refrigerator. Drain before serving. Garnish with chopped onion, apple slices, lemon juice and chives. Makes 6 servings.

Note: The dish takes its name from the 19th century statesman, Bismarck, who enjoyed eating these herring for lunch. They are usually served as a supper dish with bread or potatoes boiled in their skins and a green salad.

1/2 lb. shrimp or prawns
4 hard-cooked eggs
3 to 5 tablespoons lemon juice
1/4 cup vegetable oil
Salt
Lettuce leaves
1 tablespoon chopped chives or finely chopped parsley

Shell shrimp or prawns immediately before using. If using canned shrimp, rinse well under water. If frozen shrimp are used, thaw completely before shelling. Coarsely chop eggs. In a medium bowl, combine shrimp or prawns and chopped eggs. In a small bowl, combine lemon juice, oil and salt. Sprinkle lemon-juice mixture over shrimp mixture. Arrange lettuce leaves in a serving dish. Spoon shrimp salad over lettuce. Sprinkle with chives or parsley. Serve with freshly made toast or crackers. Makes 4 servings.

Herring Salad
Heringssalat

Multi-Colored Chicken Salad
Bunter Geflügelsalat

Salad:
4 salted herring fillets
1 to 2 boiled potatoes
3 hard-cooked eggs
1/3 cup diced pickled beets
1/4 lb. cold cooked meat, diced
1 small tart apple, diced
1 to 2 pickled cucumbers or gherkins, diced
Small piece cooked celeriac, diced, if desired
1 small onion, diced, if desired

Dressing:
3 tablespoons mayonnaise
1/4 cup dairy sour cream or plain yogurt
1/2 teaspoon prepared mustard
Pinch of red (cayenne) pepper
1 tablespoon capers
1 tablespoon finely chopped chives or parsley

To make salad, wash herring to remove excess salt; drain well. Cut herring in 1/2-inch-wide pieces. Dice potatoes and 2 hard-cooked eggs. In a medium bowl, combine herring pieces, diced potatoes and eggs, pickled beets, meat, apple and pickles or gherkins. Add celeriac and onion, if desired.
To make dressing, in a small bowl, combine mayonnaise, sour cream or yogurt, mustard, red pepper, capers and chives or parsley. Thin with a small amount of liquid from pickled beets or vinegar, if desired. Pour dressing over salad; toss well. Refrigerate for several hours for flavors to blend. To serve, adjust seasoning. Garnish with remaining hard-cooked egg, chopped or sliced, and chives or parsley. Serve as a dinner dish or on a buffet. Makes 6 servings.

Variation

Substitute coarsely chopped nuts for pickled beets.

Salad:
2 cups diced cooked chicken
1 small jar chanterelle or regular mushrooms, drained
1 cucumber, cut in thin slices
4 small tomatoes, cut in quarters

Dressing:
1/4 cup vegetable oil
1 tablespoon white-wine vinegar
Salt and pepper
Sugar
1 tablespoon finely chopped fresh dill

To make salad, in a medium bowl, combine chicken, mushrooms, cucumber and tomatoes.
To make dressing, in a small bowl, combine oil, vinegar, salt, pepper, sugar and dill. Pour dressing over salad. Toss lightly. Serve immediately or cover and refrigerate until ready to serve. Makes 4 servings.

Variation

In Germany, chicken salad is often made with pineapple chunks, button mushrooms and small pieces of asparagus.

Pickled-Tongue Salad
Ochsenmaulsalat

Salad:
1 lb. pickled tongue, fresh or canned
2 onions
1 cucumber or 1 large gherkin

Dressing:
1/4 cup vegetable oil
3 tablespoons vinegar
1/2 teaspoon prepared mustard
Salt and freshly ground pepper
Chopped chives or fresh dill

To make salad, cut tongue into thin slices or shred into thin strips. Thinly slice onions and cucumber or gherkin. Combine meat strips, onion and cucumber or gherkin in a medium bowl.
To make dressing, in a small bowl, combine oil, vinegar, mustard, salt, pepper and chives or dill. Pour dressing over meat mixture. Stir to blend. Cover and let stand 30 minutes before serving. Serve with caraway-seed bread and cold beer. Makes 4 servings.

Variation

If pickled tongue is not available, other types of processed meats can be used or several different types of cooked meats can be combined. Ordinary pressed tongue can also be used.

Asparagus Salad
Spargelsalat Schloss Schwetzingen

1-3/4 lbs. fresh asparagus
1 teaspoon salt
Pinch of sugar
1/3 cup whipping cream
3 tablespoons mayonnaise
1/3 cup orange juice
1 teaspoon grated orange peel
Salt and white pepper
Finely chopped parsley

Trim asparagus, cutting off woody ends and peeling stems; rinse well. Break asparagus into 2- to 3-inch pieces. In a medium saucepan, cook asparagus over low heat in a small amount of water seasoned with salt and sugar. Cook until tender. Drain asparagus well. Place cooked asparagus on a plate. In a small bowl, whip cream. Fold in mayonnaise, orange juice and orange peel. Season with salt and white pepper. Spoon whipped-cream mixture over asparagus immediately before serving. Garnish with parsley. Stir together asparagus and cream mixture at the table. Serve with French bread or toast and butter. Best accompanied by a dry white wine. Makes 4 to 6 servings.

Variation

Substitute 1 large can white asparagus for fresh asparagus, omitting salt and sugar. Drain canned asparagus well. It is not necessary to cook canned asparagus. Continue as directed above.

Note: In most European countries, asparagus is picked when green. But in Germany, it is picked before the shoot has emerged from the soil and the asparagus is still white.

Mixed-Vegetable Salad with Eggs
Bunter Gemüsesalat mit Eiern

Stuffed Eggs
Gefüllte Eier

Salad:
1/2 lb. young carrots
2 cups fresh green peas (about 1/2 lb.)
1 cucumber
4 hard-cooked eggs
1/3 cup alfalfa sprouts, if desired

Dressing:
3 tablespoons vegetable oil
3 tablespoons white-wine vinegar
1 small onion, finely chopped
3 tablespoons mayonnaise, if desired
Salt and pepper
Pinch of sugar

To make salad, cut carrots into thin slices. In a medium saucepan with a small amount of salted water, cook carrot slices and peas until tender. Drain well, reserving cooking liquid. Peel cucumber; cut lengthwise in half. Scoop out seeds, if desired, with a teaspoon. Slice cucumber. Slice hard-cooked eggs or cut each egg into 8 wedges. In a large glass salad bowl, combine cooked carrots and peas, cucumber, eggs and sprouts, if desired.

To make dressing, in a small bowl, combine oil, vinegar, onion, a little reserved cooking liquid from peas and carrots and mayonnaise, if desired. Season with salt, pepper and sugar. Pour dressing over salad. Cover and let stand. Stir well immediately before serving. Makes 4 to 6 servings.

Variation

Different vegetables can be used depending on what is available. For a quick, last-minute preparation, use frozen or canned vegetables. If alfalfa sprouts are not available, substitute parsley, chives or dill.

6 hard-cooked eggs
1 teaspoon lemon juice
1 tablespoon mayonnaise
Flavorings: anchovy paste, tomato paste, curry powder, minced fresh herbs, finely grated fresh horseradish, paprika
Salt and white pepper
Lettuce leaves
Garnishes: anchovies, radishes, stuffed green olives, cucumber, tomatoes, canned peppers, chives, parsley

Shell eggs carefully. Cut eggs in half lengthwise; remove yolks. Press egg yolks through a sieve into a small bowl. Stir in lemon juice, mayonnaise and a choice of flavorings. Season with salt and white pepper. Omit salt if anchovy paste is used. Sprinkle egg-white halves lightly with salt. Fill a piping bag with seasoned egg yolks. Force egg-yolk mixture through piping bag into each egg white. Garnish stuffed eggs as desired. Arrange on a lettuce-lined plate. Stuffed eggs make a very good light supper dish or can be served as part of a buffet meal. Makes 4 to 6 servings.

Liver Pâté
Landleberwurst

Mecklenburg Goose Fat
Mecklenburger Gänseschmalz

2 lb. pork liver
2 lb. fresh pork belly
small onion
alt and freshly ground pepper
ried leaf marjoram
round nutmeg
teaspoon grated lemon peel
4 lb. thin-sliced bacon, if desired
or 2 bay leaves

reheat oven to 300F (150C). Grind liver and pork belly twice,
sing a fine disk, until a smooth paste. Finely chop onion. In a
edium bowl, combine ground meat, onion, salt, pepper,
arjoram, nutmeg and lemon peel. Line a medium soufflé dish
ith bacon slices, if desired. Press liver mixture into lined dish or
to a heatproof jar. Place bay leaves on pâté surface. Set dish or jar
a shallow pan of water. Bake 45 minutes. Cool before using.
erve as a snack, starter or supper dish with gherkins, homemade
read or French bread accompanied by wine or cold beer. Makes 4
8 servings.

1 lb. goose fat
1 lb. fresh pork fat
2 to 3 small onions
1 small apple, peeled

This multi-purpose German specialty is made with yellow solid fat
pulled from inside uncooked geese. Wash fat well; pick off any
foreign particles or membrane. Cut fat into small pieces. Heat
gently in a heavy saucepan until fat has liquefied. Remove any
fiberous residue. Finely dice pork fat, onions and apple. Add pork
fat to saucepan; continue heating gently. When pork fat has melted,
add onions and apple; cook until pale golden brown. Remove from
heat before onion and apple color too much and before apple is
mushy. For storage, transfer mixture to an earthenware pot. Once
solidified, it is called *Schmalz*. It may be used as a spread on bread
like butter, on its own or with cottage cheese. It can be used in place
of butter on potatoes boiled in their skins. It is also very good for
cooking purposes and, if strained while still liquid, for pastry
making.

Steak Tartare
Steak Tartare

Onion Tart
Zwiebelkuchen

1-1/4 lbs. lean beef sirloin or tenderloin
4 egg yolks
1 large onion, finely chopped
3 tablespoons capers
2 small gherkins, sliced
4 anchovies, chopped
1/3 cup sliced pimientos
1/3 cup chopped chives
Salt
Red (cayenne) pepper
Paprika
Brandy, if desired

Tear beef into fine shreds or grind using a fine disk. Divide ground beef into 4 portions. Make a well in center of each beef portion. Place an egg yolk in well of each beef portion. Surround with small portions of onion, capers, gherkins, anchovies, pimientos, chives, salt, red pepper and paprika. Each person may then flavor their tartare as desired. Brandy may be included, if desired. Serve with crusty homemade bread and cold beer. Makes 4 to 6 servings.

1/2 cup plus 1 tablespoon butter
1-3/4 cups all-purpose flour
1 egg
3 to 5 tablespoons half and half
Salt
3 large or 4 medium onions
4 bacon slices, diced
Generous 1/2 cup whipping cream
2 eggs
Salt and pepper

Preheat oven to 400F (205C). Lightly grease an 11-inch quiche pan; set aside. Using a pastry blender or fork, work butter into flour. Stir in 1 egg, half and half and salt to make a dough. Let stand in a cool place a few minutes. Thinly slice onions. Fry bacon in a small skillet over medium heat until golden brown. Add onion rings; sauté 2 to 3 minutes. Drain off excess fat. In a medium bowl, beat together whipping cream, 2 eggs, salt and pepper. On a lightly floured surface, roll out pastry. Line greased pan with pastry. Prick pastry surface with a fork. Spread cooked bacon and onions over pastry. Pour in cream mixture. Cover with foil. Bake 20 minutes. Remove foil; bake 10 to 15 minutes longer or until set. Cut in squares or wedges. Serve warm. When cooking for large numbers, double the quantities given. Bake on a large baking sheet with sides or jelly-roll pan. Puff pastry or pizza dough can be substituted for pie pastry. Serve with chilled white wine. Makes 8 servings.

Ham & Cheese Toast
Käse-Schinkentoast

Baked Cheese Slices
Übergrillter Käsetoast

4 slices bread
3 tablespoons butter
4 cooked-ham slices
2 cups shredded Emmentaler cheese (8 oz.)
2 eggs
1/3 cup whipping cream
Salt and pepper
Ground nutmeg

Preheat oven to 400F (205C). Spread each slice of bread thinly with butter on both sides. Arrange slices flat in a deep rectangular baking dish. Dice ham. Sprinkle diced ham and shredded cheese over buttered bread. In a small bowl, beat together eggs, whipping cream, salt, pepper and nutmeg. Pour egg mixture evenly over bread. Bake 20 minutes. Serve slices right from the dish at the table. Serve with a green salad and cold beer or white wine. Makes 4 servings.

4 slices bread
2 tablespoons butter or mayonnaise
4 cooked-ham slices
4 Emmentaler-cheese slices
1 tomato, cut in wedges
Parsley
Red (cayenne) pepper, if desired

Preheat oven to 350F (175C). Toast bread lightly on both sides. Spread each slice of bread thinly with butter or mayonnaise. Arrange bread slices on a broiler pan or baking sheet. Top bread with ham slices, trimmed to fit bread. Top ham with cheese slices, trimmed to fit. Bake until cheese melts. Do not broil because the cheese should not brown. Garnish with tomato and parsley. Sprinkle with red pepper, if desired. Serve immediately. Makes 4 servings.

Variation

To make this snack more exotic, place a well-drained slice of canned pineapple or pear on the buttered toast before topping with ham and cheese.

Soups

German children grow up hearing Hoffmann's tale of *Suppenkaspar*—the story of a little boy who refused to eat his soup. As a result, the boy wasted away until he was as thin as a rake. The tale ends with the child's death and the touching scene of a soup bowl being placed on his tomb.

If good health was solely dependent on the intake of large quantities of soup, there would be some cause for concern. Nowadays, most German families have dropped the once-customary clear soup from everyday meals. This is now served only on special occasions or in restaurants. Rather more substantial soups are very often served for the evening meal or offered to guests as a late-evening snack. The German culinary repertoire includes a wide variety of meat broths, containing a variety of garnishes such as delicate noodles, flour dumplings, strips of pancake or toasted cheese on small pieces of toasted bread. These warming, comforting soups are low in calories. They do not dull the appetite. The widespread use of blenders means that smooth, creamy vegetable soups have become much more popular and leftovers can be pureed and transformed into a meal with little or no effort. A delicate cream-of-shellfish or seafood soup is a treat which every gourmet is sure to appreciate.

Substantial soups of peas, beans or lentils are still very popular and are great favorites for lunch or dinner. Potato soup with small pieces of cooked or cured meat or sausage, or a flavorsome chicken soup with noodles or rice, is served as a main dish. Quick and easy to prepare, they appeal to the whole family. Plus, there's the advantage that they can be prepared in advance and heated before serving.

Creamy Apple Soup
Apfelweinsuppe

East Prussia Prune Soup
Ostpreussische Schmandsuppe

Soup:
2 cups water
2 cups white wine
1 small piece of lemon peel
1 small cinnamon stick
3 medium, sweet apples
Juice of 1 lemon
1/4 cup cornstarch
Water
1/3 cup sugar

Meringue Drops:
1 egg white
2 tablespoons sugar
1/4 teaspoon vanilla extract

To make soup, in a medium, enamel-lined saucepan, heat 2 cups water, wine, lemon peel and cinnamon stick over low heat 10 minutes. Remove and discard lemon peel and cinnamon. Peel and core apples; finely slice. Add apples to warm liquid; poach briefly, being careful not to overcook. In a small cup, combine lemon juice and cornstarch. Add a little water. Stir mixture into apple and wine mixture. Add sugar, stirring until dissolved.

To make meringue, in a small bowl, beat egg white until nearly stiff. Gradually beat in sugar and vanilla. Drop by spoonfuls onto surface of hot but not boiling soup. Cover and cook 3 to 5 minutes or until set. Using a slotted spoon, carefully remove Meringue Drops; set aside on a plate. Transfer apple soup into individual bowls or a terrine. Garnish with Meringue Drops. Serve in winter with toasted bread or Melba toast or in summer as a cold soup. Toasted almonds are particularly good sprinkled over the soup. Makes 4 to 6 servings.

Soup:
1/2 lb. pitted prunes
1 qt. water
1 tablespoon dark corn syrup or molasses
1/4 cup all-purpose flour
Water
Pinch of salt
Generous 1/2 cup dairy sour cream

Dumplings:
Generous 1 cup all-purpose flour
1 egg
Salt
Water

To make soup, rinse prunes under cold running water. Soak prunes in a small saucepan of cold water overnight. Next day, cook soaked prunes in 1 quart water until tender. While prunes are still hot, stir in corn syrup or molasses. In a small cup, combine flour with a little water to make a paste. Stir flour mixture and salt into soup. Cook until slightly thickened.

To make dumplings, in a small bowl, combine flour, egg and salt. Add enough water to make a smooth, firm mixture. Let stand 10 minutes. Shape dumplings using a teaspoon. Add each dumpling to soup; poach over low heat. Dumplings are done when they float to the surface. Remove soup from heat. Carefully swirl in sour cream. Serve immediately. Makes 4 to 6 servings.

Sweet Milk Soup
Milchsuppe

Meat Broth with Pancake Strips
Flädlesuppe

Soup:
1 qt. milk
1 small piece of lemon peel
1/4 cup cornstarch or 1/4 cup rolled oats
3 to 5 tablespoons sugar
1 egg yolk
Pinch of salt
3 tablespoons toasted chopped almonds

Meringue Drops:
1 egg white
2 tablespoons sugar
1/4 teaspoon vanilla extract

To make soup, scald milk and lemon peel by heating in a medium saucepan over low heat until bubbles appear around edge of pan. Remove and discard peel. If using cornstarch, blend with a little cold milk to make a paste. Stir into hot milk. Or, sprinkle rolled oats into milk when it comes to a boil. Cook 10 to 15 minutes, stirring constantly, until oats are cooked or milk has thickened. Add sugar to taste. Remove from heat. In a small bowl, combine egg yolk and salt. Add a small amount of hot milk mixture, blending well. Immediately stir egg-yolk mixture into remaining hot milk mixture. Stir over low heat 1 minute. Do not boil because egg yolk will curdle. Sprinkle with almonds.
To make meringue, in a small bowl, beat egg white until nearly stiff. Gradually beat in sugar and vanilla. Bring 2 inches of water to a boil in a deep skillet. Reduce heat to a simmer. Poach small spoonfuls of meringue mixture 3 to 5 minutes. Add poached meringues to warm milk soup. Makes 4 to 6 servings.

Note: This soup is often served at breakfast and also as a supper dish for children.

1 egg
3 tablespoons all-purpose flour
1/3 cup milk
Salt
Oil for frying
1 qt. meat stock
3 tablespoons dry sherry
1 tablespoon minced chives

In a small bowl, beat together egg, flour, milk and salt. Let stand 15 minutes. Heat a small amount of oil in a large shallow skillet. When oil is very hot, cook 1 or more thin pancakes; remove from skillet. Roll up cooked pancakes and let cool. Using a sharp knife, cut pancake rolls into thin slices. Place in a large soup tureen. In a medium saucepan, combine stock and sherry. Place over medium heat until steaming. Pour hot stock mixture over pancake strips. Sprinkle with chives. Leftover pancakes can be used for this soup. Makes 4 servings.

Variation

For extra color and flavor, add minced herbs or spinach to the pancake mixture before frying.

Meat Broth with Herb Dumplings
Brühe mit Kräuterklösschen

Vegetable Soup with Dumplings
Gemüsesuppe Klärchen mit Schwemmklösschen

2 tablespoons butter, room temperature
1 egg
2/3 cup fresh breadcrumbs
3 tablespoons minced herbs, such as: parsley, chives or basil
Salt
Ground nutmeg
1 qt. meat stock
3 tablespoons dry sherry

In a small bowl, beat butter until light and creamy. Beat in egg, breadcrumbs, herbs, salt and nutmeg to make a light, smooth mixture. Let stand 15 minutes. In a medium saucepan, heat stock and sherry over medium heat. Using a teaspoon or your hands, shape dough into small dumplings. Rinse your hands in cold water to prevent sticking. Gently poach dumplings in heated stock over low heat about 3 minutes. Makes 4 servings.

1 qt. meat stock
1 tablespoon dry sherry
Finely chopped parsley or 3 lettuce leaves
Generous 1 cup water
Scant 1 tablespoon butter
Salt
Pinch of ground nutmeg
1/2 cup all-purpose flour
1 egg

In a medium saucepan, heat stock, sherry and parsley or lettuce over medium heat. In a small saucepan, combine water, butter, salt and nutmeg. Bring to a boil. Gradually sift flour into boiling water, stirring rapidly and thoroughly. Stir until mixture forms a ball. Remove from heat; cool slightly. Work in egg. Using 2 teaspoons rinsed in cold water, shape mixture into small oval dumplings. Add dumplings to hot stock. Simmer about 5 minutes. As dumplings cook, they will swell and become firm. Add more stock, if needed. Makes 4 servings.

Broth with Cheese Croutons
Brühe mit Käsecroutons

Beef & Vegetable Soup
Bunte Gemüsesuppe mit Rindfleisch

1/2 cup grated Swiss or Tilsit cheese (2 oz.)
3 to 5 tablespoons milk
Salt and pepper
2 white-bread slices
1 qt. meat stock
4 eggs
Minced chives

In a small bowl, combine cheese, milk, salt and pepper to make a smooth paste. Lightly toast bread. Spread toasted bread with cheese mixture. Place under a medium-hot broiler until cheese is melted and golden brown. Cut each slice into 8 small squares. Bring stock to a boil in a medium saucepan. Pour stock into 4 soup bowls. Break an egg into each bowl. Quickly add cheese croutons. Sprinkle with chives. Serve immediately. Makes 4 servings.

1 qt. beef stock
1/4 to 1/2 lb. boiled beef
1 to 1-1/2 cups frozen mixed vegetables
1 small tomato, peeled, diced
Finely chopped chives
Freshly grated Parmesan cheese, if desired

Bring stock to a boil in a medium saucepan. Trim any fat from beef; slice or dice beef. Add beef and frozen vegetables to boiling stock. Cook 5 minutes. Vegetables should be slightly crisp but tender. Add tomato and chives to taste. Ladle hot soup into 4 soup bowls. Sprinkle with Parmesan cheese, if desired. Serve with fresh crusty French bread. Makes 4 servings.

Variation

For a more substantial soup, add pieces of boiled potato, leftover pasta, rice or small flour dumplings.

Cream of Chervil Soup
Kerbelcremesuppe

1/4 cup butter
1/4 cup all-purpose flour
3 cups hot meat stock
Generous 1 cup milk
1/3 cup whipping cream
Salt and white pepper
Ground nutmeg
1 cup chopped fresh chervil

Melt butter in a heavy saucepan. Add flour, stirring constantly. Stir in stock. Add milk, cream, salt, white pepper and nutmeg, stirring constantly 5 minutes. Add chervil to soup immediately before serving. Chervil will lose its color and flavor if subjected to heat too long. Serve with crusty white bread or toast. Makes 4 servings.

Note: Chervil is an aromatic herb. It is bright green and looks like parsley. Its pleasant mild flavor resembles anise seed. Fresh chervil can be found in early summer and fall. Grow it in window-boxes or the garden.

Clear Soup with Liver Dumplings
Leberspätzlesuppe

3 tablespoons butter, room temperature
1 egg
1/2 cup fresh breadcrumbs
1 small onion, finely chopped
1/4 lb. calves' liver, finely chopped or ground
Salt
Pinch of dried leaf marjoram
1 tablespoon finely chopped parsley or chives
1 qt. meat stock
Additional finely chopped parsley or chives

In a small bowl, beat butter until creamy. Add egg, breadcrumbs, onion, liver, salt, marjoram and 1 tablespoon parsley or chives. Let stand 30 minutes. Bring stock to a boil in a medium saucepan. Reduce heat and simmer. Press dumpling mixture through a ricer or food mill so small particles fall directly into simmering stock. Simmer 5 minutes. Sprinkle with additional parsley or chives. Serve immediately. Makes 4 servings.

Flour Soup with Cheese
Basler Mehlsuppe

1/4 cup butter
1/2 cup all-purpose flour
1 qt. hot meat stock
Ground nutmeg
1 cup grated Emmentaler or Gruyère cheese (4 oz.)

Melt butter in a heavy saucepan over low heat. Add flour, stirring constantly until light brown. Be careful not to burn flour. Pour in stock, stirring until well blended. Cook 10 minutes, stirring occasionally. Season with nutmeg. Pour into 4 soup bowls. Sprinkle with grated cheese. Serve immediately. Makes 4 servings.

Note: Although this soup combines simple ingredients, it has an excellent flavor.

Swabian Onion Soup
Schwäbische Zwiebelsuppe

4 medium onions
3 tablespoons vegetable oil
1 cup meat stock
Salt and white pepper
Pinch of red (cayenne) pepper
3 tablespoons brandy, if desired
4 French-bread slices, toasted
1/3 cup grated Emmentaler cheese (1-1/2 oz.)
1/3 cup freshly grated Parmesan cheese (1-1/2 oz.)

Slice onions into very thin rings. Heat oil in a large saucepan over medium heat. Add onions; sauté until pale golden brown, 15 to 20 minutes. Add stock, salt, white pepper and red pepper. Cover and simmer about 30 minutes. Add brandy, if desired, for additional flavor. Add additional stock, if needed. Preheat broiler. Ladle soup into 4 individual heatproof dishes. Place 1 slice of toasted bread in each bowl. Sprinkle each slice with a little of each cheese. Place bowls under broiler until cheese melts. Serve immediately. Makes 4 servings.

Cream of Cauliflower Soup
Blumenkohlcremesuppe

3 cups water
1 chicken bouillon cube
1/2 small head cauliflower
3 tablespoons butter
1/4 cup all-purpose flour
1 cup milk or cream, or a combination
Salt
Ground nutmeg
Minced chives, if desired
Croutons, if desired

Place water and bouillon cube in a medium saucepan. Heat until bouillon cube dissolves. Break cauliflower into flowerets. Cook in bouillon until tender. Drain cauliflower, reserving cooking liquid. Select flowerets that are most intact; set aside. Chop remaining cooked cauliflower or, puree in a blender or food processor. Melt butter in a medium saucepan. Add flour, stirring constantly. Cook 1 to 2 minutes. Add hot cauliflower puree, reserved cooking liquid, milk or cream, salt and nutmeg. Simmer 3 to 5 minutes. Add reserved whole flowerets; heat through. Pour soup into a warm tureen. Sprinkle with chives and croutons, if desired. Serve immediately. Makes 4 servings.

Variation

For a richer, creamier soup, stir 1 or 2 egg yolks beaten lightly with a little cream into soup immediately before serving. Do not boil soup after these have been added.

Cream of Leek Soup
Lauchcremesuppe

1/2 lb. leeks
3 cups meat stock
3 tablespoons butter
1/4 cup all-purpose flour
2 tablespoons milk
1 cup grated or diced processed cheese, preferably German Schmelzkäse
   (4 oz.)
Salt and white pepper
Ground nutmeg
1 egg yolk
1/3 cup whipping cream
4 white-bread slices
1/4 cup butter

Trim leeks; wash thoroughly. Slice leeks into thin rings. In a medium saucepan, combine sliced leeks and stock. Cook until tender. Puree leeks with cooking liquid in a blender or food processor. Melt 3 tablespoons butter in a medium saucepan. Stir in flour. Add pureed leek mixture and milk. Simmer 3 to 5 minutes. Add cheese, salt, white pepper and nutmeg. Remove from heat when cheese is melted. In a small bowl, beat together egg yolk and whipping cream; stir into hot soup. Cut bread into small cubes. Melt 1/4 cup butter in a medium skillet. Sauté bread cubes in hot butter. Do not reheat soup; serve immediately with croutons. Makes 4 servings.

Cream of Tomato Soup
Tomatencremesuppe

Potato Soup
Kartoffelsuppe

1 small onion
3 tablespoons butter or margarine
1/4 cup all-purpose flour
1 qt. meat stock
1/3 cup tomato paste
Salt and white pepper
Fresh or dried leaf oregano, basil, rosemary and thyme to taste
1/3 cup whipping cream
Flaked cooked fish, small cooked shrimp or diced cooked chicken, if
  desired
Minced chives, if desired

Thinly slice onion. Melt butter or margarine in a medium skillet. Add onion; sauté until tender. Add flour, stirring constantly 1 to 2 minutes. Add stock. Bring liquid to a boil, stirring constantly; reduce heat and simmer 3 to 5 minutes. Stir in tomato paste. Season to taste with salt, white pepper and herbs. Simmer 3 to 5 minutes longer. To serve, pour into soup bowls. Pour about 1 tablespoon cream onto surface of each serving. Add flaked fish, shrimp or diced cooked chicken, if desired. Sprinkle with chives, if desired. Makes 4 to 6 servings.

4 bacon slices, diced
1 large onion, chopped
4 to 8 potatoes
1 celery stalk
1/2 small leek
1 carrot
3 cups meat stock
Salt
Dried leaf marjoram
4 frankfurters
Finely chopped parsley

In a medium saucepan, sauté bacon briefly. Add onion; sauté 2 to 3 minutes. Peel potatoes. Dice potatoes, celery, leek and carrot. Add vegetables to saucepan. Pour in stock. Season with salt and marjoram. Bring to a boil. Reduce heat and simmer 20 minutes. If a thicker soup is desired, crush potatoes with a potato masher. Before serving, cut frankfurters into small pieces. Add to soup; heat through. Sprinkle with parsley. Makes 4 servings.

Chicken Soup
Geflügelsuppe

Hamburg Eel Soup
Hamburger Aalsuppe

Garnish:
2 eggs
1/2 cup milk
Salt
Ground nutmeg
1 tablespoon minced mixed fresh herbs

Soup:
1 qt. chicken stock
1 (10-oz). pkg. frozen mixed vegetables
1/4 to 1/2 lb. cooked chicken

To make garnish, grease an 8- or 9-inch cake pan. In a small bowl, beat together eggs, milk, salt, nutmeg and herbs. Pour egg mixture into greased pan; cover with foil. Set pan in a larger saucepan or skillet of hot water. Simmer 30 to 40 minutes or until herb custard is firm. Do not allow water to boil. Slide cooked custard out of pan. Cut into strips or shapes using a fluted pastry cutter. Place pieces in individual bowls.
To make soup, in a medium saucepan, bring stock to a boil. Add frozen vegetables; cook 5 minutes or until crisp-tender. Add chicken; heat until warmed through. Pour stock mixture over custard pieces in soup bowls. Serve immediately. Makes 4 servings.

1 eel (1-1/2 to 2 lbs.)
Coarse salt
1 qt. water
Salt
Few black peppercorns and mustard seeds
1 bay leaf
1 small onion
3 tablespoons vinegar
2/3 cup pitted prunes
6 oz. frozen mixed vegetables
Fresh basil

Clean and skin eel; rub with coarse salt. Wash eel thoroughly. Cut into 1-1/4- to 1-1/2-inch pieces. In a large saucepan, combine water, salt, peppercorns, mustard seeds, bay leaf, onion and vinegar. Bring to a boil. Add eel pieces; simmer about 25 minutes. Strain stock; return stock to pan. Add prunes; cook 10 minutes or until soft and tender. Add frozen vegetables; cook 5 to 10 minutes. Return eel pieces to saucepan. Heat through. Garnish with fresh basil; serve immediately. Makes 4 to 6 servings.

Variation

If a richer, slightly thicker soup is desired, remove pan from heat. Stir in 2 beaten egg yolks.

Note: The preparation of this soup varies between regions. For example, the soup served in Bremen is slightly different from that served in Holstein. Small pears and little flour dumplings are often added. Sometimes a ham bone is cooked in the stock to add flavor.

Saffron Seafood Soup
Sylter Fischsuppe

Cream of Mussel Soup
Muschelcremesuppe

1 lb. fish trimmings or small fresh fish
3 tablespoons vinegar
1/2 small leek
1 celery stalk
1 carrot
3 tablespoons vegetable oil
1 small onion, diced
1 qt. hot water
1 cube or small packet fish bouillon
Salt
1/4 teaspoon saffron
White pepper
1 to 2 tablespoons dry white wine
8 to 12 fresh mussels
2 tablespoons margarine
3 tablespoons all-purpose flour
1/2 lb. thin fish fillets
4 to 8 shrimp
1/3 cup dairy sour cream

Rinse fish trimmings or small fresh fish; sprinkle with vinegar. Cut leek, celery and carrot into small pieces. Heat oil in a large saucepan. Add leek, celery, carrot and onion; sauté until nearly tender. Add fish trimmings or fish; cook over low heat 5 minutes. Add hot water, bouillon cube or packet, salt, saffron, white pepper and white wine. Cover and simmer 30 minutes. Scrub mussels; discard any that are open or damaged. Strain fish stock. Add water, if necessary, to make 1 quart liquid. In a medium saucepan, melt margarine over medium heat. Add flour, stirring constantly. Cook 2 to 3 minutes. Then stir in fish stock. Cut fish fillets in medium pieces. Add fillets, one at a time. Add mussels. Simmer soup very gently. Add shrimp before fish is tender or fish will become too soft. Discard any mussels that do not open. Season to taste. Immediately before serving, swirl in sour cream. Serve with fresh white bread and a chilled dry white wine. Makes 4 servings.

1 teaspoon vegetable oil
1 small onion, diced
1 celery stalk, diced
1 leek, diced
1 carrot, diced
3 black peppercorns
3 mustard seeds
3 pimiento seeds
2 juniper berries
1 bay leaf
1/4 lemon
2 cups water
2-1/4 lbs. fresh mussels
3 tablespoons butter
1/4 cup all-purpose flour
Salt
Pinch of saffron
6 tablespoons half and half
1 egg yolk
1 to 2 tablespoons dry white wine
1 tablespoon finely chopped parsley

Heat oil in a heavy saucepan. Add diced vegetables; sauté until nearly tender. Add peppercorns, mustard seeds, pimiento seeds, juniper berries, bay leaf, lemon and water. Simmer about 15 minutes. Scrub mussels; discard any that are open or damaged. Add mussels to saucepan. Cook 5 minutes over high heat, shaking pan once or twice. Discard any mussels that do not open. Strain mixture through a colander. Add enough water to make 2 cups liquid. In a medium saucepan, melt butter. Add flour, stirring constantly 1 to 2 minutes. Add liquid, stirring constantly. Simmer 3 to 4 minutes. Add salt, saffron and 3 tablespoons half and half. Add mussels; remove from heat. In a small bowl, beat together egg yolk, remaining 3 tablespoons half and half and white wine. Stir egg-yolk mixture into soup. Season to taste. Ladle into soup bowls. Sprinkle each serving with parsley. Makes 3 to 4 servings.

Meats & Sausages

The most popular meats in Germany are fresh pork, smoked or cured ham or bacon. They're followed closely by veal and beef, then by lamb and mutton. Germans use every part of meat animals.

Most meats are prepared by braising. Meat is browned slowly on all sides in hot fat with onions. Other vegetables and broth or liquid are added later. This mixture is covered and simmered until tender.

German meats are traditionally cured using only natural ingredients. They are pickled in brine or salted or both and then cold- or warm-smoked. Cured meats include:

Kasseler—a delicious pork loin, soaked in brine and then smoked.

Knochenschinken—ham on the bone, dry-salted, air-dried and cold-smoked.

Lachsschinken—eye of pork loin, milk-cured, warm-smoked and encased in bacon.

Westphalian Ham—boned, skinned, cured with rubbed salt and brine, then smoked over a wood fire to which juniper berries are added. The smoking process can take up to five weeks and produces the dark color and smoky flavor.

Germany produces an astonishingly wide range of sausages. Here are some of the better-known ones:

Blood Sausage or Blutwurst—blood sausage, a category which includes *Speckwurst,* made of cooked blood with diced fat bacon and *Zungenwurst,* a dark sausage containing tongue and pork fat, medium-spiced with black pepper.

Bockwurst—like Vienna sausages but much larger, made from finely ground beef and pork, smoked until they turn the traditional pink color. Sold in cans. Heat in hot but not boiling water.

Bragenwurst—a delicate smoked sausage made with pork and brains. A specialty of lower Saxony.

Bratwurst or frying sausage—spicy links made from pork or pork and beef.

Frankfurter Wurstchen—given this name if they come from the Frankfurt area. They look like Vienna sausages and are made from prime, lean pork that is ground to a fine paste and cold-smoked.

Hirnwurst—made with veal, pork and brains. A Bavarian specialty.

Jadwurst or Hunter's Sausage—made of finely ground meat flecked with small pieces of pork and fat bacon; firm in texture and eaten cold.

Knockwurst or Knackwurst—fat and about 4 inches long. Made of beef or beef and pork and seasoned with coriander, garlic, nutmeg and other seasonings.

Landjager—small slightly flat sausages that are eaten out of hand rather than sliced.

Leberkase—a Bavarian specialty made from beef and pork.

Mettwurst or teewurst—short, stubby sausage made from smoked pork; sometimes contains beef. Completely cooked. Spread on breads. Hard mettwurst has been cooked longer and can be sliced. Varying types come mainly from Hamburg, Westphalia, Hanover and Rugenwald.

Pinkelwurst—a Bremen specialty containing pork, pork fat and cereal. Serve with cabbage or kale.

Thuringer—available fresh, smoked and semi-dry. Mild-flavored fresh thuringer is made from finely ground pork or pork and veal, dry milk and spices. Cooked, smoked thuringer is made from coarsely ground beef and pork and seasoned with mustard, garlic and other spices. The semi-dry sausage is the most tangy.

Weisswurst—small, delicately flavored, white sausages from Bavaria. They must be eaten within 12 hours of purchase since the veal, brains and herbs they are made from deteriorate quickly.

Broiled German Sausages
Bratwurst

Pork & Beef Patties
Frikadellen

1 lb. bratwurst
Milk
Vegetable oil
Margarine, if desired

Raw sausage has a reddish-pink color. Before broiling, boil sausages gently in water a few minutes. This will prevent them from bursting in broiler. Place boiled sausages in a bowl of milk. Sucrose in milk will cause sausages to turn golden brown when broiled. After soaking 2 to 3 minutes in milk, drain well. Sprinkle or brush sausages with oil. Place under broiler. Broil gently or, fry in a skillet with a little margarine or oil. Add a little water to skillet when starting to cook, if desired. Cover skillet. Sausages can be left to fry over a low heat without bursting. Serve with mustard, sauerkraut, potato salad or bread rolls and plenty of chilled beer. Makes 4 servings.

Note: Bratwurst are fairly small fresh sausages with a coarser texture than many other German sausages. There are a great number of different varieties: fat, thin, short, long, veal, pork and sometimes a mixture of pork and veal. They are all highly seasoned and are sold raw, cooked, canned and frozen. They are extremely simple to prepare and can be broiled or barbecued.

1 cup dry breadcrumbs
1 small onion, finely chopped
1 lb. mixed ground pork and beef
1 egg
Salt and pepper
Butter or vegetable oil

Soak breadcrumbs in cold water. Squeeze to remove excess water. In a small bowl, combine soaked breadcrumbs, onion, ground meats, egg, salt and pepper. Shape into 4 firm patties; flatten slightly. In a medium skillet, fry patties in hot butter or oil. Or, sprinkle with oil and cook under a broiler. Brown patties well on both sides. Do not overcook or they will be hard and dry. Serve hot with tomatoes, sauerkraut, cabbage and creamed potatoes or fresh crusty bread. Also use cold as fillings for rolls. Makes 4 servings.

Königsberg Meatballs in Caper Sauce
Königsberger Klopse

1 cup dry breadcrumbs
1 teaspoon vegetable oil
1 small onion, finely chopped
1 to 2 sardines
1 lb. mixed ground pork and beef
1 egg
Salt and pepper
3 tablespoons butter
2 tablespoons all-purpose flour
1 cup hot meat stock
1 cup half and half
3 tablespoons capers
Prepared mustard, to taste
1 egg yolk, if desired

Soak breadcrumbs in hot water. Squeeze to remove excess water. In a small skillet, heat oil. Add onion; sauté until tender. Rinse sardines; chop finely. In a large bowl, combine soaked breadcrumbs, sautéed onion, chopped sardines, ground meats, egg, salt and pepper until thoroughly blended. Rinse your hands in cold water; with wet hands, shape mixture into 2-inch balls. Rinsing your hands helps keep meatball surface smooth. Bring a large saucepan of salted water to a simmer. Place meatballs in gently simmering water. Cook, uncovered, 10 minutes. When cooked, meatballs will float to the surface. Drain; set aside, keeping warm. Melt butter in a medium skillet. Add flour; stir well. Stir in hot stock. Cook, stirring constantly, until slightly thickened. Stir in half and half, capers, salt, pepper and mustard. Add meatballs to sauce. If sauce is not thick enough, remove from heat. Stir in 1 beaten egg yolk. Cook about 2 minutes before adding meatballs. Serve with boiled potatoes and a fresh green salad. Makes 4 to 6 servings.

Mock-Hare Meat Loaf
Falscher Hase

1-1/4 cups dry breadcrumbs
1 tablespoon vegetable oil
1 large onion, finely chopped
2 lbs. mixed ground pork and beef
2 eggs
Salt and pepper
Paprika, rosemary or thyme, if desired
2 hard-cooked eggs, if desired
1 tablespoon margarine

Preheat oven to 375F (190C). Soak breadcrumbs in cold water. Squeeze to remove excess water. In a small skillet, heat oil. Add onion; sauté until tender. In a medium bowl, combine soaked breadcrumbs, sautéed onion, ground meats, 2 eggs, salt and pepper. Season with paprika, rosemary or thyme, if desired. Shape meat mixture into a firm, slightly elongated, flattened shape to resemble the body of a hare. Enclose 2 hard-cooked eggs in center of meat loaf, if desired. Rinse your hands in cold water. Smooth surface of meat loaf with wet hands. Place shaped meat loaf in a baking dish. Dot with small pieces of margarine. Bake 50 to 60 minutes. Let stand 5 to 10 minutes before slicing. Serve with a mustard sauce or Horseradish Cream, page 94. Use leftover meat loaf as a sandwich filling or, slice and serve with potato salad. Makes 4 to 6 servings.

Vienna-Style Veal Cutlets
Wiener Schnitzel

Veal Cutlets Holstein
Holsteiner Schnitzel

4 veal cutlets
Lemon juice
Salt
All-purpose flour
1 egg
3 tablespoons water
Fine dry breadcrumbs
Butter
4 lemon slices
4 anchovy fillets, if desired

Pound cutlets lightly; trim meat as needed. Clip or slash edges to prevent curling during cooking. Sprinkle each cutlet lightly with lemon juice and salt; coat with flour. In a small shallow bowl, beat together egg and water. Dip cutlets in egg mixture; coat with breadcrumbs. Melt butter in a medium skillet. Fry cutlets in butter until golden brown. Garnish with lemon slices and anchovy fillets, if desired. Serve immediately with potatoes, lettuce and tomato wedges. Makes 4 servings.

Note: This method of cooking veal did not originate in Austria but was introduced from Italy about 100 years ago. The Milanese took the idea from the Spanish when the Duchy of Milan formed part of the Spanish-Hapsburg Empire. Despite this, every visitor to Vienna seems to make a special point of ordering a crisp and juicy Wiener Schnitzel, one of the city's specialties.

4 veal cutlets
Lemon juice
Salt
All-purpose flour
1/4 cup butter
4 eggs
4 anchovy fillets
2 to 4 tomatoes, sliced
Parsley

Pound cutlets lightly; trim meat as needed. Clip or slash edges to prevent curling during cooking. Sprinkle each cutlet lightly with lemon juice and salt; coat with flour. Melt 2 tablespoons butter in a large skillet. Fry cutlets in butter until golden brown. Remove from pan; keep warm. Melt remaining butter in skillet. Add eggs; fry gently. Top each cooked cutlet with a fried egg. Garnish with anchovy fillets, tomato slices and a sprig of parsley. Makes 4 servings.

Cutlets with Paprika Sauce
Paprikaschnitzel

Pepper Steak
Pfeffersteak

4 veal or pork cutlets
Lemon juice
Salt
Vegetable oil
1 shallot, finely chopped
3 tablespoons all-purpose flour
Generous 1/2 cup meat stock
3 tablespoons white wine
1/4 cup half and half
1 teaspoon paprika

Pound cutlets lightly; trim meat as needed. Clip or slash edges to prevent curling during cooking. Sprinkle each cutlet lightly with lemon juice and salt. Heat a little oil in a medium skillet. Fry cutlets until golden brown on both sides. Remove from skillet; keep warm. Add shallot; sauté lightly. Add flour to sautéed shallot. Cook, stirring constantly, until light golden brown. Stir in stock and wine; cook gently, stirring constantly. Add half and half and paprika. Season with salt, if needed. Return cutlets to skillet to coat with sauce; heat through. Serve immediately with green beans, salad and boiled potatoes, rice or noodles. Makes 4 servings.

Variation

Stir 1 to 2 tablespoons canned chopped pimiento into sauce.

4 (1-1/2- to 2-inch-thick) beef sirloin steaks
Lemon juice
Vegetable oil
Salt
Coarsely crushed black peppercorns
1/2 lb. mushrooms, cut in halves
1 onion, cut in rings
4 tomatoes

Trim beef, if necessary; pound slightly to tenderize. Sprinkle lightly with lemon juice. In a heavy, cast-iron skillet, heat a little oil until very hot. Fry steaks in hot oil over medium heat, turning once. Frying time will depend on thickness, but beef should be quite pink inside when done. Season with salt and peppercorns. Meanwhile, in a medium skillet, sauté mushrooms briefly in oil; remove and keep warm. In the same skillet, sauté onion rings. Garnish steaks with mushrooms, onion rings and tomato slices. Serve with French-fried potatoes or rice and salad. Also delicious with béarnaise sauce or Horseradish Cream, page 94. Makes 4 servings.

Pork Chops Hubertus
Koteletts Hubertus

Lamb Chops with Herbs
Hammelkoteletts

Generous 1/2 cup Burgundy or other red wine
1 tablespoon tomato paste
Salt and pepper
4 pork loin chops
Vegetable oil
1 onion, cut in rings
3 to 4 tomatoes, peeled, sliced
Chanterelle or regular mushrooms
Basil, preferably fresh
Generous 1/2 cup half and half

In a large nonmetal or earthenware bowl, combine wine, tomato paste, salt and pepper; add pork chops. Cover and refrigerate 24 hours, turning occasionally and spooning marinade over chops so they absorb flavor evenly. Remove chops from marinade; drain well, reserving marinade. Heat oil in a heavy skillet. Brown chops on both sides. When chops are cooked, remove and keep warm in a deep serving dish. Sauté onion rings in oil and meat juices. Add tomato slices; heat through. Add mushrooms, basil, remaining marinade and half and half. Season to taste with salt and pepper. Pour sauce over chops. Serve with creamed potatoes or a green salad. Makes 4 servings.

8 lamb chops
Lemon juice
1 garlic clove, cut in half
Vegetable oil
Fresh thyme, basil, rosemary and oregano, coarsely chopped
Salt and pepper

Remove bones from lamb chops, if desired. Pound chops lightly with your fist. Sprinkle lightly with lemon juice. Cover and let stand 30 minutes. Rub chops with cut surfaces of garlic halves. Sprinkle lightly with oil. For best results, cook over a barbecue grill or broil in the oven, turning several times so chops cook evenly and remain moist. While cooking, combine fresh herbs, salt and pepper. When chops are nearly cooked, sprinkle with herb mixture. By adding salt near end of cooking time, meat remains more moist and juicy. Herbs will also keep their full aroma. Serve with tomatoes and baked onions, green beans and French-fried potatoes or hot cooked rice and garlic-flavored butter. Makes 4 servings.

Pork Tenderloin Steaks
Schweinemedaillons

4 (1/2-inch-thick) pork tenderloin steaks
Vegetable oil
Salt and pepper
4 thick slices white bread, cut in 3-inch rounds
1 small can goose-liver pâté (pâté de fois gras)
4 cooked-ham slices
4 Gruyère-cheese slices
4 pineapple slices
8 canned pitted cherries or maraschino cherries

Lightly pound pork steaks. Heat oil in a large skillet. Fry steaks in hot oil until golden brown on both sides. Season with salt and pepper. Preheat oven to 425F (220C). Spread each bread round with liver pâté. Remove any fat from ham. Place a pork piece on each bread round. Top each with slices of ham, cheese and pineapple. Secure with a cocktail pick. Arrange carefully in a shallow casserole dish. Bake until cheese is melted. Remove cocktail stick; place a cherry in center of each pineapple slice. Serve immediately. Makes 4 servings.

Pork Spareribs in Herb Sauce
Schweinerippchen in Kräutersosse

2-1/4 lbs. pork spareribs
Generous 1 cup dry rosé wine
1/3 cup apricot jam
Salt and pepper
Vegetable oil
Generous 1/2 cup meat stock
1/3 cup half and half
3 tablespoons all-purpose flour
4 canned pear halves, drained
4 canned peach halves, drained
3 tablespoons toasted slivered almonds
3 tablespoon finely chopped parsley, if desired

Trim ribs; cut into 4 to 8 sections. Arrange ribs in a shallow dish. In a small bowl, combine wine, apricot jam, salt and pepper. Pour wine mixture over ribs. Cover and refrigerate overnight, turning occasionally and spooning marinade over ribs so they absorb flavor evenly. Remove ribs from marinade; drain well, reserving marinade. Heat oil in a large deep skillet; brown drained ribs on both sides. Add reserved marinade and stock. Cover and bring to a boil; reduce heat. Simmer 1-1/2 hours. Remove ribs from pan; keep warm. In a small bowl, combine half and half and flour; stir into sauce. Cook, stirring constantly, until thickened. Cut fruit into small pieces. Add to sauce; stir until warmed through. Add cooked ribs; spoon sauce over ribs. Transfer to a warm serving dish. Sprinkle with almonds and parsley, if desired. Serve with hot rice and a green salad. Makes 4 to 6 servings.

Variation

After adding fruit, add mustard, ginger or curry powder to the sauce. Jam can be omitted, if desired, because the dish is sweetened by the addition of canned fruit.

Stuffed Cabbage Leaves
Kohlrouladen

Stuffed Red-Cabbage Leaves
Rotkohlrouladen

1 medium head green cabbage
3 tablespoons cooking fat or vegetable shortening
2 onions, finely chopped
Generous 1/2 cup dry breadcrumbs
1 lb. mixed ground pork and beef
1 egg
Salt and pepper
2 bacon slices, finely diced
3 tablespoons all-purpose flour
Generous 1 cup meat stock
1/3 cup tomato paste
Paprika
Generous 1/2 cup dairy sour cream, if desired

Clean cabbage; use a sharp knife to remove main stem. Bring a large saucepan of salted water to a boil. Plunge cabbage into boiling water. After 4 to 5 minutes, carefully remove outer leaves. Repeat 2 to 3 times or until all leaves have been removed. In a small skillet, heat fat or oil. Add half the onion; sauté until transparent. In a medium bowl, combine breadcrumbs, ground meats, egg, salt and pepper. Divide stuffing mixture into 8 portions. Taking 2 cabbage leaves at a time, roll or pound gently to soften ribs. Place leaves, 1 inside the other. Spread 1 portion of stuffing over surface, stopping well short of edges. Roll leaves up neatly into a little package. Repeat with remaining cabbage leaves and stuffing. In a large saucepan, sauté bacon. Add cabbage rolls and remaining onion. Cook until onion is transparent. Dissolve flour in stock. Add to saucepan along with tomato paste, salt and pepper. Cover and cook 1 hour over low heat. Adjust seasoning, if necessary. Place on a warm serving dish. Pour sauce over cabbage rolls. Sprinkle with paprika. Top with dollops of sour cream, if desired. Makes 8 cabbage rolls.

1 medium head red cabbage
2 tablespoons margarine
2 onions, finely chopped
1 cup dry breadcrumbs
1 lb. mixed ground pork and beef
1 egg
Salt and pepper
3 tablespoons cooking fat or vegetable shortening
1/4 lb. mushrooms, if desired
3 to 4 tablespoons all-purpose flour
2 cups meat stock
1/3 cup half and half

Clean cabbage; use a sharp knife to remove main stem. Bring a large saucepan of salted water to a boil. Plunge cabbage into boiling water. After 4 to 5 minutes, carefully remove outer leaves. Repeat 2 to 3 times or until all leaves have been removed. In a small skillet, melt margarine. Add half the onion; sauté until transparent. In a medium bowl, combine breadcrumbs, ground meats, sautéed onion, egg, salt and pepper. Divide stuffing into 8 portions. Taking 2 cabbage leaves at a time, roll or pound gently to soften ribs. Place leaves, 1 inside the other. Spread 1 portion of stuffing over surface, stopping well short of edges. Roll leaves up neatly into a little package. Repeat with remaining cabbage leaves and stuffing. Heat fat or shortening in a large skillet. Add cabbage rolls; sauté gently. Add remaining onion and mushrooms, if desired. Dissolve flour in stock; add to skillet. Cover and cook gently over low heat 40 minutes; stirring occasionally. Season with salt and pepper. Add half and half; stir to blend. Place on a warm serving dish. Spoon sauce over cabbage rolls. Serve with creamed potatoes and a salad. Makes 8 cabbage rolls.

Beef Rolls
Rindsrouladen

Swallows' Nests
Schwalbennester

4 (1/2-inch-thick) slices beef top round
Salt and pepper
Prepared mustard
3 onions, finely chopped
3 bacon slices, chopped
1 pickled cucumber or gherkin, sliced
1 tablespoon cooking fat or vegetable shortening
1 teaspoon tomato paste
1 generous cup meat stock
1 tablespoon all-purpose flour
Dry red wine

Season beef with salt and pepper; spread thinly with mustard. Using about 2/3 the onion, sprinkle onion, bacon and pickle over beef. Roll up slices and secure with skewers, cocktail picks or thread. Heat fat or shortening in a medium skillet. Add beef rolls; sauté until well browned, turning occasionally. Add remaining onion; sauté until light golden brown. Add tomato paste and stock. Season to taste with salt and pepper. Cover and simmer about 1 hour. To thicken sauce, combine flour and a small amount of wine. Stir flour mixture into cooking liquid. Cook, stirring, until slightly thickened. Remove skewers, cocktail picks or thread. Serve beef rolls and sauce with hot cooked rice, noodles, or boiled or creamed potatoes. Serve with salad or other vegetables in season and chilled lager beer. Makes 4 servings.

4 boneless veal leg or round cutlets
Lemon juice
Salt
4 bacon slices
4 cooked-ham slices
4 hard-cooked eggs
3 tablespoons butter
Generous 1/2 cup white wine
Generous 1/2 cup meat stock
Generous 1/2 cup dairy sour cream
Pepper

Pound cutlets lightly; trim meat as needed. Clip or slash edges to prevent curling during cooking. Sprinkle each cutlet lightly with lemon juice and salt. Place 1 bacon slice and 1 ham slice on each veal cutlet. Place 1 shelled hard-cooked egg in center of each. Roll up meat layers, enclosing egg. Secure with small skewers, cocktail picks or thread. Melt butter in a small skillet; add meat rolls. Sauté until light golden brown, turning frequently. Add wine and stock. Cover and simmer 40 minutes or until meat is tender. Add water occasionally to keep from boiling dry. Stir in sour cream; season with salt and pepper. Remove skewers, cocktail picks or thread before serving. Serve with fresh vegetables or salad and rice, noodles or creamed potatoes. Makes 4 servings.

Peppered Beef Casserole
Pfefferpotthast

Stuffed Peppers
Gefüllte Paprikaschoten

2 lbs. beef for stew
3 tablespoons butter or vegetable shortening
3/4 lb. small onions or shallots, coarsely chopped
1 bay leaf
1/2 lemon, sliced
2 whole cloves
1 tablespoon coarsely crushed black peppercorns
Salt
1 qt. beef stock
3 tablespoons fresh breadcrumbs
1 tablespoon capers

Trim beef; cut in bite-size pieces. Melt butter or shortening in a large saucepan over medium heat. Add beef and onions or shallots. Sauté until onions are tender and beef is browned. Add bay leaf, lemon slices, cloves, peppercorns, salt and stock. Cover and bring to a boil. Reduce heat and simmer 1-1/2 hours. Beef should be very tender. Remove cloves and bay leaf; discard. Thicken juices by adding breadcrumbs. Stir in capers. Season to taste with salt. Pickled cucumbers or gherkins and boiled potatoes are usually served with this dish. Makes 4 to 6 servings.

4 large or 8 small red peppers
Salt
2 to 3 cups fresh breadcrumbs or 1 cup cooked rice
1 medium onion, finely chopped
1 lb. mixed ground beef and pork
1 egg
Pepper
Thyme
Oregano or basil
4 bacon slices, diced
1 onion, finely chopped
1/2 cup meat stock
3 tablespoons tomato paste

Preheat oven to 400F (205C). Remove stalk and surrounding hard flesh from peppers. Or, cut peppers in half lengthwise. Wash, remove seeds and membrane. Boil 5 minutes in salted water; drain. Soak breadcrumbs in cold water. Squeeze to remove excess water. In a small bowl, combine breadcrumbs or rice, 1 onion, ground meats, egg, salt, pepper, thyme and oregano or basil. Sprinkle peppers lightly with salt; fill each with stuffing. Sauté bacon in a medium skillet. Add onion; sauté until tender. Add stock, tomato paste, salt and pepper. Pour mixture into a casserole dish. Arrange peppers, stuffing side up, in dish. Cover and bake 30 minutes. Remove lid and bake 10 minutes longer or until lightly browned. If rice was not used in stuffing, serve peppers with hot cooked rice. Or serve with a salad. Makes 4 servings.

Zurich-Style Veal
Zürcher Geschnetzeltes

Fricassee of Veal
Kalbsfrikassee

1-1/2 lbs. boneless veal round
3/4 lb. button mushrooms
Lemon juice
1/3 cup vegetable oil or butter
1 tablespoon all-purpose flour
1/2 cup meat stock
White wine
Half and half
Salt and white pepper

For ease in slicing, wrap veal in plastic wrap. Place in a freezer until nearly firm. Remove wrapping; thinly slice using a sharp knife. Trim off excess fat, if necessary. Clean mushrooms; cut into thin slices. Sprinkle mushrooms with lemon juice to prevent darkening. Heat oil or butter in a large skillet over high heat. Add veal slices; sauté until lightly browned on all sides. Remove veal from skillet. Sauté sliced mushrooms in fat and juices in skillet. Sprinkle with flour. Stir in stock, wine to taste and a little half and half. Cook, stirring constantly, until thickened. Return veal to skillet. Heat in sauce, seasoning to taste with salt and white pepper. Serve immediately so veal does not lose its delicate flavor and consistency. Grated Potato Cake, page 116, usually accompanies this dish. Makes 4 to 6 servings.

Water
1 small onion
1 bay leaf
1 whole clove
Pinch of ground nutmeg
Salt
2-1/2 to 3 lbs. veal shoulder or leg
1/3 cup butter or margarine
1/4 cup all-purpose flour
3 tablespoons white wine
1 teaspoon lemon juice
1 egg yolk
1/2 cup half and half

Bring 1 quart water to a boil in a medium saucepan. Add unpeeled onion, bay leaf, whole clove, nutmeg and salt. Add veal; simmer 1-1/2 hours or until tender. Remove veal from stock; strain and reserve stock. Cool veal; cut into 1-inch cubes. Melt butter or margarine in a saucepan. Add flour, stirring well. Add 2 cups hot strained stock, a little at a time, stirring constantly. Bring mixture to a boil. Reduce heat; add salt, wine and lemon juice. Add veal; heat until warmed through. Remove from heat. In a small bowl, combine egg yolk and half and half. Briskly stir egg-yolk mixture into veal mixture. Serve veal fricassee with rice or pasta. Makes 4 to 6 servings.

Variation

Add sautéed mushrooms, cooked asparagus tips or tiny cooked veal meatballs to fricassee.

Bavarian Goulash
Bayerisches Gulasch

Braised Beef
Rinderschmorbraten

1-1/2 lbs. beef for stew
1/4 cup vegetable oil or butter
4 onions, finely chopped
2 tomatoes, peeled, chopped
Salt and pepper
Paprika
Bay leaf
1-1/2 cups meat stock
2 tablespoons all-purpose flour
Burgundy or other red wine

Trim beef, if necessary. Cut in bite-size pieces. Heat oil or butter in a heavy saucepan. Add beef; sauté until evenly browned on all sides. Add onions; sauté until nearly translucent. Add tomatoes; season to taste with salt, pepper and paprika. Add bay leaf. Pour in stock; stir well. Cover and simmer 1 to 1-1/2 hours or until beef is tender. In a small bowl, combine flour and small amount of wine. Stir into goulash. Cook over low heat until thickened. Serve goulash with potato dumplings or white-bread dumplings. Boiled or pureed potatoes, pasta or rice may also be served. Makes 4 to 6 servings.

Variation

Stir 1/4 cup whipping cream and 1/2 teaspoon ground cumin into thickened goulash. Heat through but do not boil.

1 (3- to 3-1/2-lb.) beef rump roast
Salt and pepper
1 tablespoon prepared mustard
8 bacon slices, diced
3 tablespoons vegetable oil
2 large onions, coarsely chopped
Thyme, bay leaf and parsley, coarsely chopped
Paprika
1 teaspoon tomato paste
1/2 cup dry red wine
1 cup beef stock
2 tablespoons all-purpose flour
Water
1/2 cup whipping cream or dairy sour cream

Rub beef generously with salt, pepper and mustard. Sauté bacon in a large heavy saucepan; remove bacon. Add oil. When hot, add beef. Brown beef evenly all over. Add onions and herbs. Cook until onions are nearly tender. Add paprika, tomato paste, wine, stock and sautéed bacon. Cover and simmer 1-1/2 to 2 hours or until tender. Let stand 5 to 10 minutes before carving. Strain cooking liquid through a fine sieve; if it has reduced too much, add a little stock. Return cooking liquid to saucepan. Dissolve flour in a small amount of water. Stir into hot cooking liquid. Cook, stirring constantly, until slightly thickened. Stir in whipping cream or sour cream. Serve with pasta, rice or potatoes or almost any type of vegetable or salad. Heat leftover beef in sauce. Makes 6 to 8 servings.

Rhenish Braised Beef
Rheinischer Sauerbraten

Cured Spit-Roasted Ham
Schweinenacken am Spiess

3-1/3 cups water
1 cup red-wine vinegar
1 onion, chopped
1 whole clove
1 bay leaf
1 teaspoon black peppercorns
1 teaspoon mustard seeds
1 teaspoon whole allspice
1 (3- to 3-1/2-lb.) beef chuck roast or beef round roast
Salt
Prepared mustard
1/3 cup vegetable oil
1 slice pumpernickel or honey bread
1/2 cup red wine
3 tablespoons golden raisins, if desired
3 tablespoons cornstarch
1/3 cup dairy sour cream

In a large nonmetal or earthenware bowl, combine water, vinegar, onion, clove, bay leaf, peppercorns, mustard seeds and allspice. Add beef. Cover and refrigerate 3 to 4 days, turning occasionally and spooning marinade over beef so it absorbs flavor evenly. Remove beef from marinade; drain well, reserving marinade. Rub beef with a little salt and mustard. Heat oil in a large heavy saucepan. Add beef; brown evenly in hot oil. Cut bread in cubes; add bread cubes, wine and a little reserved marinade. Simmer 1-1/2 hours or until beef is tender, adding marinade as needed. Let beef stand 5 to 10 minutes before carving. Soak raisins in a small bowl of water 10 to 15 minutes, if desired. Strain cooking juices; return to saucepan. Add soaked raisins and cornstarch dissolved in a small amount of water. Cook, stirring constantly, until mixture begins to thicken. Gradually stir in sour cream. Pass sauce to serve over beef. Serve with dumplings, potatoes, vegetables or a mixed salad. Makes 6 to 8 servings.

3 tablespoons vegetable oil
Salt and pepper
1 tablespoon prepared mustard
1 tablespoon grated horseradish
1 garlic clove, crushed
1 onion, finely chopped
1/2 cup beer
1 (2-1/2-lb.) boned cured ham
Bay leaf
Parsley
Thyme
1/2 cup meat stock

Preheat oven to 400F (205C). In a small bowl, combine oil, salt, pepper, mustard, horseradish, garlic, onion and beer. Place ham in a roasting pan. Pour mixture over ham. Coarsely chop bay leaf, parsley and thyme. Add chopped herbs and stock to roasting pan. Bake ham 45 minutes. Remove from oven and take from roasting pan, reserving marinade. Preheat rotisserie. Slide ham carefully onto spit for rotisserie. Be sure weight of ham is evenly balanced. Place ham on rotisserie. Baste frequently with reserved marinade. After 45 minutes, test by inserting a skewer into ham. If juices run clear with no hint of pink, ham is done. Remove from spit. Slice with a sharp knife. Serve with potato salad, sauerkraut and beer. Makes 4 to 6 servings.

Note: This method of first baking the ham and then spit roasting it makes the ham more flavorful.

Roast Loin of Veal
Kalbsnierenbraten

Smoked Pork Loin en Croûte
Kasseler in Teig

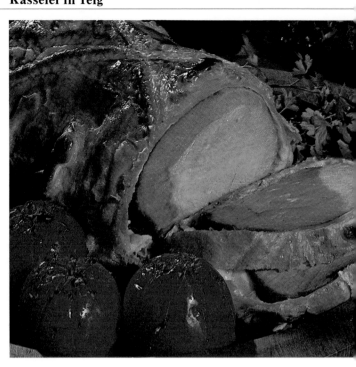

1/3 cup vegetable oil
1 (2-1/2-lb.) veal loin
1 small leek, finely chopped
1 celery stalk, finely chopped
1 carrot, finely chopped
1 onion, finely chopped
1 tablespoon all-purpose flour
Salt and white pepper
Paprika
Sage
Ground nutmeg
Rosemary
2 cups meat stock
White wine
1 tablespoon tomato paste
1/2 cup half and half or dairy sour cream

Heat oil in a large heavy saucepan. Add veal; brown evenly. Before completely browned, add leek, celery, carrot, onion, flour, salt, white pepper, paprika, sage, nutmeg and rosemary. Stir to blend well. Stir in stock, wine and tomato paste. Cover and simmer 1 to 1-1/2 hours, turning from time to time. Pierce veal with a fork to test doneness. If juices run clear, meat is cooked. If there is any hint of pink or red juice, continue cooking until juice is clear. Remove veal. Let stand 5 to 10 minutes before carving. Strain cooking juices; return to saucepan. Stir in half and half or sour cream. Serve with veal. Makes 4 to 6 servings.

1 (2-1/2-lb.) smoked pork loin or Canadian bacon
1-1/2 pkgs. frozen patty shells (9 shells), thawed
1 egg white
Water

Preheat oven to 400F (205C). Oil a large sheet of foil. Wrap pork in oiled foil, folding to make airtight so moisture will not escape. Bake 30 minutes; cool. On a lightly floured board, arrange patty shells, slightly overlapping, in 3 rows of 3 shells. Roll pastry shells into an 18-inch square. Cut a 4-inch strip off 1 side. Place cooled pork on large rolled pastry. Brush pastry edges with egg white. Bring 2 longest sides over top of pork. Press firmly to seal. Close and seal ends. Cut remaining pastry into strips and diamond shapes for decoration. Brush with egg white so shapes will adhere to pastry. Arrange on pastry-covered pork. Combine remaining egg white with a small amount of water. Brush pastry crust and decoration with egg-white and water mixture. Place on a nonstick baking sheet. Preheat oven to 425F (220C). Place a large baking pan in bottom of oven. Pour in 2 cups water. Bake pork about 40 minutes or until pastry is crisp and golden brown. Grilled tomatoes, mustard and horseradish are usually eaten with this dish. Makes 4 to 6 servings.

Grilled Leg of Mutton
Gegrillte Hammelkeule

Pork Hocks
Schweinshaxe

1 leg of lamb or mutton
3 to 4 garlic cloves
Vegetable oil
Salt and pepper
1/2 cup meat stock

Preheat oven to 400F (205C). Trim excess fat or skin from lamb. Cut garlic into slivers. With the point of a very sharp knife, make small incisions below skin of lamb. Insert garlic slivers. Sprinkle lamb with oil and season to taste with salt and pepper. Place lamb in oven, resting it directly on oven rack. Place a drip pan directly below lamb. Pour in stock so juices and fat that drip from lamb will not burn. Add a little hot water to drip pan from time to time. Roast 60 to 75 minutes. Remove lamb from oven. Carefully thread lamb on spit or place on a barbecue grill. Cook, uncovered. If cooking on a barbecue grill, turn meat occasionally. Lamb should be slightly pink and very tender. Serve with potatoes, rice, green beans or broiled tomatoes. Makes 4 to 6 servings.

Note: Leg of mutton or mature lamb may be difficult to obtain. It is especially flavorful when grilled.

1 small leek
1 celery stalk
1 carrot
1 onion
1 to 2 meaty pork hocks
Salt
Black peppercorns
2 tablespoons cooking fat or vegetable shortening
Beer or water
Cumin, if desired

Clean and dice leek, celery, carrot and onion. Cook pork hocks, diced vegetables, salt and peppercorns in water to cover 2 to 3 hours or until tender. Avoid overcooking. Remove from water; drain well reserving vegetables and cooking liquid. Preheat oven to 425F (220C). Melt fat or shortening in an enamel-lined, cast-iron pan. Add drained pork hocks, cooked vegetables and a small amount of cooking liquid. Bake 30 minutes. Moisten meat frequently with more cooking liquid. Before meat is fully cooked, sprinkle with beer or water in which a good amount of salt has been dissolved. Add cumin to increase flavor, if desired. Serve with potato or white-bread dumplings or sauerkraut salad. Makes 3 to 4 servings.

Note: In Bavaria, the juices and cooking liquid are strained and served as an accompanying sauce.

Boiled Beef Brisket
Gesottene Rinderbrust

1 tablespoon vegetable oil
1 onion, cut in quarters
1 leek, chopped
1 celery stalk, chopped
1 carrot, chopped
Water
Salt
1 bay leaf
1/2 teaspoon mustard seeds
1/2 teaspoon black peppercorns
1 whole clove
1 (2-1/4-lb.) beef brisket

Heat oil in a large skillet. Add onion, leek, celery and carrot. Sauté until nearly tender. Add 2 to 3 cups water or enough to cover meat. Add salt, bay leaf, mustard seeds, peppercorns and clove. Bring to a boil. Place beef in boiling stock. Boil gently 1-1/2 to 2 hours or until tender. Let beef stand 5 to 10 minutes before carving in thin slices. Use stock to make a delicious soup. Makes 4 to 6 servings.

Variation

Add peeled potatoes to dish 15 to 20 minutes before beef is done.

Note: Recipes for classic accompaniments of Horseradish Cream and Mustard & Egg Sauce are given on pages 94 and 96. When herbs are at their freshest and most tender, Frankfurt Green-Herb Sauce, page 94, would be more suitable.

Leg of Pork
Eisbein

1 (4-1/2-lb.) pork leg, or fresh or brined knuckle
1 onion, cut in quarters
1 bay leaf
1 whole clove
1 teaspoon black peppercorns
1 small piece leek
1 small celery stalk, cut in half
1 carrot, cut in half
Water

Place pork in a large saucepan or cooking pot. Add onion, bay leaf, clove, peppercorns, leek, celery and carrot. Cover with cold water. Bring to a boil. Reduce heat and cook 2 to 2-1/2 hours or until tender. Pig's knuckle is nearly always served with sauerkraut and creamed or boiled potatoes. In Berlin, a traditional accompaniment is a puree of green peas that can be purchased in cans or as a packet mix, although homemade is preferred. Makes 4 to 6 servings.

Note: The amount of flesh on knuckles, between the thigh or haunch and the foot, varies. In Bavaria, it is sold salted in brine. This particular cut of pork has a high proportion of bone and fat. Try to choose knuckles that have a fairly even distribution of meat, fat and bone.

Mixed Cured Meats & Sauerkraut
Schlachtplatte

Beef Fondue
Fondue Bourguignonne

2 tablespoons margarine or vegetable shortening
1 onion, chopped
1-3/4 to 2 lbs. sauerkraut
2 cups water or meat stock
Salt and pepper
1 teaspoon juniper berries
1 bay leaf
2 blutwurst
2 liverwurst
2 pairs mettwurst
3/4 to 1 lb. ham or Canadian bacon, thickly sliced
1/2 lb. thick-sliced bacon

Melt margarine or shortening in a large heavy pan. Add onion; sauté until tender. Add sauerkraut, water or stock, salt, pepper, juniper berries and bay leaf. Cover and simmer 1 hour, occasionally shaking pan sharply from side to side to prevent sticking. Shortly before serving, warm sausages in a pan of hot, **NOT** boiling, water. They will be ruined if they boil. Serve sauerkraut mixture with ham or Canadian bacon and sausages on a warmed dish. Also serve dumplings, prepared mustard and chilled German or lager beer. Makes 4 servings.

1-3/4 to 2-1/4 lbs. beef tenderloin or sirloin
1 qt. peanut oil or vegetable oil
Mushrooms
1 jar pickled small onions

Marinate beef 2 to 3 days in a light covering of oil in the refrigerator. Shortly before using, cut beef into 3/4- to 1-inch cubes. Heat oil in a fondue pot. Be sure oil is hot enough, but the flame below it is not too high. Arrange mushrooms, drained pickled onions and beef in small dishes around fondue pot. Serve a variety of cold sauces in small bowls, including recipes on pages 94 through 97. Be sure to use sauces with contrasting and fairly pronounced flavors. Serve fresh, crusty white bread, such as French bread, and a mixed salad to complement the meal. Each guest spears a piece of beef with a long fondue fork. Then meat is cooked in oil to desired doneness. To eat meat, guests transfer cooked meat to their dinner forks because the shaft of the fondue fork becomes very hot and can burn. Mushrooms are cooked in the same way. Makes 4 to 6 servings.

Variation

A variety of spices and herbs can be used to add flavor while beef is marinating: salt, freshly ground pepper, paprika, curry and dried or chopped fresh herbs, such as tarragon, thyme or basil.

Ham en Croûte
Schinken in Teig

1 (2-1/2- to 3-lb.) cooked boneless ham
Prepared mustard
Salt and pepper
1-1/4 lbs. bread dough, frozen or homemade
1 egg white, slightly beaten

Preheat oven to 400F (205C). Trim ham into a neat oblong or rectangular shape. Season with mustard, salt and pepper. Thaw frozen bread dough. Roll out dough on a lightly floured surface. Moisten edges of dough with water. Carefully wrap ham with dough, sealing well by pinching edges together. Use scraps of dough to make decorations. Brush surface of wrapped ham with egg white. Arrange decorative dough pieces on surface. Brush decorative pieces with egg white. Prick dough at intervals with a fork so steam can escape during cooking. Place dough-wrapped ham on a lightly floured baking sheet. Bake 1-1/2 to 2 hours or until pastry is golden brown. Serve very hot. Makes 4 to 6 servings.

Note: This dish is a specialty of Baden, a town near the French border. Some residents still follow the old custom of taking their ham in its bread "case" to the baker to have it baked in his oven. The baker's wood-fired oven gives much better results than an electric or gas oven. This is partly due to the moister heat and the aroma of the wood fire.

Ham & Mushroom Rolls au Gratin
Schinkenrollen

3/4 lb. button mushrooms
1 tablespoon lemon juice
2 tablespoons butter
2 tablespoons all-purpose flour
1/2 cup dry white wine
Whipping cream
Salt and white pepper
4 large cooked-ham slices
2 egg yolks, slightly beaten
2 tablespoons grated Sbrinz, Asiago or Romano cheese

Preheat oven to 425F (220C). Butter a shallow baking dish. Clean mushrooms; slice thinly. Sprinkle mushrooms with lemon juice to prevent darkening. Melt butter in a medium saucepan. Sauté mushrooms gently in butter. Remove mushrooms when done, leaving as much butter as possible in saucepan. Stirring constantly, combine flour with melted butter over low heat. Add wine, stirring well. Stir in a little whipping cream. In a small bowl, combine half the sauce with half the mushrooms. Season with salt and white pepper. Spread 3 to 4 tablespoons mushroom-sauce mixture on each ham slice. Roll up slices; secure with a wooden pick. Arrange in buttered baking dish. Add remaining mushrooms to remaining sauce. Stir in egg yolks. Spoon evenly over ham rolls. Sprinkle cheese evenly over top. Bake 10 minutes or until cheese is melted and lightly browned. Serve with rice, lettuce and a light, dry white wine. Makes 4 servings.

Calves' Kidneys
Kalbsnieren

Grilled Calves' Hearts with Herbs
Gegrilltes Herz

1-1/2 lbs. calves' kidneys
2 tablespoons butter
2 small apples, peeled, sliced
1 small jar chanterelle or regular mushrooms, drained
1/2 cup light meat stock
Sage
Rosemary
Parsley
Salt and white pepper
4 bacon slices, diced

Remove thin outer skin or membrane from kidneys. Slice kidneys in half lengthwise; trim away any fat. Wash thoroughly. Soak kidneys 30 minutes in cold water. Pat dry with a cloth or paper towels. Cut kidneys in thin crosswise slices. Melt butter in a large skillet until butter begins to foam. Add kidney slices; sauté briefly, turning once. Remove kidneys from skillet; keep warm. Sauté apples briskly, turning constantly, in butter remaining in skillet. While apples are still very firm, add mushrooms, stock, sage, rosemary, parsley, salt and white pepper. Return sautéed kidney slices to skillet before serving. If dish continues to cook for any length of time, apples will become mushy and kidneys will toughen. Meanwhile, sauté bacon in a small skillet until slightly crisp; remove bacon with a slotted spoon and drain on paper towels. Sprinkle bacon over kidneys. Serve with rice, creamed potatoes or Swabian Noodles, page 129. Makes 4 to 6 servings.

2 calves' hearts
Vegetable oil
Rosemary
Thyme
Oregano
Marjoram
Salt and pepper

Trim fat from hearts. Remove any arteries or tendons; wash well. Use a sharp knife to cut hearts into rings or slices about 1 to 1-1/2 inches thick. Brush or sprinkle all over with oil. Let stand 30 minutes. Place under a broiler or on a grill, 6 to 8 inches from flame on an oiled pan or oiled grate. Heart grilled over too high heat will become tough and dry. Turn frequently, basting with oil. Sprinkle with herbs and seasoning but do not salt until immediately before serving. Serve with grilled mushrooms, onions and tomatoes and rice or fresh white bread. Makes 4 to 6 servings.

Note: Calf heart is excellent when grilled. However, ox or pig heart is too tough for grilling. If calf heart is unobtainable, precook an ox heart in stock in a pressure cooker, if possible. Drain and prepare as directed above.

Berlin-Style Liver
Leber Berliner Art

Sautéed Liver with Wine & Herb Sauce
Lebergeschnetzeltes

2 crisp apples
2 large onions
1/4 cup butter
Salt
4 slices calves' liver
3 tablespoons all-purpose flour
Pepper
4 cherry tomatoes, if desired

Core apples; wash, dry and cut into rounds 1/4 to 1/2 inch thick. Cut onions into very thin slices. Separate into rings. Heat 2 tablespoons butter in a large skillet. Fry apple rings in hot butter, 1 to 2 minutes. Remove apple rings; keep warm. Add onion rings, adding more butter, if needed. Fry onion rings until golden brown and crisp. Season with salt; remove from skillet and keep warm. Remove any skin or fibers from liver; coat lightly with flour. Melt remaining butter in skillet. Sauté liver very briskly in butter, turning once. Season with pepper. Arrange on a warm serving plate. Top with fried apple and onion rings. Grill tomatoes; add as a garnish, if desired. Serve with creamed potatoes. Makes 4 servings.

Note: This is an extremely popular Berlin specialty. Pork or beef liver can be used instead of calves' liver, but before cooking, they should be soaked in milk 30 minutes.

1-1/4 to 1-1/2 lbs. calves' liver or beef liver
1/2 cup milk, if using beef liver
3 tablespoons all-purpose flour
1/3 cup vegetable oil
1 large onion, chopped
4 bacon slices, diced
1/2 cup Burgundy or other red wine
1/3 cup meat stock
Salt and pepper
Thyme or rosemary
3 tablespoons finely chopped parsley

Remove thin skin from liver. If beef liver is used, soak in milk 30 minutes. Place liver in freezer until firm. Thinly slice liver using a sharp knife. Coat liver slices lightly with flour. Heat oil until very hot in a large skillet. Fry liver 3 to 4 minutes, stirring constantly. Do not overcook. Remove from pan with a slotted spoon; set aside. Fry onion and bacon in remaining oil. Reduce heat; add wine, stock, salt, pepper, thyme or rosemary. Return cooked liver slices to pan. Cook until heated through, 1 to 2 minutes. Do not overcook or liver will be hard and tasteless. Season to taste. Transfer to a warm deep serving dish. Sprinkle with parsley. This quick dish is usually served with dumplings or pasta. Makes 4 to 6 servings.

Liver Dumplings
Leberknödel

Lungs in Sweet & Sour Sauce
Lungenhaschee

1 tablespoon vegetable oil
1 onion, chopped
5 slices stale white bread
1/3 cup milk
About 1 lb. calves' liver or beef liver
2 oz. kidney suet or fresh unsmoked salt-pork fat
2 small eggs, slightly beaten
Salt
Marjoram or parsley

Heat oil in a large skillet. Add onion; sauté until tender. Soak bread in milk. Remove skin or membrane from liver. Put bread, liver and suet or fat through a grinder with a fine disc to make a smooth-textured paste. In a medium bowl, combine liver paste, eggs, salt, marjoram or parsley and sautéed onion. If mixture is too moist, add 2 to 3 tablespoons fine breadcrumbs. Using a spoon, shape mixture into small balls. Bring a large pot of salted water to a boil. Drop liver dumplings into boiling salted water. Cook 10 to 15 minutes. Do not overcrowd pot with dumplings; if necessary, cook in batches. Dumplings may be served as a starter, in soup or as a main dish with sauerkraut, serving 1 large dumpling to each person. Makes 4 to 6 servings.

Note: Liver Dumplings are a specialty of Bavaria, and Munich in particular.

1-3/4 lbs. calves' lungs
Water
1/2 cup vinegar
Salt
1 carrot, chopped
1 celery stalk, chopped
1 leek, chopped
1 onion, chopped
1/4 cup margarine
1/4 cup all-purpose flour
1/2 cup red wine
3 tablespoons vinegar
Sweet red peppers or powdered paprika, if desired
1 tablespoon sugar
2 pickled cucumbers or gherkins, chopped

Wash lungs thoroughly; place in an enamel-lined, cast-iron pan. Cover with water. Add 1/2 cup vinegar, salt, carrot, celery, leek and onion. Boil gently 45 minutes. Remove lungs; allow to cool. Strain and reserve cooking liquid. Thinly slice cooled lungs. In a small saucepan, melt margarine. Add flour, stirring constantly. Cook 1 to 2 minutes. Add wine, 3 tablespoons vinegar, 1 cup strained cooking liquid and red peppers or paprika, if desired. Add salt and sugar. Stir in chopped cucumbers or gherkins and sliced lungs. Season to taste before serving. Serve with dumplings. Makes 4 servings.

Variation

Fry 1 small finely chopped onion in butter or margarine before adding flour.

Poultry & Game

As in most industrialized nations of Western Europe, a great deal of poultry is eaten in Germany. Besides the traditional roast chicken, boiled chicken is also a favorite. And it gives the delicious bonus of wholesome chicken stock which is so important in good homecooking. On special occasions or holidays, German families will often sit down to a mouth-watering chicken fricassee. Well before Christmas, at Martinmas, November 11th, goose appears as the main item in a festive meal. Each German family orders a good goose well in advance of Christmas. First it is baked until the skin is crisp and the meat tender. Then it is carved by the man of the house and served piping hot. Duck and turkey are also very popular.

Venison is usually reserved for important occasions. The numbers of such game as hare, pheasant and partridge have decreased dramatically in recent years. Demand for these sought-after delicacies far exceeds supply.

Nearly all these meats are roasted and then served in or with a highly seasoned sauce containing fresh or sour cream.

Traditional accompaniments to poultry and game are mainly winter vegetables, such as red cabbage, Brussels sprouts and sauerkraut. Jellies or sauces made from apples and cranberries, and potato or flour dumplings are also served.

A red wine is the ideal accompaniment to these delicious dishes.

Chicken Fricassee
Hühnerfrikassee

Chicken Paprika
Paprikahuhn

1 stewing chicken
Cold water
Salt
1 leek
1 celery stalk
1 carrot
1 whole clove
1 bay leaf
1 small onion, cut in half
1 small jar button mushrooms, drained
1/4 to 1/3 cup butter or margarine
1/4 cup all-purpose flour
Pinch of ground nutmeg
1 teaspoon Worcestershire sauce
Dry white wine
1 teaspoon lemon juice
1 small can green peas, drained
1 egg yolk
6 tablespoons whipping cream

Cut chicken into pieces. Place chicken in a deep saucepan; cover with cold water. Add salt, leek, celery, carrot, whole clove, bay leaf and onion. Bring to a boil; reduce heat. Simmer 1 to 2 hours, depending on size and tenderness of chicken. When joints linking thigh portions to main body move easily and seem flexible, chicken will be done. Remove chicken from cooking liquid; cool slightly. Remove skin and fat; cut flesh from bones in large pieces. Strain liquid. Cut mushrooms in thin slices. Sauté in a small amount of butter in a medium skillet. Melt butter or margarine in a large skillet. Stir in flour. Cook, stirring constantly, until light golden brown, about 3 minutes. Add a small amount of hot cooking liquid. Season with salt, nutmeg, Worcestershire sauce, wine and lemon juice. Place chicken pieces, sautéed mushrooms and peas in sauce; warm gently over low heat. When all ingredients are hot, turn off heat. Let stand 3 to 4 minutes. Before serving, blend egg yolk and whipping cream in a small bowl. Stir egg-yolk mixture into sauce to make it smooth and rich. Serve hot with rice. Makes 4 to 6 servings.

1 roasting chicken
Lemon juice
All-purpose flour
4 bacon slices, diced
1 cup chicken stock
1 large red bell pepper, chopped
1 large green bell pepper, chopped
Salt
Paprika
1 tablespoon tomato paste
White wine
1/2 cup dairy sour cream

Cut chicken in 4 to 8 portions. Pat chicken pieces dry with paper towels. Sprinkle chicken with lemon juice; coat with flour. In a medium skillet, sauté bacon lightly. Add chicken pieces; brown slightly. Add stock, red and green peppers, salt and paprika. Cover and cook 20 to 40 minutes, depending on size of chicken pieces. When chicken is tender, stir in tomato paste, wine and sour cream. Heat through. Serve immediately. Makes 4 to 6 servings.

Viennese Fried Chicken
Wiener Backhendl

Bavarian-Style Roast Chicken
Bayerisches Brathuhn

2 (3-lb.) frying chickens
Lemon juice
Salt
Paprika
All-purpose flour
2 eggs
1 tablespoon vegetable oil
3 tablespoons water
Dry breadcrumbs
Butter or margarine
Parsley sprigs
Lemon wedges

Cut chicken in serving pieces. Sprinkle with lemon juice; let stand 15 minutes. Sprinkle with salt and paprika; coat with flour. In a small bowl, beat together eggs, oil and water. Dip chicken pieces in egg mixture until well coated. Coat with breadcrumbs. Shake off any excess breadcrumbs. Let chicken pieces stand 15 to 20 minutes before frying. Melt enough butter or margarine in 1 or 2 large skillets to make 2 inches of fat. Carefully place coated chicken pieces in hot fat. Brown lightly on both sides. Reduce heat and cook gently until tender, about 20 minutes. Remove from skillet with a slotted spoon or kitchen tongs; drain on paper towels. Preheat oven to 350F (175C). Arrange chicken in an open baking pan. Bake 10 to 15 minutes or until breadcrumb coating is very dry and crusty. Arrange chicken on a warm serving dish. Garnish with parsley and lemon wedges. Serve with a green salad and potatoes. Makes 6 to 8 servings.

1 large roasting chicken
Lemon juice
1 leek
1 celery stalk
1 carrot
4 bacon slices, diced
Salt
2 cups chicken stock or water
6 to 12 potatoes, if desired
White wine
3 tablespoons all-purpose flour, if desired
1/2 cup whipping cream or half and half, if desired

Preheat oven to 375F (190C). Pat chicken dry with paper towels; sprinkle with lemon juice. Clean and finely chop leek, celery and carrot. Sauté bacon in a small skillet. In a large casserole dish, place chicken, chopped vegetables and sautéed bacon. Sprinkle chicken with salt. Add half the stock or water. Bake 1 to 1-1/4 hours, basting chicken with stock or water. Add more stock or water as necessary. Slice or dice potatoes, if desired. After about 30 minutes, arrange potatoes around chicken. Cook 30 to 45 minutes or until potatoes and chicken are tender. Before serving, stir in wine. If desired, stir flour into cream or half and half, then into sauce. Cook 3 to 4 minutes or until thickened. Serve hot. Makes 4 to 6 servings.

Stuffed Pigeons
Gefüllte Tauben

Partridges with Red Wine
Geschmorte Rebhüner

4 young plump pigeons
Salt
1/2 lb. lean ground beef
1/2 lb. chopped liver
2 eggs
About 1/2 cup dry breadcrumbs
1/2 cup whipping cream or half and half
Salt and pepper
Basil
4 bacon slices
1/2 cup vegetable oil
2 tablespoons butter
3 tablespoons cognac
About 1 cup chicken stock
1 tablespoon all-purpose flour
1/2 cup half and half
Red wine, if desired

Clean pigeons; pat dry with paper towels. Salt pigeons lightly. In a large bowl, combine ground beef, liver, eggs, breadcrumbs, 1/2 cup whipping cream or half and half, salt, pepper and basil. Stuff pigeons with beef mixture. Truss birds as securely as possible. Wrap bacon around breast of each bird; secure with skewers or wooden picks. Heat oil and butter in a large skillet. Gently fry pigeons in oil and butter until evenly browned. Sprinkle cognac over chicken; allow to evaporate. Add 1 cup stock. Cover and simmer 30 to 40 minutes, adding more stock if necessary. Shortly before serving, place pigeons on a serving dish. Remove and discard bacon. In a small bowl, combine flour and 1/2 cup half and half; stir into cooking liquid to thicken. Cook gently, stirring constantly, 5 minutes. Add a little wine to the sauce, if desired. Serve with creamed potatoes and fresh green vegetables. Makes 4 to 8 servings.

4 partridges
Salt and pepper
8 bacon slices
4 bacon slices, diced
3 tablespoons butter or margarine
1/2 cup red wine
About 1 cup chicken stock
2 to 3 slices white bread, cut in cubes
1/3 cup golden raisins
1 tablespoon cognac
1 tablespoon all-purpose flour
1/2 cup dairy sour cream

Clean partridges; pat dry with paper towels. Season with salt and pepper. Wrap 2 bacon slices around breast of each bird; secure with wooden picks or skewers. In a medium skillet, sauté diced bacon. Add butter or margarine; when foaming, add partridges. Brown partridges on all sides. Add wine and a little stock. Cover and simmer about 15 minutes. Add bread cubes. If necessary, add a little more butter or margarine. In a small bowl, combine raisins and cognac. Strain cooking liquid and juices to make sauce; return to skillet. Add soaked raisins. In a small bowl, combine flour and sour cream. Stir into sauce; cook and stir until thickened. Season to taste. Suitable accompaniments are red cabbage cooked in wine, pineapple or Brussels sprouts and potato dumplings or creamed potatoes. Makes 4 servings.

Variation

If a very flavorful sauce is desired, add a bay leaf, 2 to 3 juniper berries and a few sliced, sautéed mushrooms to the liquid at the beginning of cooking.

Stuffed Turkey
Gefüllte Pute

1 apple, peeled, chopped
1 celery stalk, chopped
3/4 lb. mixed ground beef and pork
1 cup cranberries, coarsely chopped
1/3 cup fresh breadcrumbs
1 cup whipping cream or half and half
1 teaspoon salt
1 (9- to 11-lb.) turkey
Salt
8 to 10 thin bacon slices
About 1 cup chicken or turkey stock
1 leek, chopped
1 celery stalk, chopped
1 carrot, chopped
1 small onion, chopped
1/2 cup half and half

Preheat oven to 425F (220C). In a medium bowl, combine apple, 1 chopped celery stalk, ground meat, cranberries, breadcrumbs, whipping cream or half and half and 1 teaspoon salt. Clean turkey; pat dry with paper towels. Season lightly with salt. Stuff turkey with apple mixture; truss to secure. Cover turkey breast with bacon slices; secure with string or thread. Place stuffed turkey, breast-side up, in a roasting pan. Roast turkey 40 minutes. Baste turkey with stock. After about 1 hour, sprinkle leek, 1 chopped celery stalk, carrot and onion around turkey. Roast turkey about 2 hours longer. About 30 minutes before turkey is done, remove bacon. When skin is golden brown, remove turkey from oven. Let stand 5 to 10 minutes. Cook juices, stock and vegetables over medium heat. Add 1/2 cup half and half. Cook, stirring constantly, until thickened. Carve turkey; arrange on a large platter. Brussels sprouts, red cabbage, creamed potatoes or potato croquettes are typical accompaniments to roast turkey. Makes 8 servings.

Note: Cooking time will depend on size of the turkey. Allow 20 minutes per pound plus 20 minutes.

Pheasant with Sauerkraut
Fasan auf Weinkraut

2 to 3 tablespoons pork fat or lard
1 small onion, chopped
1-1/4 to 1-3/4 lbs. sauerkraut
1 teaspoon juniper berries
1/2 cup dry white wine
1 (2- to 3-lb.) pheasant
Lemon juice
Salt and white pepper
4 bacon slices
1/4 lb. dark-purple grapes or 1/3 to 1/2 cup diced pineapple, if desired
18 oysters

Soak a large clay roaster in cold water 15 minutes. In a large, heavy enamel-lined saucepan, heat fat or lard. Add onion; sauté lightly. Stir in sauerkraut, juniper berries and wine. Drain clay roaster. Transfer sauerkraut mixture to clay roaster. Clean pheasant; pat dry with paper towels. Sprinkle with lemon juice; season with salt and white pepper. Wrap bacon slices around bird, covering breast; secure with wooden picks or metal skewers. Place bacon-wrapped pheasant on top of sauerkraut. Cover and place in a cold oven. Set oven to 425F (220C). Bake 1-1/2 hours or until pheasant is tender. Remove and discard bacon. Season sauerkraut to taste, adding grapes or pineapple, if desired. Arrange sauerkraut on a warm platter. Place pheasant on sauerkraut. If oysters are used, clean thoroughly, dip in egg, then in breadcrumbs. Fry in very hot oil. Serve with creamed potatoes. Makes 3 to 4 servings.

Roast Goose
Gänsebraten

Duck with Cherries
Ente mit Sauerkirschen

1 (8-1/2- to 11-lb.) goose
Salt
1 to 1-1/4 lbs. cooked chestnuts, peeled
4 to 6 small apples, cut in quarters
2/3 cup golden raisins
Several fresh tarragon leaves or 1 teaspoon dried leaf tarragon
3 cups light stock
1 tablespoon cornstarch

Preheat oven to 400F (205C). Clean goose; remove any excess fat. Pat dry with paper towels. Sprinkle generously with salt. Coarsely chop chestnuts. In a medium bowl, combine chopped chestnuts, apples and raisins. Use to stuff goose. Securely truss goose. Scatter tarragon over bird. With a carving fork, prick skin, especially in fatty parts, to let fat escape. Place goose, breast-side down, directly on middle oven shelf. Place a large drip pan directly under goose. Or, place goose on a roasting rack in a large roasting pan. Bake goose 2 to 3 hours, depending on size. Or, roast 3 to 4 hours at 325F (165C). Baste goose frequently with stock and cooking juices from drip pan or roasting pan. Twenty minutes before goose is done, turn breast-side up so skin can brown. Baste with hot salty water to help make a crisp skin. Leave oven door slightly ajar while skin browns. When tender, place goose on a warm platter. Cool 5 to 10 minutes before carving. Strain juices from drip pan. Remove excess fat. Add a little more stock to juices, if necessary. In a small bowl, combine cornstarch and a little cold water or stock; stir into juices. Cook over low heat until thickened, stirring constantly. Serve with potatoes, green vegetables, red cabbage or celery salad. Makes 8 servings.

1 duck
Salt and pepper
4 to 5 apples, cut in quarters
4 to 6 carrots
1 leek
1 celery stalk
1 cup chicken stock or water
1 jar or can red tart cherries
1 tablespoon brandy or schnapps
1 tablespoon kirsch

Preheat oven to 350F (175C). Clean duck; pat dry with paper towels. Season duck with salt and pepper; stuff with apple quarters. Truss duck; then prick all over with a fork or sharp knife. This lets fat escape during roasting. Place carrots, leek, celery and duck in a baking dish or roasting pan. Pour in stock or water. Roast 1-1/2 to 1-3/4 hours. Cooking time will vary according to size of duck. Place foil loosely over bird to keep moist and to reduce amount of grease spattered on oven walls. Baste with a little boiling water from time to time. This also helps keep flesh moist. Cook until juices run clear when duck is pricked with a fork. Transfer duck to a large deep skillet. Strain juices into a small saucepan; skim off fat. Heat cherries in cooking juices. Pour over roast duck. Heat brandy or schnapps and kirsch in a small pan. Pour over duck. Carefully ignite to burn off alcohol. Serve with potato croquettes or creamed potatoes. Makes 4 to 6 servings.

Duck with Orange Sauce
Ente mit Orangen

Quail
Wachteln

1 (4- to 5-lb.) duck
Salt
5 small tart apples
2/3 cup golden raisins
3 to 4 tablespoons sugar
1 tablespoon freshly squeezed orange juice
1 to 2 teaspoons thin orange-peel strips
3 tablespoons white wine
1/4 to 1/3 cup fresh breadcrumbs
2 cups water
3 to 4 tablespoons freshly squeezed orange juice
1 tablespoon cornstarch
2 oranges

Clean duck; pat dry with paper towels. Season with salt. Preheat oven to 350F (175C). Peel and thinly slice apples. In a small saucepan, combine apple slices, raisins, sugar, 1 tablespoon orange juice, orange peel and wine. Bring to a boil. Stir in breadcrumbs. Season with salt; combine well. Stuff duck with hot apple mixture. Truss duck and place in a deep roasting pan or oven dish. Add a little water. Roast 1-1/2 to 1-3/4 hours or until tender. Occasionally baste with a little more boiling water during cooking. Place cooked duck on a warm platter. Remove as much fat as possible from cooking juices. In a small bowl, combine 3 to 4 tablespoons orange juice and cornstarch; stir into cooking juices. Cook, stirring constantly, until thickened. Using a peeler, cut only colored peel from 1 orange. Cut peel into short thin strips. Blanch peel strips in boiling water, 2 minutes. Add blanched peel to sauce. Remove trussing thread. Pour a little sauce over duck. Serve remaining sauce separately. Slice remaining orange into rounds. Garnish duck with orange slices. Serve with dumplings or creamed potatoes. Makes 4 to 6 servings.

4 quail
Salt and pepper
1 cup fresh breadcrumbs
1/2 lb. ground veal
1 egg
1 tablespoon finely chopped onion
1 tablespoon finely chopped parsley
Salt and pepper
Basil
Rosemary
Vegetable oil
4 bacon slices, cooked

Clean quail; pat dry with paper towels. Season quail with salt and pepper. In a medium bowl, soak breadcrumbs in a little cold water; squeeze to remove excess moisture. In medium bowl, combine ground veal, egg, onion, parsley, salt, pepper, basil and rosemary. Add soaked breadcrumbs. Stuff quail with breadcrumb mixture; truss quail. Heat oil in a deep skillet to 350F (175C) or until a 1-inch cube of bread turns golden brown in 65 seconds. Carefully add quail, one at a time, maintaining temperature of oil. Fry 20 minutes. Remove quail; drain well. Place on a warm serving dish. Season with salt. Garnish with cooked bacon slices. Serve with vegetables in season, creamed potatoes and fried onion rings. Makes 4 servings.

Game Goulash
Wildgulasch

Braised Rabbit with Prunes
Hase mit Backpflaumen

1 cup red wine
3 tablespoons wine vinegar
1-1/4 to 1-3/4 lbs. rabbit, wild boar or venison, boned, diced
4 bacon slices, diced
1 onion, finely chopped
Salt and pepper
1 bay leaf
2 mustard seeds
2 juniper berries
About 1 cup meat stock
2 to 4 oz. fresh or canned mushrooms
1 small pkg. frozen green peas
1 tablespoon cornstarch
6 tablespoons half and half

In a medium bowl, combine wine and vinegar. Add game; cover and marinate overnight in refrigerator. Drain well, reserving marinade. Sauté bacon in a large skillet. Add marinated meat pieces; brown evenly on all sides. Add onion before meat has completely browned. Add salt, pepper, bay leaf, mustard seeds and juniper berries. Add reserved marinade and a little stock. Cook meat over low heat 1-1/2 hours or until tender, stirring occasionally. Add remaining stock, if needed. Add mushrooms with juice and peas. Cook 5 to 10 minutes. Before serving, remove bay leaf. In a small bowl, combine cornstarch and half and half. Stir into sauce. Cook over medium heat, stirring constantly, until thickened. Serve with potato dumplings. Makes 4 to 6 servings.

1 lb. pitted prunes
2-1/2 cups Burgundy or other red wine
1 rabbit or hare
2 onions, finely chopped
1 carrot, thinly sliced
1 teaspoon black peppercorns
Thyme
Rosemary
Marjoram
2 bay leaves
Salt
6 bacon slices, diced
1/2 cup half and half, if desired
1 teaspoon cornstarch, if desired

In a small bowl, combine prunes and wine. Cover and let stand overnight. Soak a large clay roaster in cold water 15 minutes. Cut rabbit or hare in serving pieces; pat dry with paper towels. Place onions, carrot, peppercorns, thyme, rosemary, marjoram and bay leaves in soaked clay roaster. Arrange rabbit or hare pieces on top of vegetables. Drain prunes, reserving marinade. Add prunes and half the reserved marinade to roaster. Season with salt. Cover and place in a cold oven. Set oven to 450F (230C). Bake 2 hours or until tender. Add a little marinade if contents become dry. Sauté bacon in a small skillet until crisp. Scatter bacon over cooked rabbit or hare. It is not usually necessary to thicken sauce because it reduces and thickens during cooking. To thicken sauce, if necessary, transfer sauce to a small saucepan. Combine half and half and cornstarch in a small bowl. Add to sauce. Cook over medium heat, stirring constantly, until slightly thickened. Serve with ribbon noodles or small flour dumplings. Makes 4 to 6 servings.

Braised Wild Boar
Wildschweinbraten

Leg of Venison
Rehkeule

1 (1-3/4- to 2-1/4-lb.) wild-boar leg
1 onion, chopped
1 garlic clove, crushed
1 small carrot, chopped
1 celery stalk, chopped
2 cups red wine
6 tablespoons red-wine vinegar
1 bay leaf
4 whole mustard seeds
4 black peppercorns
4 juniper berries
6 to 8 bacon slices, diced
3 tablespoons butter
Salt
1/2 cup meat stock
1 tablespoon cornstarch
1/2 cup half and half
Mushrooms, if desired

Clean meat thoroughly; place in a large earthenware dish or pot. Add onion, garlic clove, carrot and celery. In a small bowl, combine wine, vinegar, bay leaf, mustard seeds, peppercorns and juniper berries. Pour mixture over meat and vegetables. Cover and refrigerate 1 to 3 days, turning occasionally. Drain off and reserve marinade. Sauté bacon in a large heavy saucepan. Add butter and drained meat. Salt lightly. Brown meat well on all sides, then add stock and some marinade. Cover and cook over medium-low heat 1-1/2 to 2-1/2 hours or until tender. Turn at intervals during cooking and add marinade, if necessary. Cool 10 minutes before carving. Strain cooking liquid into a saucepan. In a small bowl, combine cornstarch and half and half; stir into cooking liquid. Cook over medium heat, stirring constantly, until thickened. Season to taste. Sauce will be greatly enhanced with addition of a few mushrooms. Before adding to sauce, sauté mushrooms in butter. Serve sauce separately. Makes 4 to 6 servings.

1 (2-1/4-lb.) leg of venison
Salt and pepper
4 juniper berries, crushed
Thyme
Marjoram
1/4 cup butter
2 tablespoons finely chopped onion
1 cup red wine
3 tablespoons red-wine vinegar
1 tablespoon black-currant juice or red-currant jelly
1 cup dairy sour cream
Mushrooms, if desired

Clean venison; pat dry with paper towels. Season with salt and pepper. Rub juniper berries, thyme and marjoram vigorously into venison. Melt butter in a large heavy saucepan. Add venison; brown evenly on all sides. Add onion before meat has completely browned. Add wine, vinegar and, if needed, a small amount of hot water. Cover and simmer 1-1/2 hours or until tender, basting at frequent intervals. Remove venison from pan; keep warm. Strain cooking liquid into a saucepan. To remove deposits on bottom of pan in which venison has cooked, pour in some boiling water. Scrape up caramelized juices with a wooden spoon. Add this liquid to juices in saucepan. Cook 3 to 4 minutes. Add juice or jelly. Remove from heat and stir in sour cream. If desired, sauté mushrooms separately in butter, then add to sauce. Serve with potato croquettes, ribbon noodles, red cabbage, Brussels sprouts, chestnuts or cranberries. Makes 4 to 6 servings.

Ragout of Venison
Rehragout

Venison Cutlets with Mushrooms
Rehschnitzel mit Pfifferlingen

1-3/4 lbs. venison shoulder, neck or breast
Water
1 onion, cut in quarters
Few black peppercorns
Few mustard seeds
Several juniper berries
1 bay leaf
Salt
4 bacon slices, diced
1 small onion, chopped
1/3 cup all-purpose flour
Red wine
1/2 cup dairy sour cream
Chopped parsley

Place venison in a large heavy cooking pot; cover with water. Add quartered onion, peppercorns, mustard seeds, juniper berries, bay leaf and a little salt. Bring to a boil; reduce heat and simmer 1 to 1-1/2 hours, depending on tenderness of meat. Let cool in cooking liquid. Remove cooled meat. Strain and reserve cooking liquid. Remove thin membrane or skin from venison. Cut meat into thin slices or small cubes. To prepare sauce, sauté bacon in a large saucepan. Add chopped onion; sauté until transparent. Add flour; cook, stirring constantly, until a light golden color. Slowly stir in hot cooking liquid. Bring to a boil; reduce heat and simmer until thickened. Stir in venison pieces. Add wine. Season to taste with salt. Spoon sour cream over top before serving and sprinkle with parsley. Makes 4 to 6 servings.

Variation

Add a little thyme and 1/2 cup sautéed mushrooms to sauce for additional flavor.

8 venison cutlets or chops
Vegetable oil
1/2 cup red wine
4 bacon slices, diced
About 3 tablespoons all-purpose flour
1 large onion, finely chopped
1/2 lb. mushrooms, sliced
1/2 cup half and half
Thyme
Juniper berries, crushed
Salt and pepper

Pound venison lightly with a meat mallet. Brush with oil on both sides. Arrange venison in a shallow baking dish. Pour wine over venison. Cover and refrigerate overnight. Sauté bacon in a large skillet until fat is translucent. Remove bacon; keep warm. Drain venison, reserving marinade. Coat venison with flour; fry briskly over high heat in bacon fat, turning once during cooking. Add extra oil, if needed. Turn once during cooking. Do not overcook or meat will become hard and dry. Remove from skillet; set aside on a warm plate. Sauté onion in remaining fat and cooking juices in pan until pale golden brown. Add mushrooms, half and half, thyme, juniper berries and a little reserved marinade. Simmer sauce 4 to 5 minutes. Season to taste with salt and pepper. Return venison to sauce. Heat through. Garnish with bacon. Serve with potato croquettes or boiled or creamed potatoes, potato dumplings and red cabbage or Brussels sprouts and cranberries. Makes 6 to 8 servings.

Venison Liver
Geschmorte Rehleber

Goose-Liver Pie
Gänseleberpastete

1-1/2 lbs. venison liver
1/2 cup red wine
All-purpose flour
8 bacon slices
1 small jar mushrooms, drained
Thyme
2 crushed juniper berries
Salt and pepper
6 tablespoons half and half

Remove thin skin or membrane from liver; pat dry with paper towels. Place liver in a bowl. Cover with wine. Let stand 30 minutes. Drain liver, reserving marinade. Coat liver lightly with flour. Fry bacon slices in a large skillet until nearly crisp; remove and set aside. Sauté liver briskly on both sides over high heat; remove and set aside, keeping warm. Sauté mushrooms, thyme and juniper berries in fat and juices in pan. Add a little marinade; season with salt and pepper. Simmer a few minutes. Stir in half and half. Salt liver lightly, then heat in sauce a few minutes. Place liver on a warm platter. Pour sauce and mushrooms over liver. Garnish with bacon slices. Makes 4 to 6 servings.

Variation

Substitute calves' liver for venison liver.

1-1/2 pkgs. frozen patty shells (9 shells), thawed
1/2 lb. goose fat
1/2 lb. lean veal
1/2 lb. goose liver
1 goose heart
1 small onion
1 egg
Salt and pepper
Marjoram
Few chopped tarragon leaves
5 tablespoons port or cherry brandy
1 bay leaf
1 egg, separated
Water
1/2 (1/4-oz.) pkg. unflavored gelatin
1/2 cup meat stock
3 tablespoons sherry
Orange segments, apple pieces or Cumberland Sauce, page 95

Preheat oven to 400F (205C). On a lightly floured surface, arrange 6 patty shells, slightly overlapping, in 2 rows of 3 shells. Roll shells out to about 1/4 inch thick. Line a 9'' x 5'' loaf pan with pastry. Roll remaining 3 patty shells for top crust. Finely chop goose fat, veal, liver, heart and onion. Place in a medium bowl. Stir in egg, salt, pepper, marjoram, tarragon and port or brandy. Turn into lined pan, gently pressing down filling to avoid air bubbles. Place bay leaf on top. Cover with top crust, moistening edges of bottom crust with egg white and pressing or pinching firmly to seal. Cut a few holes, about 1/2 inch in diameter, in top crust. From remaining pastry, cut out leaves to garnish top. Brush surface with egg yolk beaten with a small amount of water. Bake 60 to 70 minutes. Soften gelatin in a little cold water. Heat stock until hot, not boiling. Stir in gelatin mixture and a little sherry. Refrigerate 30 to 40 minutes until gelatin begins to set. Carefully pour gelatin mixture into pie through small holes made in crust. Allow pie to cool. When cold, cut into slices about 1/2 inch thick. Garnish with orange segments or apple pieces. Or, serve with Cumberland Sauce. Makes 6 to 8 servings.

Fish & Seafood

Germany has a limited stretch of coastline and a limited number of freshwater fish in her lakes and rivers. As a result of over-fishing the world's coastal seas, fishing fleets have to sail farther and farther from Germany to make good catches. These catches must be transported over long distances. This means German people, except in the north, do not eat a great deal of fresh fish. Deep-sea fishing, as an industry, relies on deep-freezing the catch on board ship.

Connoisseurs of good fish still seek the delicacies of Germany's inland lakes and rivers. Inland you'll find rainbow trout, salmon from Bavaria's lakes, whitefish or pollan—a member of the salmon family found in the Bodensee. And, there's catfish caught in the Danube and superb pike and carp.

Baked fish is the most popular fish dish in Germany. Filleted fish is also popular. It is usually coated with egg and breadcrumbs, then sautéed in butter until golden brown. In recent years, fish sticks and fish cakes have become increasingly popular. They are made from deep-frozen, cleaned and filleted fish. They have great appeal for busy mothers and the elderly because they are quick and easy to prepare.

Any visitor to Germany will be struck by the great variety in methods of preparing herring. There are *Matjes,* small, young white herring served with thin onion rings; fried herring; rollmop herring; Bismarck herring and smoked herring. Each method of treatment imparts a characteristic and appetizing flavor. Herring, eaten as a light meal with black bread and good beer, is irresistible. The fish can be successfully canned without the flavor suffering.

Court Bouillon

Fish trimmings, if desired
1 carrot, coarsely chopped
1 leek, coarsely chopped
1 celery stalk, coarsely chopped
1 onion, cut in quarters
3 mustard seeds
3 black peppercorns

3 juniper berries
1 whole clove
1 bay leaf
1/2 lemon
Salt
1/2 cup white wine

In a large pot, combine all ingredients. Add water to cover, using at least 1 quart. Bring to a boil; skim foam from surface until surface is clear. Reduce heat and simmer, uncovered, 15 to 20 minutes. Strain well. Use in soups and sauces as directed.

Smoked Trout
Geräucherte Forellen

Fish Salad
Fischsalat

4 smoked trout
Lemon

Carefully remove backbone and skin from fish. Do not remove skin too long before serving or fish will become dry. Serve with crusty white bread and white wine or champagne. Let each guest squeeze lemon juice over fish, if desired. Also serve Frankfurt Green-Herb Sauce and Horseradish Cream, page 94. Makes 4 servings.

Note: Smoked trout make a delicious starter and are quick to prepare. Buy moist smoked trout; they are all too often dry and therefore much less appetizing. Trout acquires an exquisite flavor when smoked over juniper wood in the gentle heat of the smoke alone. There is no flame since the wood is sprinkled with water to give off plenty of smoke. Trout are strung up about 8 inches above the smoking wood. Then covered with a metal hood or inverted pail which prevents the smoke from dispersing too quickly. After about 30 minutes of smoking, the fish are allowed to cool slowly. Only freshly caught trout should be used for smoking.

1 large or 2 small oranges
1/2 jar sliced pimientos
2 to 3 pickled cucumbers or gherkins
3/4 lb. cooked filleted fish
3 tablespoons cooked green peas, if desired
1/2 cup whipping cream, whipped
3 tablespoons lemon juice
3 tablespoons finely chopped fresh dill
Salt and white pepper

Peel oranges; remove all pith. Cut each orange into halves; thinly slice. Drain pimientos; slice more finely, if necessary. Cut pickled cucumbers or gherkins into thin slices. Cut fish into large pieces. In a large bowl, combine fish pieces, orange slices, pimientos, cucumbers or gherkins and peas, if desired. In a small bowl, combine whipped cream, lemon juice, dill, salt and white pepper. Fold cream mixture into fish mixture or, mound on top ready to stir in. Refrigerate until ready to serve. Before serving, toss or stir salad to combine well. Makes 4 to 5 servings.

Variation

If fish is uncooked, sprinkle a fresh fillet of firm whitefish with white-wine vinegar and seasoned salt. Wrap in a piece of oiled foil; seal well. Place in a large skillet with about 1-inch of water. Cover and cook gently 15 minutes. When tender but firm, remove fish. Cool slightly. Cut into large pieces.

Note: This is an excellent way to use leftover fish.

Pickled Herring
Heringe Hausfrauenart

Herring Fillets with Green Beans
Matjes mit grünen Bohnen

4 salted herring or 8 small salted herring fillets
1 cup water
1 tablespoon sugar
1 tablespoon white-wine vinegar
1 small bay leaf
1 teaspoon black peppercorns
1 teaspoon mustard seeds
1 crisp apple, peeled, chopped
1 mild onion, cut in rings
1 pickled cucumber or 1 to 2 gherkins, sliced
1-1/2 cups dairy sour cream or 1 cup dairy sour cream and 6 tablespoons
    ricotta cheese
1/3 cup plain yogurt

Clean herring; remove heads. In an enamel or earthenware dish, cover herring with cold water. Refrigerate 24 to 48 hours. Change water several times during soaking. With a sharp pointed knife, slit herring along backbone. Remove backbone and as many small bones as possible. Remove skin, if possible. If fillets are used, soak 1 to 2 hours in cold water. Leave as whole fillets or cut in pieces. Poach herring gently in 1 cup water with sugar, vinegar, bay leaf, peppercorns and mustard seeds. Let stand in liquid 4 to 6 hours to cool. Drain herring. Place herring pieces on a plate or in a glazed earthenware dish. Garnish with apple pieces, onion rings and pickle or gherkin slices. In a small bowl, combine sour cream or sour cream and cheese with yogurt; pour mixture over salad. Serve cold with new potatoes boiled in their skins and butter. Makes 4 to 6 servings.

Note: This used to be a very popular "poor man's dish" widely eaten in Northern Germany. Now it is served as a specialty in the finest restaurants.

8 salted herring fillets
2 onions, diced
1-3/4 lbs. fresh green beans
Salt
Fresh savory
2 tablespoons butter

Soak herring in cold water in refrigerator 24 hours. Change water several times during soaking. Place ice cubes in a dish. Drain herring fillets. Arrange fillets on ice. Scatter onion over fillets; cover and refrigerate. Clean green beans. Bring a medium saucepan of salted water to a boil. Add green beans and a sprig of savory. Cook beans until tender but crisp. Drain beans; season with butter. Serve hot beans as an accompaniment to cold herring. May also be served with new potatoes and butter, Horseradish Cream, page 94, or Brown Sauce with Bacon, page 98. Makes 4 to 6 servings.

Fish Soup
Fischsuppe

Breaded Fish Fillets
Paniertes Fischfilet

4 bacon slices, diced
1 onion, chopped
1 qt. Court Bouillon, page 64
1 large pkg. frozen mixed vegetables or 1/4 lb. green peas, 1/4 lb. green beans and 1/4 lb. carrots, diced
1 piece cauliflower, coarsely chopped
1 turnip, coarsely chopped
1/2 lb. broad beans, if desired
1/2 lb. frozen fish fillets
Juice of 1/2 a lemon
Salt
A little white wine
Chopped parsley

Sauté bacon in a medium skillet. Add onion; sauté until translucent. Add Court Bouillon. If frozen vegetables are used, add to liquid when fish is added. If using fresh vegetables, add at this time; cook 10 minutes. Cut fish into medium pieces. Add to Court Bouillon; simmer 10 minutes longer. Avoid overcooking. Season to taste with lemon juice, salt, white wine and parsley. Serve with a garlic sauce prepared by mixing equal quantities of homemade mayonnaise and breadcrumbs with a little lemon juice and 1 crushed garlic clove. Makes 6 to 8 servings.

Note: German soup recipes call for a wide variety of vegetables. If pressed for time, use frozen vegetables.

1-3/4 lbs. whitefish fillets
White-wine vinegar
Salt
All-purpose flour
1 large egg, slightly beaten
1 teaspoon vegetable oil
1 tablespoon water
3 tablespoons finely grated Parmesan or Romano cheese
Fine dry breadcrumbs
Vegetable oil
1 lemon, cut in wedges
Parsley

Pat fish fillets dry with paper towels. Sprinkle with vinegar and salt. Dredge fillets with flour. In a shallow bowl, combine egg, oil and water. In another shallow bowl, combine cheese and breadcrumbs. Dip fillets in egg mixture, then in cheese mixture. Shake gently to remove loose breadcrumbs. Pour oil 1 to 1-1/2 inches deep in a large skillet; heat oil. Fry fillets in hot oil until golden brown. Keep oil hot and at an even temperature for all fish fillets. Drain fried fish on paper towels; transfer to a warm platter. Garnish with lemon wedges and parsley sprigs. Serve with Potato Salad, page 117, lettuce or mixed green salad and Sauce Rémoulade, page 96. Makes 4 to 6 servings.

Fish Cakes
Gebratene Fischklopse

1-3/4 to 2-1/4 lbs. fish fillets
3 tablespoons lemon juice
2 egg whites
Salt and white pepper
All-purpose flour
1 egg, slightly beaten
Dry breadcrumbs
Butter or vegetable oil
Lemon wedges

Remove as many bones as possible from fish. Mince or finely grind fish in a food processor or blender. Add lemon juice, egg whites, salt and white pepper. Shape fish mixture into small cakes. Or, work mixture into a long sausage shape; slice into rounds. Dredge fish cakes in flour. Dip in beaten egg; coat with breadcrumbs. In a large skillet, heat butter or oil until very hot. Fry fish cakes over high heat until golden brown on both sides. Serve with potato salad, cucumber or a mixed green salad. Garnish with lemon wedges. Makes 4 to 6 servings.

Note: In Germany, frozen fish balls and fish cakes are readily available in the marketplace. However, homemade ones are usually tastier, contain more fish and are quick to prepare.

Fish Fried in Batter
Fisch in Ausbackteig

1-3/4 to 2 lbs. fish fillets
White-wine vinegar
Salt
1-1/4 cups all-purpose flour
2 eggs
1 tablespoon vegetable oil
1 cup brown ale, dark-brown beer or soda water
Vegetable oil for deep-frying
4 lemon slices

Pat fish fillets dry with paper towels. Sprinkle with vinegar and salt. In a small bowl, combine flour, eggs, 1 tablespoon oil, beer or soda water and salt. Beat until batter is smooth and has the consistency of lightly whipped cream. Heat oil in a deep-fryer or deep heavy saucepan to 375F (190C) or until a 1-inch cube of bread turns golden brown in 50 seconds. Dip fish fillets in batter. Fry 2 to 3 fillets in hot oil until crisp and golden. Drain on paper towels. Repeat until all fillets are fried. Arrange cooked fillets on a warm platter. Garnish with lemon wedges. Serve with potato salad, French-fried potatoes or sautéed potatoes and Sauce Rémoulade, page 96. Makes 4 to 6 servings.

Note: Use freshwater or ocean fish or a variety of fish.

Fried Flounder
Gebratene Schollen

Meunière-Style Sole
Seezunge Müllerin Art

4 flounder fillets
White-wine vinegar
Salt
All-purpose flour
1 egg
1 teaspoon vegetable oil
1 tablespoon water
Dry breadcrumbs
Butter
4 lemon wedges
Finely chopped parsley or 8 bacon slices, cooked crisp, crumbled
Dill

Pat fillets dry with paper towels. Sprinkle with vinegar and salt. Dredge fillets with flour; shake off excess. In a small bowl, beat together egg, oil and water. Dip fillets in egg mixture, then in breadcrumbs. In a large skillet, melt a generous amount of butter. Fry fillets in hot butter, over medium-high heat, until golden brown on both sides. If butter is not hot enough, fillets will stick to the pan. Drain on paper towels. Place on a warm platter. Garnish with lemon wedges, parsley or bacon, and dill. Makes 4 servings.

Variation

If fillets are too large to fry easily, place them on buttered foil. Bake in a 400F (205C) oven 25 to 30 minutes. Turn halfway through cooking time.

4 sole fillets
White-wine vinegar
Salt
All-purpose flour
Vegetable oil
2 to 3 tablespoons butter
1/3 cup lemon juice
1/3 cup finely chopped parsley
1/2 lemon, cut in quarters
Lemon balm sprig

Remove skin from sole, if not already done. Pat fillets dry with paper towels. Sprinkle with vinegar and salt. Dredge fillets with flour; shake off excess. Heat oil in a large skillet. Fry fish until golden brown, turning once. Drain on paper towels; keep warm. Pour off oil from pan; wipe clean with paper towels. Combine butter, lemon juice and parsley in skillet. Cook over low heat. Pour butter sauce over sole. Garnish with lemon pieces and lemon balm. Makes 4 servings.

Trout with Almonds
Mandelforellen

Trout en Papillotes
Kräuterforellen in Folie

4 fresh trout
White-wine vinegar
Salt
All-purpose flour
Butter
1/3 cup sliced almonds
1/2 lemon, sliced
Parsley

Clean trout; pat dry with paper towels. Sprinkle inside and out with vinegar and salt. Dredge fish with flour. Heat butter in a large skillet until foaming. Fry fish in hot butter until browned lightly on both sides. Reduce heat; fry gently until cooked through. Drain on paper towels. Discard cooking butter; wipe skillet clean with paper towels. Add fresh butter to pan; heat gently. Add almonds; sauté until lightly browned. Garnish trout with browned almonds, lemon and parsley. Makes 4 servings.

4 fresh trout
1/2 cup white-wine vinegar
Salt
Chopped fresh parsley
Chopped fresh dill
White wine

Butter 4 large pieces of foil; set aside. Clean trout, place in a shallow baking dish. Heat vinegar to boiling; pour over trout. Let stand, uncovered, 10 minutes. Preheat oven to 400F (205C). Drain fish. Lightly salt inside of trout. Place each trout on a buttered sheet of foil. Fill trout with parsley and dill. Sprinkle fish with white wine. Fold foil around each fish, making airtight packets. Place foil packets on middle shelf of oven, leaving 1 inch or more space between packets. Place a drip pan below fish to catch any juices. Bake trout 15 to 20 minutes. To serve, cut through foil crosswise on top of each packet; turn back foil a little. Let guests unwrap their own fish at table. Serve with fresh boiled potatoes, lemon slices and Horseradish Cream, page 94, or melted butter. Makes 4 servings.

Eel in Dill Sauce
Aal in grüner Sosse

Carp au Bleu
Karpfen blau

1-3/4 to 2-1/4 lbs. eel
Salt
1/2 cup white-wine vinegar
1 qt. Court Bouillon, page 64
3 tablespoons margarine
1/4 cup all-purpose flour
1/2 cup half and half
A little white wine
Pinch of ground nutmeg
Pinch of white pepper
Pinch of sugar
1 teaspoon lemon juice
4 to 6 tablespoons finely chopped dill
3 tablespoons finely chopped parsley, if desired
Lemon slices

Remove skin from eel, if desired, by making an incision 2 inches below the head. Slit skin all around; then peel off like a glove, working from head to tail. Clean and cut eel in 2-inch pieces. Rub eel pieces with salt. Heat vinegar; sprinkle over eel. In a large saucepan, combine eel pieces, Court Bouillon and a little vinegar. Gently poach eel 20 to 30 minutes, depending on size of pieces. Melt margarine in a large heavy skillet. Stir in flour. Add 1-1/2 cups hot Court Bouillon from saucepan, half and half, white wine, nutmeg, white pepper, sugar, lemon juice and salt. Immediately before serving, sprinkle with dill and parsley, if desired. Place eel in sauce. Let stand 5 minutes. Serve directly from cooking dish or on a warm platter. Garnish with lemon slices. Sauce can also be served separately. Makes 4 to 6 servings.

1 (2-1/4- to 3-lb.) carp
White-wine vinegar
1 qt. Court Bouillon, page 64
Lemon slices
Parsley sprigs

Carp can be cooked in the oven or over direct heat. Clean carp; pat dry with paper towels. Sprinkle carp with vinegar; let stand 4 to 5 minutes.

To cook carp over direct heat, in a large saucepan, gently poach carp in Court Bouillon 25 to 40 minutes. Carp is cooked when eyes bulge and fins can be detached easily. Transfer carefully to a warm platter.

To bake carp, preheat oven to 400F (205C). Use a buttered baking dish to help carp keep its color. Prop fish up by placing 2 boiled potatoes or an over-turned eggcup inside its belly. Pour 1/2 cup Court Bouillon over carp; cover dish with foil. Tie foil tightly around baking dish. Bake 30 to 45 minutes. Before serving, draw off excess cooking liquid with a bulb-baster or paper towels. Wipe sides of dish. Garnish with lemon slices and parsley. Serve with a medley of cooked vegetables. Makes 4 to 6 servings.

Trout au Bleu
Forelle blau

Poached Fish
Kochfisch

4 fresh trout
1/2 cup white-wine vinegar
1 qt. Court Bouillon, page 64, made with allspice berries rather than juniper berries
Parsley
1/2 lemon

Clean trout. Handle as little as possible. Place in a shallow bowl. Bring vinegar to a boil; pour over trout. Let stand 4 to 5 minutes. If placed in a draft, the attractive blue color produced by the vinegar on the fresh fish will be particularly pronounced. In a large saucepan or kettle, bring Court Bouillon nearly to a boil. Reduce heat and lower trout into hot liquid. Gently poach trout 12 to 15 minutes, depending on size. Trout is cooked when dorsal or center-back fin pulls off easily. Remove from Court Bouillon; place on a warm platter. Garnish with parsley and lemon. Serve with boiled potatoes; melted butter, Horseradish Cream or Frankfurt Green-Herb Sauce, page 94; and a fresh green or cucumber salad. Makes 4 servings.

2-1/4 lbs. whiting, cod, catfish, pike or perch
White-wine vinegar
1 qt. Court Bouillon, page 64, made with 1/2 teaspoon ground allspice rather than juniper berries
Parsley
Lemon slices

Clean fish; pat dry with paper towels. Sprinkle with vinegar; let stand a few minutes. Drain fish. Place fish in a large saucepan. Add Court Bouillon. Simmer gently 25 minutes or until fins pull out easily and eyes bulge from their sockets. Remove fish carefully from cooking liquid. Drain and place on a warm platter. Garnish with parsley and lemon slices. Serve with tomatoes and cold Mustard & Egg Sauce, page 96, Horseradish Cream, page 94, or melted butter. Makes 4 to 6 servings.

Fricassee of Fish
Fischfrikassee

Poached Cod in Mustard Sauce
Kabeljau in Senfsosse

1-3/4 lbs. sole, haddock or cod fillets
White-wine vinegar
1 qt. Court Bouillon, page 64
3 tablespoons margarine
1 small onion or shallot, finely chopped
1/4 cup all-purpose flour
1/2 cup half and half
3 tablespoons white wine
1 tablespoon capers
Pinch of sugar
1 tablespoon lemon juice
Salt
Few mushrooms, sliced
Small can asparagus tips
Dill, if desired
1/4 lb. scampi, prawns or shrimp

Pat fillets dry with paper towels; sprinkle with vinegar. Place fillets in a large saucepan. Add Court Bouillon. Gently poach fillets 10 minutes. Set fish aside; strain liquid. Melt margarine in a large heavy saucepan or baking dish. Add onion or shallot; sauté until lightly browned. Stir in flour until smooth. Add half and half, wine and 2 cups strained poaching liquid. Cook 5 minutes, stirring constantly. Add capers, sugar, lemon juice and salt to taste. Add mushrooms and asparagus tips. Cut fish into large pieces. Carefully place in sauce without breaking. Spoon sauce over fish. Garnish with finely chopped or minced dill and scampi, prawns or shrimp. This dish is generally served with rice or boiled potatoes and cucumber salad. Makes 4 to 6 servings.

1-3/4 lbs. cod fillets
White-wine vinegar
1 qt. Court Bouillon, page 64
3 tablespoons margarine
1/4 cup all-purpose flour
1 tablespoon white wine
1/4 cup half and half
2 to 3 tablespoons mild prepared mustard
Salt
Pinch of sugar
1 pickled cucumber or gherkin, if desired, finely chopped
1 egg yolk, if desired
Half and half, if desired

Pat fillets dry with paper towels; sprinkle with vinegar. Place fillets in a large saucepan. Add Court Bouillon. Gently poach fillets 10 minutes. Remove fillets; strain cooking liquid. Melt margarine in a small saucepan. Stir in flour; do not brown. Add wine, 1/4 cup half and half and about 3/4 cup strained liquid. Cook sauce 5 minutes, stirring constantly. Season with mustard, salt, sugar and pickled cucumber or gherkin, if desired. For a smoother, richer sauce, combine egg yolk with a little half and half. Stir into sauce. Do not let sauce boil or it will curdle. Arrange poached fish fillets on a warm platter. Top with hot sauce. Serve with French-cut green beans, rice or new potatoes and a green salad. Makes 4 to 6 servings.

Cod in Dill Sauce
Kabeljau in Dillsosse

Sole-Fillet Roll-Ups in White Wine
Seezungenröllchen in Weissweinsosse

1-3/4 lbs. fresh or frozen cod fillets
White-wine vinegar
1 qt. Court Bouillon, page 64
3 tablespoons margarine
1/4 cup all-purpose flour
White wine
1/2 cup half and half
Few drops lemon juice
Salt
3 tablespoons finely chopped fresh dill

Thaw frozen fillets. Pat fillets dry with paper towels; sprinkle with vinegar. Place fillets in a large saucepan. Add Court Bouillon. Gently poach fillets 15 to 20 minutes. Remove fillets; keep warm. Strain cooking liquid. Melt margarine in a small saucepan. Stir in flour. Blend a little wine with enough strained cooking liquid to make 2 cups. Stir liquid mixture into flour mixture. Cook 5 minutes, stirring constantly. Add half and half. Season with lemon juice and salt. Before serving, stir in dill. Serve cod on a warm platter. Cover with sauce. Serve with boiled potatoes and a mixed salad of cooked green beans and cucumber. Makes 4 to 6 servings.

Note: Cod steaks can be used for this recipe, however, fillets are more suitable.

2 pkgs. frozen sole fillets or 10 fresh sole fillets
White-wine vinegar
1 egg white
Salt
3 tablespoons finely chopped parsley
2 tablespoons butter
3 tablespoons all-purpose flour
1/2 cup Court Bouillon, page 64
1/2 cup whipping cream or half and half
White wine
Lemon juice

Thaw frozen fillets. Butter a shallow medium baking dish; set aside. Select 8 best fillets. Pat fillets dry with paper towels; sprinkle with vinegar. Finely chop remaining fillets. In a medium bowl, combine chopped fillets, egg white, salt and parsley. Spread this mixture over 8 reserved fillets. Carefully roll up fillets; secure with wooden picks or skewers. Arrange rolled fillets in buttered baking dish. Preheat oven to 400F (205C). Melt butter in a small saucepan. Stir in flour. Stir in Court Bouillon and whipping cream or half and half. Stirring constantly, cook 2 to 3 minutes. Season with white wine, salt and lemon juice. Pour sauce over rolled fillets. Bake 15 minutes or until tender. Carefully remove skewers before serving. Serve with rice and peas or a green salad. Makes 4 to 6 servings.

Larded Pike
Gespickter Hecht

Fish with Mixed Vegetables
Fisch auf Gemüsebett

1 (2-1/2- to 3-lb.) fresh pike
White-wine vinegar
Salt
1 red bell pepper
1 green bell pepper
10 bacon slices, cut in 1/4-inch strips
Vegetable oil
4 tomatoes, if desired
Pepper
1/2 cup white wine
Parsley
Lemon slices

Oil a large shallow casserole dish; set aside. Clean fish; pat dry with paper towels. Sprinkle with vinegar and salt. Using a larding needle, thread strips of red and green pepper and bacon through pike flesh, one at a time, directly under surface. Or, place bacon on both sides of fish. However, this will not be quite as successful as the larding process. Place fish in oiled dish. If tomatoes are used, season with salt and pepper. Arrange in dish with pike. Moisten with white wine. Place casserole in a cold oven. Set oven to 400F (205C). Bake fish 30 to 50 minutes. When fish is tender, remove from oven. Garnish with parsley and lemon slices. Serve immediately with boiled potatoes and plenty of butter. Makes 6 to 8 servings.

Variation

For more flavor, sprinkle 3 tablespoons grated Emmentaler and Parmesan cheese evenly over fish as it comes out of the oven.

Leeks
3 to 4 carrots
1 bunch celery
1/2 lb. Brussels sprouts
2 to 3 tablespoons butter
Water
Salt
2-1/4 lbs. whole fish or fish steaks
White-wine vinegar
1 qt. Court Bouillon, page 64
1/2 lemon, cut in wedges or slices
Finely chopped dill or parsley

Clean and trim vegetables. Cut leeks into large pieces. Dice or thinly slice carrots and celery. Make a crisscross incision in base of each Brussels sprout. In a large, shallow skillet with a tight-fitting lid, cook or steam vegetables slowly with butter and a little water and salt. Clean fish; pat dry with paper towels. Sprinkle with vinegar and salt. Place fish in a large saucepan. Add Court Bouillon. Gently poach fish steaks 12 minutes and whole fish about 30 minutes. Fish is cooked when dorsal or center-back fin pulls off easily. Remove carefully from saucepan. Place on a warm platter with cooked or steamed vegetables. Garnish with lemon. Sprinkle dill or parsley over fish. Serve immediately. Makes 6 to 8 servings.

Baked Fish & Tomatoes au Gratin
Gratinierter Tomatenfisch

Fish Cooked on a Spit
Steckerlfische

8 tomatoes
Salt
4 fish fillets (1-3/4 lbs.)
White-wine vinegar
1/3 cup tomato paste
1/3 cup dry white wine
1/3 cup finely chopped onion
3 tablespoons finely chopped parsley
1/3 cup dry breadcrumbs
1/3 cup grated Emmentaler cheese (1-1/2 oz.)
2 tablespoons butter

Preheat oven to 400F (205C). Butter a large shallow baking dish. Slice tomatoes; sprinkle with salt. Pat fish fillets dry with paper towels; sprinkle with vinegar and salt. Arrange tomato slices and fish fillets alternately in buttered baking dish. In a small bowl, combine tomato paste, wine, onion and parsley. Season to taste with salt. Pour mixture over fish and tomatoes. Top with breadcrumbs and grated cheese. Dot surface with butter. Bake 25 minutes or until tender. Serve while hot. Makes 4 to 6 servings.

4 whole fresh fish, such as mackerel, herring, or freshwater whitefish
White-wine vinegar
Salt
Vegetable oil

Preheat barbecue grill. Rinse and remove scales from fish; do not open and clean. Pat fish dry with paper towels. Sprinkle with vinegar; let stand 5 to 10 minutes. Sprinkle with salt and oil. Thread fish onto skewers, inserting through mouth. Cook over a barbecue grill. Cook fish slowly but not too close to fire. Turn frequently, basting with oil, until tender. Makes 3 to 4 servings.

Broiled or Grilled Salmon
Gegrillter Lachs

Broiled or Grilled Halibut
Gegrillter Heilbutt

4 (1-inch-thick) fresh salmon steaks
Lemon juice
Salt
Vegetable oil
Watercress or dill sprigs
3 to 4 tablespoons Herb Butter, opposite
1 lemon, cut in wedges

If using a broiler, lightly oil a large piece of foil. If using a barbecue grill, oil rungs of grill. Preheat broiler or grill. Sprinkle salmon with lemon juice and salt. Place salmon on oiled foil or grill; sprinkle salmon lightly with oil. Broil or grill briskly, about 6 minutes on each side. Transfer carefully to a warm platter. Garnish with sprigs of watercress or dill, chilled Herb Butter and lemon wedges. Makes 4 servings.

4 fresh or frozen halibut slices (1-3/4 lbs.)
Lemon juice or white-wine vinegar
1 teaspoon Worcestershire sauce
Salt
All-purpose flour
Vegetable oil
1 lemon, cut in wedges
Parsley
Herb Butter, below

Thaw frozen halibut. If using a broiler, lightly oil a large piece of foil. If using a barbecue grill, oil rungs of grill. Preheat broiler or grill. Pat fish dry with paper towels. Sprinkle halibut with lemon juice or vinegar. Season with Worcestershire sauce and salt. Dredge halibut with flour; sprinkle lightly with oil. Place prepared halibut slices on oiled sheet of foil or on grill. Grill or broiler should be very hot to seal in juices and prevent halibut from becoming watery. Broil or grill fish 5 minutes on each side, turning fish carefully. Serve on a warm platter. Garnish with lemon wedges, parsley and Herb Butter. Makes 4 servings.

To make Herb Butter, combine room-temperature butter with finely chopped herbs of your choice, dash of lemon juice, dash of Worcestershire sauce and a little prepared mustard. Before using, refrigerate until firm. Cut butter in round pats or use special butter molds. Store in refrigerator up to 4 weeks.

Broiled or Grilled Fish
Gegrillte Fische

Broiled or Grilled Trout
Gegrillte Speckforellen

4 whole fresh herring, trout or mackerel
White-wine vinegar
Salt
8 to 12 bacon slices, if desired
Vegetable oil

If using a broiler, lightly oil a large piece of foil. If using a barbecue grill, oil rungs of grill. Preheat broiler or grill. Clean fish; pat dry with paper towels. Sprinkle with vinegar; let stand 10 minutes. Season with salt. Wrap bacon in a spiral around fish, securing with small metal skewers, if desired. Brush fish with oil. Place fish on grill or under broiler. Cook each side 12 to 15 minutes, depending on size of fish. Makes 4 to 6 servings.

4 whole fresh trout
White-wine vinegar
Salt
Vegetable oil
8 thin lean bacon slices

If using a broiler, lightly oil a large piece of foil. If using a barbecue grill, oil rungs of grill. Preheat broiler or grill. Clean fish; pat dry with paper towels. Sprinkle with vinegar and salt. Sprinkle lightly with oil. Cook trout 7 to 8 minutes on each side. Fish is cooked when dorsal or center-back fin pulls off easily. Meanwhile, sauté bacon in a skillet or broil in oven until crisp and lightly browned. When the trout is nearly done, place 2 bacon slices on each fish. Serve with potatoes and parsley, fresh green salad and Horseradish Cream, page 94. Makes 4 servings.

Shrimp Soup with Dill
Krabbensuppe mit Dill

Shrimp au Gratin
Gratinierte Krabben

3 tablespoons butter
1/4 cup all-purpose flour
1 qt. hot Court Bouillon made with fish trimmings, page 64
1/2 cup half and half
Lemon juice
White wine
8 to 12 large shrimp or 1 cup small shrimp or cooked crabmeat
Chopped fresh dill

Melt butter in a large saucepan. Add flour, stirring well. Gradually blend in hot Court Bouillon. Simmer 3 minutes. Stir in half and half, lemon juice and wine. Add shrimp; cook briefly. Or, stir in crabmeat. Pour into a soup tureen. Sprinkle with dill. Makes 5 to 6 servings.

3/4 lb. large shrimp
1 tablespoon lemon juice
2 tablespoons butter
3 tablespoons all-purpose flour
1/2 cup water
1/2 cup half and half
White wine
1/2 teaspoon lemon juice
Salt
1/4 cup dry breadcrumbs
1/4 cup finely grated Parmesan or Romano cheese (1 oz.)
Butter

Preheat oven to 400F (205C). Sprinkle shrimp with 1 tablespoon lemon juice; place in ramekin dishes or scallop shells. Melt 2 tablespoons butter in a small saucepan; stir in flour. Gradually add water, half and half and wine, stirring constantly. Cook 5 minutes. Season with 1/2 teaspoon lemon juice and salt. Spoon or pour sauce over shrimp. In a small bowl, combine breadcrumbs and cheese; sprinkle mixture over sauce-coated shrimp. Dot with butter. Bake 12 to 15 minutes or until topping forms a golden crust. Serve hot as an appetizer or snack. Makes 4 servings.

Rhineland Mussels
Muscheln Rheinische Art

Helgoland Lobster
Helgoländer Hummer

4-1/4 lbs. mussels
1 qt. Court Bouillon made with 1 red chili pepper, page 64
3-1/2 tablespoons butter, if desired
1/2 cup half and half, if desired
2 to 3 tablespoons finely chopped parsley, if desired

Scrub mussels; discard any that are open or damaged in any way. Place closed mussels in a large cooking pot; add Court Bouillon. When fresh mussels are used, they will add their own liquor to liquid in pan. Bring to a simmer. Cook mussels 5 minutes; shake pot. Cook 3 to 5 minutes longer. Discard any mussels that do not fully open. Serve mussels in Court Bouillon. Or, serve mussels separately on plates. Strain Court Bouillon and serve in small soup bowls with butter, half and half and chopped parsley. Fresh, crusty white bread and white wine should be served with this dish. Makes 6 to 8 servings.

1 fresh live lobster
3 tablespoons white-wine vinegar
1 carrot, coarsely chopped
1 onion, cut in quarters
1 tablespoon black peppercorns
1/2 teaspoon ground cumin
Salt

The main pincer claws of a lobster should be tied together, preferably when bought. Scrub lobster under cold running water. Bring a large pot of water to a boil. Add vinegar, carrot, onion, peppercorns, cumin and salt. Boil 10 minutes. Plunge lobster, head first, into rapidly boiling water. After about 1 minute, reduce heat. Simmer 20 to 30 minutes, depending on lobster size. Cut lobster in half lengthwise; remove claws. Serve claws and lobster halves with fresh, homemade mayonnaise or lemon butter and white bread or toast. A good sparkling dry Riesling goes well with this dish. Makes 2 servings.

Eggs & Cheese

Germans appreciate eggs and eat many of them. The average German eats about 280 eggs a year—a good laying hen's entire production. Quick and easy to prepare, the most popular dish is certainly fried eggs, followed by scrambled eggs and hard-cooked eggs. A great many eggs are used for omelets and desserts such as Kaiserschmarren, the golden-raisin or apple scrambled pancakes. This delicious spicy German specialty is usually served topped with whipped cream or sour cream. Eggs play a vital role and are included in many different dishes.

Many people are astonished to learn that such a highly industrialized country as Germany is the world's third-largest cheese exporter, producing over 700,000 tons a year. Bavarians claim to account for two-thirds of the national output. The most popular cheese is *Speisequark,* known all over the world as *Quark.* With its low-fat content and high-protein quota, it is an extremely wholesome and versatile product. It can be made with buttermilk, whole milk, milk and cream or skim milk. Germany has also learned how to emulate some of her neighbors' most outstanding cheeses. There's *Emmentaler,* a hard cheese; the mild and tasty *German Camembert;* and the *German Gouda* cheese, pale in color but full-flavored. *Tilsit* cheese is a purely German creation, creamy-yellow in color, smooth and mildly pungent with tiny irregular holes. *Curd* cheeses are widely popular in Germany. They are low in fat and therefore recommended for low-calorie diets. *Limburger* cheese is soft and spicy with a robust taste and smell. The curd is formed into fairly large rectangular slabs, drained, rubbed with salt and ripened four to eight weeks. *Romadur käse* bears a close resemblance to Limburger, but has a higher fat content, being a half-fat cheese. It is pale yellow in color with few holes and is softer than Limburger. All these cheeses are delicious eaten with fresh bread and beer.

Berlin-Style Hard-Cooked Eggs
Berliner Soleier

Hard-Cooked Eggs with Herb Sauce
Eier mit Kräutersahne

1 qt. water
1/2 cup salt
1 bay leaf
1 teaspoon black peppercorns
Small piece of onion
8 eggs, room temperature
3 tablespoons vegetable oil
3 tablespoons white wine
1 tablespoon vinegar
2-1/2 teaspoons prepared mustard
Salt

In a medium saucepan, combine water, 1/2 cup salt, bay leaf, peppercorns and onion. Simmer 20 minutes; cool slightly. Remove and discard onion. Place eggs in seasoned water; simmer 10 to 12 minutes. Remove eggs from cooking liquid; reserve liquid. Immediately plunge eggs into cold water to stop yolk discoloration. Roll and press eggs against a hard surface to crack and loosen shells but do not peel. Place cooled cooking liquid in a glass or earthenware jar or narrow, deep dish. Place cooled eggs in cool cooking liquid. Refrigerate at least 24 hours but preferably 2 to 3 days. In a small bowl, combine oil, white wine, vinegar, mustard and salt to taste. Drain eggs shortly before serving. To serve, let each person shell his or her own. Cut eggs in half; remove yolks. Pour sauce into well of egg white. Return yolk to well. The flavorful result should be eaten in 1 mouthful. Serve with whole-wheat bread and beer. Makes 4 servings.

8 eggs
Salt
1 cup dairy sour cream
1/2 cup plain yogurt
1/3 cup quark, sieved ricotta cheese or cottage cheese
1 small onion, finely chopped
Choice of mixed finely chopped fresh herbs, such as: parsley, chervil, chives, basil, borage, savory, anise, dill
White pepper
1/2 teaspoon prepared mustard

Place eggs in a medium saucepan; cover with cold water. Simmer eggs 10 to 12 minutes. Immediately plunge eggs into cold water to stop yolk discoloration. Remove shells. Sprinkle eggs lightly with salt; cool. In a small bowl, combine sour cream, yogurt, cheese, onion, herbs, salt, white pepper and mustard. Adjust seasonings as needed. Place spoonfuls of sauce on individual plates. Cut eggs in half; press gently into sauce. Serve with boiled new potatoes and lettuce lightly tossed in a lemon and oil dressing. Makes 4 servings.

Eggs with Shrimp & Asparagus
Rührei mit Krabben und Spargel

Scrambled Eggs with Mushrooms
Rührei mit Champignons

1 small can asparagus spears
1/2 cup small shelled shrimp
4 eggs
3 tablespoons water
Salt and white pepper
3 tablespoons butter
1 tablespoon finely chopped chives

Drain asparagus; if the spears are thick, cut diagonally in half. Rinse shrimp. In a small bowl, beat together eggs, water, salt and white pepper. Add asparagus and shrimp. In a large skillet or omelet pan, melt butter. Add egg mixture. Cook over medium heat until eggs begin to set, stirring gently. Do not overcook. Sprinkle with chives. Serve immediately with fresh white bread and a green salad. Makes 2 servings.

1/2 lb. small mushrooms
1 tablespoon lemon juice
4 bacon slices, diced or 1/4 cup butter
4 eggs
3 tablespoons water
Salt and white pepper
Finely chopped parsley

Clean mushrooms; pat dry with paper towels. Quarter or slice mushrooms. Sprinkle with lemon juice to prevent discoloration. In a large skillet or omelet pan, lightly sauté bacon or melt butter. Add sliced mushrooms; sauté lightly. In a small bowl, beat together eggs, water, salt and white pepper. Add egg mixture to mushrooms. Stir to combine. Cook over medium heat until eggs begin to set, stirring gently. Do not overcook. Egg mixture should not brown. Sprinkle with parsley. Serve immediately. Makes 2 servings.

Farmer's Wife Cheese Omelet
Käseomelette nach Bäuerinnenart

Leek Omelet
Omelett mit Lauchringen

4 bacon slices, diced
3 tablespoons butter
2 small cooked potatoes, diced
5 to 6 tablespoons cocktail onions
1/4 lb. fresh or canned mushrooms
6 eggs
1 cup grated Emmentaler cheese (4 oz.)
Salt

Sauté bacon in a skillet or omelet pan. Add butter and potatoes. Drain onions and canned mushrooms. Slice onions into halves. Cut mushrooms into slivers. Add onions and mushrooms to skillet. Sauté over medium-high heat 1 to 2 minutes. In a small bowl, beat together eggs, cheese and salt, beating in as much air as possible. Pour egg mixture into skillet or omelet pan. Reduce heat and cook until set. Serve immediately. Makes 3 to 4 servings.

1 small leek
4 bacon slices, diced or 1/4 cup butter
4 eggs
Salt and white pepper

Trim leek discarding tough outer layer and extreme root and top ends. Wash thoroughly to remove all dirt. Slice into thin rings. Sauté bacon or melt butter in a skillet or omelet pan. Add leek slices; sauté 10 minutes over low heat. Leek should be tender but firm and should not be allowed to color. In a small bowl, beat together eggs, salt and white pepper, beating in as much air as possible. Pour egg mixture into skillet or omelet pan. Cook gently until set. Serve immediately. Makes 2 servings.

Fluffy Omelet with Ham & Vegetables
Omelett mit bunter Füllung

Savory Bacon Pancake
Speckpfannkuchen

1/4 lb. canned asparagus tips or spears
1/4 lb. canned button mushrooms
1/4 lb. frozen green peas
1/4 lb. frozen green beans, if desired
2 tablespoons butter
2 tablespoons all-purpose flour
1/2 cup meat stock
A little white wine
Salt and white pepper
1/4 to 1/2 lb. cooked ham, shredded
4 eggs, separated
All-purpose flour
1/4 cup butter
Chopped parsley

Drain asparagus and mushrooms; slice into small pieces. Cook peas and green beans, if desired; drain well. Melt 2 tablespoons butter in a small saucepan; stir in 2 tablespoons flour. Add stock; cook, stirring constantly, until slightly thickened. Flavor with wine, taking care not to make sauce too thin. Season with salt and white pepper. Cook 1 to 2 minutes, stirring constantly. Add asparagus, mushrooms, peas and green beans, if desired. Add ham. Cook gently until warmed through. Keep hot while preparing omelet. In a small bowl, beat egg whites until stiff but not dry. In another small bowl, beat a little flour and salt into yolks; then whisk yolks into whites. Melt 1/4 cup butter in a large omelet pan or heavy skillet; pour in egg mixture. Smooth surface with a spatula. Cover and cook over low heat 5 minutes. Remove lid. Place under a medium-hot broiler for a few minutes until top is cooked. Slide omelet half onto a warm serving plate. Spoon in ham and vegetable filling and fold other omelet half over to cover. Sprinkle with parsley. Serve immediately. Makes 1 to 2 servings.

3 eggs
1 cup milk
Salt
1-1/2 cups all-purpose flour
1/2 to 3/4 cup diced bacon

In a medium bowl, beat together eggs, milk, salt and flour. Or, process mixture in a blender. Let stand 20 minutes. Sauté about 1/4 of the bacon in a large heavy skillet until slightly colored. Add about 1/4 of the batter to skillet. Cook over medium heat, tilting skillet so pancake is thin and well spread out. Turn pancake when underside is cooked and has a lacy golden-brown pattern. When done, slide pancake carefully onto a warm plate. Repeat cooking bacon and batter 3 more times. Serve with a green salad. Makes 4 servings.

Note: In the Rhineland, these pancakes are usually served with iced coffee, but a glass of wine or beer goes as well with them. In the region of Germany near the Dutch border, these pancakes are served with maple syrup.

Eggs in Curry Sauce
Eier mit Currysosse

Strammer Max
Strammer Max

Curry Sauce, page 98
8 eggs
Salt
1/4 lb. frozen green peas

Prepare Curry Sauce; keep hot. Place eggs in a medium saucepan; cover with cold water. Simmer eggs 10 to 12 minutes. Immediately plunge eggs into cold water to stop yolk discoloration. Remove shells. Sprinkle eggs lightly with salt. Immediately place hot eggs in hot curry sauce. Cook peas in a little salted water until tender; drain. Add cooked peas to sauce. New potatoes, rice, a green salad or tomato salad are good side dishes to serve with this dish. Makes 4 servings.

Variation

Eggs can also be served in mustard sauce, dill sauce, bacon sauce or parsley sauce.

3 tablespoons butter
4 eggs
Unsalted butter
4 slices black bread or whole-wheat bread
4 large thin slices smoked ham, such as: Westphalian, Parma or Virginia ham
Salt and pepper
1 tablespoon finely chopped chives

Melt butter in a large heavy skillet. Carefully break eggs into skillet; cook gently over low heat. If cooked too fast, egg whites will become brown and crisp. While eggs are cooking, spread butter on bread. Top each with a slice of ham. Once eggs are ready, remove carefully from skillet; place on ham slices. Season with salt and pepper. Sprinkle with chives. Serve immediately with a glass of beer. Makes 4 servings.

Note: The origin of this substantial snack's intriguing name is unknown, although it suggests its undoubted fortifying qualities. I is a typical Rhineland specialty and when served in that region, the ham is often diced and placed on the bread, rather than being sliced.

Fränkischer Obatzter
Fränkischer Obatzter

Cheese with Mixed Herbs
Kräuterquark

1/4 lb. ripe Camembert cheese
1/3 cup cream cheese, room temperature
3 tablespoons butter, room temperature
1 medium onion, finely chopped
1 tablespoon beer
Salt and pepper
Caraway or cumin seeds
Paprika

Using a fork, combine Camembert, cream cheese and butter. Add onion, beer, salt, pepper, caraway or cumin seeds and paprika; combine well. Serve with fresh rolls or bread, and dry wine or beer. Makes 2 servings.

Note: The word *Batz*, which forms the root of this dish's name, is the dialect word for the thick, firm mixture resulting from blending cheeses and butter, referred to as *Pamp* in Rhineland. When prepared in this way, Camembert loses its slightly sour taste.

1 lb. quark, cottage cheese or Neufchâtel cheese
1 small onion, cut in thin rings
Salt and white pepper
Choice of mixed finely chopped fresh herbs, such as: parsley, chives,
    basil, summer savory, borage, winter savory, lovage
1 cup half and half

In a medium bowl, combine cheese, onion, salt, white pepper and herbs. Blend until mixture is smooth and creamy, adding half and half as necessary. Let stand about 1 hour. Serve with new potatoes boiled in their skins. Makes 4 to 6 servings.

Note: This makes a nourishing light meal because the cheese contains so much protein. For a slightly more elaborate presentation, add fresh butter to the potatoes and serve a green salad, cucumber salad or sweet-red-pepper and tomato salad. This mixture of cheese and herbs is also very good as a spread on whole-wheat or rye bread.

Cheese Pie
Ramequin

8 white-bread slices
8 Emmentaler-cheese slices
8 cervelat-sausage slices
16 tomato slices
2 eggs
2 cups milk
Salt
Ground nutmeg
1-1/2 tablespoons butter

Preheat oven to 400F (205C). Lightly oil or butter a shallow rectangular baking dish. Arrange bread, cheese, sausage and tomatoes in alternate layers in baking dish. In a medium bowl, beat eggs with milk, salt and nutmeg. Pour mixture evenly over layered items in baking dish. Dot surface with butter. Bake 30 minutes. Serve immediately with a green or mixed salad. Makes 4 servings.

Note: This Swiss-German dish is a good way to use stale bread and takes very little time to prepare. Do not allow to cool before serving. The classic Swiss Ramequin is made without tomatoes and sausage, but these make a more substantial and tasty meal.

Cheese, Ham & Herb Soufflé
Käseauflauf mit Schinken und Kräutern

1/4 lb. cooked ham
2 tablespoons butter
1/4 cup all-purpose flour
1 cup milk
1 cup grated cheese, such as Emmentaler (4 oz.)
2 eggs, separated
3 tablespoons finely chopped parsley
Choice of mixed finely chopped fresh herbs, such as: basil, dill, chervil, chives
Salt and white pepper
Pinch of grated nutmeg
Pinch of red (cayenne) pepper
Fresh breadcrumbs

Preheat oven to 400F (205C). Butter a large soufflé dish or individual ramekins. Shred ham; sauté lightly in a medium saucepan with 1 tablespoon butter. Add remaining butter. When melted, stir in flour. Cook, stirring constantly, 3 minutes. Gradually add milk, stirring until thickened. Remove from heat. Stir in cheese until melted. In a small bowl, combine egg yolks and a small amount of sauce. Stir egg-yolk mixture, herbs, salt, white pepper, nutmeg and red pepper into sauce. Beat egg whites until stiff but not dry; fold into sauce carefully but thoroughly with a metal spoon. Turn into a large soufflé dish or ramekins. Sprinkle top lightly with breadcrumbs. Place in oven. If baking a large soufflé, do not open oven door during first 20 minutes of baking. For individual ramekins, do not open door during first 7 to 8 minutes. Bake large soufflé 25 to 30 minutes and ramekins 10 to 12 minutes or until a fine skewer or knife inserted in center of soufflé comes out clean. Cheese soufflé is best if the center is creamy and moist. Do not overbake. Serve immediately with a salad, tomato sauce and fresh white bread. Makes 4 servings.

Cheese Fondue
Käsefondue

About 2 lbs. white bread
1/2 lb. Emmentaler cheese
3/4 lb. Gruyère cheese
1 garlic clove, cut in half
1-1/3 cups dry white wine, warmed
1 teaspoon lemon juice
2 tablespoons kirsch
1 teaspoon cornstarch
Ground nutmeg
Pepper

Cut bread in 3/4-inch cubes; set aside. Coarsely grate or finely dice cheese. Rub inside surface of fondue pot with cut surfaces of garlic halves. Place cheese, wine and lemon juice in fondue pot. Warm over heat source, stirring constantly until melted and smooth. In a small bowl, combine kirsch, cornstarch, nutmeg and pepper. Stir kirsch mixture into cheese mixture. Each person then spears a bread cube with a fondue fork and dips it into the cheese mixture. Stir fondue frequently to keep it creamy. Makes 6 servings.

Raclette
Raclette

2 lbs. raclette cheese

Cut cheese in half. Hold cut surface near a heat source until an even layer of surface has melted. Using a special raclette knife or the blunt edge of a bread knife, scrape melted cheese directly onto individual plates. Repeat until all cheese is melted. Raclette is usually served with new potatoes boiled in their skins, pickled onions and small gherkins. Freshly ground pepper can be used to season cheese. Makes 6 servings.

Note: Raclette cheese is a special variety, ideally suited to this dish. This is a very old traditional Swiss dish. It originated with shepherds who used to melt cheese by the fire in their Alpine huts. To this day, the best way of eating raclette is sitting around a roaring wood fire and melting cheese by its heat.

Sauces

Although French cuisine has developed a wide and elaborate repertoire of sauces, there are some excellent German creations. Among the most successful are those served with succulent roast meats. Any cook who sets a prime roast of meat on the table will feel a glow of satisfaction when the accompanying sauce turns out dark, rich and flavorful. Obviously, each individual adds his or her own distinctive touches to the sauce or gravy. They also know of special tricks and tips when it comes to the subtle variations in flavorings and seasoning.

Meat should always be of the best quality affordable so it will be juicy, flavorful and tender. The German cooking method involves browning and sealing the outside of the meat in butter in a large, heavy cooking pot or roasting pan. Then it is placed in the oven and cooked very slowly. While the choice of spices, seasonings and herbs varies greatly, these should usually be added to the meat when it is nearly done. High temperatures tend to destroy or alter the aromas and tastes. A little wine is sometimes used to add extra flavor to these sauces.

Preferences for different recipes and methods vary from one region to another. In Bavaria, the gravy or sauce served with pork is never thickened, whereas this is done as a matter of course in northern Germany. German braising sauces are very distinctive. In the case of braised beef, the sauce would be slightly sour in taste if it wasn't balanced by the addition of seedless golden raisins and other dried fruit. As for cold sauces, the Franconia specialty of horseradish sauce, made with or without cream, is one of the most popular. And, the green sauce from Hesse always becomes a favorite with visitors to Germany. It is served with boiled beef and sometimes hard-cooked eggs.

Horseradish Cream
Meerrettichsahne

Frankfurt Green-Herb Sauce
Frankfurter grüne Sosse

1 cup whipping cream
3 to 6 tablespoons finely grated fresh horseradish
1 teaspoon lemon juice
Salt and white pepper

In a medium bowl, whip cream. Carefully fold in horseradish, lemon juice, salt and white pepper. Serve with broiled fish or boiled meat or tongue. Makes 4 servings.

Note: A great deal of horseradish is grown in the Franconia region. In the spring, the dark roots with their distinctive aroma are dug up and taken to market by old women dressed in traditional costumes. To prevent the roots from drying out and becoming hard, they are stored in cool cellars in earthenware pots or packed into very large earthenware jars with plenty of damp sand. The roots must be well washed and peeled before they are grated—a process which makes the eyes water since they react to the oil contained in the roots. If fresh horseradish cannot be found, it can usually be bought ready-grated in jars, in which case it will have a slightly sweeter taste.

3 hard-cooked eggs
1/2 cup vegetable oil
3 to 5 tablespoons white-wine vinegar
Salt and pepper
Pinch of sugar
1/2 teaspoon prepared mustard
1/3 cup dairy sour cream, if desired
1 small onion, finely chopped, if desired
Choice of the following fresh herbs: borage, chives, cress, parsley, chervil, sorrel, small quantity of winter savory or lovage, anise, dill, tarragon, summer savory, fennel seeds, basil

Finely chop eggs; reserve 2 tablespoons for garnish. In a medium bowl, combine remaining chopped eggs, oil, vinegar, salt, pepper, sugar and mustard. Stir in sour cream and onion, if desired. Use as many of the fresh herbs listed as possible; the greater the variety, the better the sauce. Wash herbs; trim and chop very finely. Pour egg mixture into a blender or food processor. Add herbs; process briefly until smooth. Season to taste. Place in a small serving bowl. Let stand 1 hour before serving. Garnish with reserved chopped egg and a little minced fresh herbs. This sauce goes very well with potatoes boiled in their skins, boiled meat or fish and hard-cooked or poached eggs. Makes 4 servings.

Variation

For a sauce with a less sharp taste, substitute whipping cream for dairy sour cream.

Cumberland Sauce
Cumberlandsosse

Maltese Sauce
Malteser Sosse

1 orange
1/3 cup port
1/3 cup full-bodied red wine
1-1/4 cups red-currant jelly
2 teaspoons dry mustard
1 teaspoon lemon juice
Few drops of Worcestershire sauce
Salt and pepper

Cut peel from half the orange, removing only the colored portion. Cut peel into fine narrow strips. Place in a small saucepan with port; simmer 5 minutes. Cool slightly. In a medium bowl, combine port mixture, wine, jelly, mustard, lemon juice, Worcestershire sauce, salt and pepper. Let stand 24 hours before serving. This sauce will keep up to 1 week if refrigerated. Cumberland Sauce is a classic sauce that goes well with game pies, roast beef and almost any cold cooked meat. Makes 4 servings.

1/2 a blood orange or regular orange
1 green onion, finely chopped
1 tablespoon dry white wine
1 tablespoon white-wine vinegar
3 tablespoons chicken stock
2 egg yolks, slightly beaten
1/2 cup butter, cut in small pieces
1 teaspoon lemon juice
Salt and white pepper
3 to 5 tablespoons whipped cream

This sauce needs to be made with extra care. Cut peel from half the orange, removing only the colored portion. Cut peel into fine narrow strips. Blanch peel briefly in boiling water, if desired. Finely chop peel, if desired; set aside. Juice orange; set juice aside. In a small skillet, simmer green onion 5 minutes over low heat in wine, vinegar and stock. Strain well, discarding green onion; cool slightly. Place egg yolks and wine mixture in a small enamel-lined saucepan. Place over hot water or use a double boiler. Water should be barely simmering at any time. If mixture is overheated, it will curdle and sauce must be remade with new ingredients. Add butter, 1 piece at a time, mixing well and making sure each piece is fully incorporated before adding the next. If desired, use a whisk to beat butter into yolk mixture. When all butter has been added, sauce should be fairly thick and creamy. Add lemon juice, salt, white pepper, blanched orange peel and juice. Fold in whipped cream before serving. Serve immediately to prevent sauce from separating. This sauce is perfect with delicate fish or vegetable dishes, such as asparagus. It is also very good with broiled meat. Makes 4 servings.

Mustard & Egg Sauce
Senf-Eiersosse

Sauce Rémoulade
Remouladensosse

4 hard-cooked eggs
1/2 cup vegetable oil
1/3 cup lemon juice
1/3 cup prepared mild or sweet mustard
1/2 teaspoon grated fresh horseradish
Salt and white pepper
Pinch of sugar
3 tablespoons orange juice
1/2 cup whipping cream

Coarsely chop eggs. In a medium bowl, combine chopped eggs, oil, lemon juice, mustard, horseradish, salt, white pepper, sugar and orange juice. In a small bowl, whip cream; fold egg mixture into whipped cream. Season to taste. Serve with boiled or broiled beef or fish. It is also delicious with hard-cooked eggs and new potatoes in their skins. Makes 4 servings.

1 hard-cooked egg
1 pickled cucumber or gherkin
1 anchovy or 1 teaspoon anchovy paste
1 tablespoon capers
1/4 onion
3 tablespoons finely chopped mixed fresh herbs
1 tablespoon lemon juice
1 cup mayonnaise
3 tablespoons yogurt, ricotta cheese or cottage cheese, if desired

Finely chop egg, gherkin, anchovy, capers and onion. In a medium bowl, combine with herbs, lemon juice and mayonnaise. For a lighter, milder sauce, yogurt, ricotta or cottage cheese may be stirred in at this stage. Let stand 1 hour in the refrigerator before serving. Leftover sauce will keep 3 to 4 days in the refrigerator. Makes 4 servings.

Note: Sauce Rémoulade is one of the Germans' favorite sauces. It is eaten with roast beef, cold meats, sliced processed meats and certain types of sausage, ox tongue, brains and is most popular with fish fillets.

Tomato Sauce
Tomatensosse

lb. tomatoes
small onion
tablespoons vegetable oil
Salt and pepper
Pinch of sugar
Rosemary
Basil
Marjoram
/2 bay leaf
tablespoon cornstarch, if desired
Water, if desired

Quarter tomatoes. Finely dice onion; sauté in oil in a medium saucepan over low heat. When onion is transparent, add tomatoes, salt, pepper, sugar and herbs. Simmer about 30 minutes. Then press mixture through a sieve or food mill. For a smoother sauce, cool sieved sauce slightly. Then process in a blender or food processor. If a thicker sauce is required, return sieved puree to saucepan. In a small bowl, combine cornstarch and a small amount of water. Stir cornstarch mixture into sauce. Cook over medium heat, stirring occasionally, until slightly thickened. Season to taste. Makes 4 servings.

Note: Tomato Sauce is probably the most popular of all sauces in Germany. It goes with almost any type of noodle or pasta dish and dumplings. It is a valuable accompaniment to such dishes as meat rissoles or meat balls and many types of fish.

Cheese Sauce
Käsesosse

2 tablespoons butter
1/4 cup all-purpose flour
1-1/3 cups milk
1/2 cup grated Sbrinz, Asiago or Romano cheese (2 oz.)
1 egg yolk, slightly beaten
3 tablespoons half and half
Salt and pepper
Prepared mustard

Melt butter in a medium saucepan; stir in flour. Cook, stirring constantly, 1 to 2 minutes. Do not allow it to color. Add milk, stirring constantly. Continue to cook 2 to 3 minutes. Stir in cheese. Continue heating, stirring constantly, over low heat until cheese has melted. Remove from heat. In a small bowl, combine egg yolk and half and half; quickly whisk mixture into sauce. Do not return to heat or it will curdle. Season to taste with salt, pepper and mustard. Serve immediately. Makes 4 servings.

Variations

If a cheese and wine sauce is required, substitute an equal quantity of dry white wine for milk and add nutmeg and Worcestershire sauce to taste.

Imperial Cheese Sauce: Add 3 to 5 tablespoons coarsely chopped toasted almonds when adding seasonings.

Brown Sauce with Bacon
Braune Specksosse

6 bacon slices, diced
1 small onion, finely chopped
1/4 cup all-purpose flour
2 cups meat stock, heated
Salt and pepper
1 whole clove
1/2 bay leaf
Pinch of sugar

Sauté bacon in a medium, heavy saucepan until golden brown. Add onion; sauté until lightly colored. Sprinkle in flour. Cook, stirring constantly, until pale golden. Avoid overbrowning bacon. Stir in hot stock. Season to taste with salt, pepper, clove, bay leaf and sugar. Simmer 5 to 10 minutes, stirring frequently. Makes 4 servings.

Variation

Small pieces of cooked beef, ox tail, heart or tongue are often added to the sauce. The flavor can also be heightened by adding a little red wine or Madeira.

Curry Sauce
Currysosse

3 tablespoons margarine
1 small onion, finely diced
1/4 cup all-purpose flour
2 cups meat stock, heated or 2 cups half and half
1/4 tart apple, peeled
1 teaspoon lemon juice
2 to 3 teaspoons curry powder

Melt margarine in a medium saucepan. Add onion; sauté over medium heat until golden brown. Sprinkle in flour. Cook 5 minutes over low heat, stirring constantly. Do not allow to color. Stir in hot stock or half and half. Cook gently 5 to 10 minutes. Grate apple into sauce. Add lemon juice and curry powder to taste. Serve with boiled fish, chicken, beef or lamb. This sauce is also good with hard-cooked eggs and shrimp. Makes 4 servings.

Rich Brown Onion Sauce
Dunkle Zwiebelsosse

1 large onion or 2 small onions
3 tablespoons margarine
1/4 cup all-purpose flour
2 cups meat stock or 1-1/2 cups stock and 1/2 cup whipping cream
1 tablespoon white wine
Salt and pepper
Pinch of sugar

Coarsely chop onion. Melt margarine in a medium, heavy saucepan. Add onion; sauté over medium heat until golden brown. Sprinkle in flour. Cook over low heat, stirring constantly, until golden brown. Stir in stock or stock and cream. Season with wine, salt, pepper and sugar. Simmer 5 to 10 minutes. For a very smooth sauce, cool slightly. Then process in a blender or food processor. Serve with potatoes, rice, noodles or vegetables. Also good with small meat rissoles or certain types of filleted fish. Makes 4 servings.

German-Style Sauce Bourguignonne
Burgundersosse

3 tablespoons sugar
1 cup Burgundy or other red wine
2 shallots or 8 green onions, chopped
3 tablespoons margarine
1/4 cup all-purpose flour
1/2 cup Burgundy or other red wine
1 tablespoon meat essence or extract
1 teaspoon lemon juice
Salt and pepper
Pinch of sugar

Heat 3 tablespoons sugar in a small heavy saucepan until it has caramelized. Pour in 1 cup wine. A great deal of steam will be produced and this can burn if the hands are not protected and face averted. Add shallots or onions; simmer 15 minutes. Heat margarine in a medium saucepan. Stir in flour; cook over low heat until pale golden brown, stirring constantly. Add 1/2 cup wine and onions in caramel liquid. Season sauce with meat essence or extract, lemon juice, salt, pepper and a pinch of sugar. Serve with pickled tongue, roast beef, liver or kidneys. Makes 4 servings.

Vegetables

No visitor to Germany should miss seeing the colorful array of vegetables displayed in stalls at the weekly market. Some street markets have occupied the same site for more than a thousand years. Stalls are set up in time-honored fashion in the oldest quarter of the city, usually near the cathedral or the old town hall. Fruit and vegetable vendors arrange their produce with the greatest skill, contrasting the fresh green of lettuces with radishes, pale horseradish roots and cucumbers, and bunches of fresh herbs. In springtime, mounds of glistening spinach are heaped beside kohlrabi, which vary in color from pale green to lilac. Fresh peas nestle next to sweet, tender carrots and white asparagus. In summer, there is an even greater profusion: cauliflower, beans, tomatoes and sweet bell peppers. In fall and winter, there's small white turnips together with black-skinned oyster plant or *salsify,* a popular and typical German vegetable. Every imaginable variety of cabbage is available: Savoy cabbage, red cabbage, white cabbage, Brussels sprouts and cauliflower. A considerable proportion of the cabbages grown is processed by the food industry—finely shredded and pickled to produce sauerkraut. Sometimes packed and stored in large barrels, sauerkraut is more commonly sold in jars or cans.

Green Salad
Kopfsalat

Mixed Raw Vegetables
Rohkostteller

1 head or bunch of lettuce
1 small onion
5 to 6 tablespoons finely chopped fresh herbs, such as: parsley, chives,
    dill, lemon balm, basil, anise
1/2 teaspoon prepared mustard
5 to 6 tablespoons vegetable oil and 3 tablespoons white-wine vinegar, or
    1/2 cup dairy sour cream
Salt and pepper
Pinch of sugar

Wash lettuce thoroughly, shaking to remove as much water as possible. Tear lettuce into small pieces. Place in a large bowl. Finely chop onion or cut into thin rings; add to bowl along with herbs. In a small bowl, combine mustard, oil and vinegar or sour cream. Add salt, pepper and sugar. Toss salad with dressing immediately before serving. Makes 4 to 6 servings.

Note: In Germany, lettuce is the most popular of all the salad vegetables and it is said that the best test of a good cook is the quality of his or her salads—particularly the quality of the dressing. Certainly a great deal of care and imagination are needed to produce a first-class salad.

1/2 lb. carrots, kohlrabi, celery or beets
2 to 3 tomatoes
1/2 cucumber
1 red bell pepper
1 green bell pepper
Lettuce or spinach leaves
Chopped fresh herbs
Sautéed diced onion and crisp bacon, if desired
Dressing of your choice

Select a variety of fresh vegetables. Trim vegetables. Coarsely grate carrots. Parboil kohlrabi or beets in water seasoned with a little lemon juice. Then cut in thin slices or coarsely grate. Cut celery in matchstick pieces. Cut tomatoes into quarters, eighths or thin slices. Slice cucumber into thin rounds. Cut peppers into rings or matchstick pieces. Arrange vegetables in small portions on lettuce or spinach leaves on individual plates or in mounds on a large platter, making an attractive color scheme. Sprinkle with herbs, onion and bacon, if desired. One or more types of dressing can be used including vinaigrette, garlic-flavored mayonnaise or a yogurt or sour-cream dressing. These can be added to the various salad vegetables before serving or each person can serve himself. Makes 4 servings.

Cucumber & Dill Salad
Gurkensalat mit Dill

Lambs' Lettuce & Orange Salad
Feldsalat mit Orangen

/2 cup dairy sour cream or, 1/2 cup vegetable oil and 3 tablespoons wine
 vinegar
/2 teaspoon prepared mustard
alt and white pepper
 inch of sugar
ew drops of Worcestershire sauce
 cucumbers
 small onion
 tablespoons finely chopped fresh dill

n a small bowl, combine sour cream or oil and vinegar, mustard,
alt, white pepper, sugar and Worcestershire sauce. Blend mixture
ell. Use a mandoline cutter or thin blade on a food processor to
lice cucumbers and onion thinly. In a medium bowl, combine
liced cucumbers and onion and salad dressing. Toss to coat lightly.
prinkle with dill. Serve immediately. Makes 4 servings.

2 bunches lambs' lettuce or young spinach
1 large mild onion
2 oranges
1 cup plain yogurt (8 oz.)
1 tablespoon vegetable oil
3 tablespoons lemon juice
2-1/2 teaspoons sugar
Salt and white pepper
1 cup walnut halves, if desired

Wash lettuce or spinach, shaking to remove as much water as
possible. Thinly slice onion; separate into rings. Peel oranges,
removing all the pith. Slice oranges into rounds. Place lettuce or
spinach, onion and orange slices in a large bowl. In a medium bowl,
beat or whisk together yogurt, oil, lemon juice, sugar, salt and white
pepper. Pour dressing over salad before serving. Sprinkle with
walnut halves, if desired. Toss lightly. Makes 4 servings.

Note: If lambs' lettuce is difficult to find, Belgian endive can be
substituted because it has a similar, slightly bitter taste. Another
name for lambs' lettuce is *corn salad*.

Beet Salad
Rote-Bete-Salat

Tyrolean White-Cabbage Salad
Krautsalat Tiroler Art

1 lb. small beets
1 piece fresh horseradish root or 1 tablespoon prepared horseradish
1 onion
5 tablespoons vegetable oil
3 to 5 tablespoons vinegar
1/2 teaspoon cumin or caraway seeds
Salt and pepper
Pinch of sugar
1/2 teaspoon mustard seeds, crushed, if desired
Chopped fresh parsley
1 bay leaf

Wash beets thoroughly but do not remove leaves and roots. Boil in plenty of water 30 to 50 minutes, depending on size. When beets are tender, plunge into cold water. Let stand to cool. Trim beet roots and tops. Peel and dice or thinly slice beets. Peel horseradish root; finely grate. Finely chop or thinly slice onion. In a medium bowl, combine beets, grated horseradish and onion. In a small bowl, combine oil, vinegar, cumin or caraway seeds, salt, pepper, sugar and mustard seeds, if desired. Pour dressing over beet mixture. Garnish with parsley and bay leaf. Let stand 1 hour before serving. This salad will keep well up to 7 days if covered and refrigerated. Serve salad at room temperature with new potatoes boiled in their skins and boiled meat. Makes 4 servings.

4 bacon slices
1 lb. white cabbage
1 teaspoon salt
1 teaspoon cumin or caraway seeds, if desired
1 tablespoon vinegar
1/2 teaspoon sugar

Cook bacon until crisp; drain and cool. Crumble bacon. Remove outer leaves of cabbage. Finely shred remaining cabbage. Place shredded cabbage in a heavy saucepan. Pound cabbage, preferably with a wooden pestle or mallet, 10 to 15 minutes. This breaks down cabbage fibers and softens them. It will make the cabbage more juicy. In a medium bowl, combine cabbage, salt, cumin or caraway seeds and crumbled bacon. In a small bowl, combine vinegar and sugar. Pour vinegar mixture over cabbage mixture; toss to coat lightly. Makes 4 servings.

Note: This salad is a great favorite in Bavaria and the Tyrol and is often served with slices of roast meat and dumplings.

Celery Salad
Selleriesalat

Braised Leeks
Gedünstetes Lauchgemüse

1 celeriac (celery root) or 4 to 5 celery stalks
Juice of 1 lemon
1/3 cup vegetable oil
3 tablespoons white-wine vinegar
Salt and white pepper
3 to 6 tablespoons mayonnaise or dairy sour cream, if desired

Peel celeriac. Cut celeriac or celery into matchstick strips or very thin slices. Sprinkle with lemon juice to prevent discoloration. Boil in plenty of salted water until almost tender but still crisp; drain well. In a small bowl, combine oil, vinegar, salt and white pepper. Pour dressing over celeriac or celery while still warm. Stir until well coated. Let stand to absorb dressing while it cools. For a richer dish, stir in mayonnaise or sour cream. Makes 4 servings.

Note: In those parts of Germany where celeriac is not readily available, celery is used instead.

2 lbs. young tender leeks
Water
1 tablespoon lemon juice
Salt
3 tablespoons all-purpose flour
1/2 cup milk, half and half or whipping cream
White pepper
Ground nutmeg

Trim leeks, removing dark-green upper leaves; slit open lengthwise. Wash leeks thoroughly. Cut each leek in 3 pieces. Cook gently over low heat in a little water with lemon juice and salt. In a small bowl, combine flour and milk, half and half or cream; stir into cooking liquid in saucepan. Cook, stirring constantly, until thickened. Season with white pepper and nutmeg. Leeks make a good winter-vegetable dish to go with meat. Makes 4 servings.

Fava Beans in Bacon Sauce
Dicke Bohnen in Specksosse

Fennel in Cream Sauce
Fenchel in Sahnesosse

4-1/4 lbs. fresh fava beans
Salt
Water
1 small bunch summer savory
4 bacon slices, diced
1-1/2 tablespoons margarine
1/4 cup all-purpose flour
1/2 cup milk
Pepper

Remove fava beans from pods. Boil beans in salted water with a sprig of savory, 12 to 25 minutes, depending on size. When beans are tender but still slightly firm, drain, reserving cooking liquid. Finely chop remaining savory. Sauté bacon in a small skillet until crisp. Drain off drippings. Add margarine to bacon. When melted, sprinkle in flour. Stir to combine. Add milk and 1-1/2 cups reserved cooking liquid. Cook, stirring constantly, until slightly thickened. Season with salt and pepper. Stir in cooked fava beans. Makes 4 to 6 servings.

Note: These beans are often cooked with *Mettwurstchen*, small smoked sausages, or with *Kasseler*, smoked pickled pork, and served with new potatoes. A glass or two of light beer complements the meal. While these beans are very popular in the Rhineland and throughout north Germany, they are hardly ever eaten in southern Germany.

4 medium fennel
Salt
Water
3 tablespoons butter or margarine
1/4 cup all-purpose flour
1/2 cup half and half
Ground nutmeg
4 bacon slices, cooked crisp, crumbled, if desired

Trim stems and any discolored parts from fennel. Reserve leaves. Cut fennel in half or into slices. Place in a medium saucepan; cover with lightly salted water. Bring to a boil; boil 8 to 15 minutes, depending on how young and tender they are. When fennel are tender, drain, reserving cooking liquid. In a medium saucepan, melt butter or margarine. Add flour, stirring constantly. Gradually add half and half and 1 cup reserved cooking liquid. Cook over medium heat, stirring constantly, until slightly thickened. Season with salt and nutmeg. Chop a few reserved fennel leaves; stir into sauce along with hot cooked fennel and bacon, if desired. Makes 4 servings.

Cauliflower au Gratin
Überbackener Blumenkohl

Brussels Sprouts with Cheese Sauce
Rosenkohl mit Käsesosse

medium head cauliflower
alt
Water
tablespoons butter
/4 cup all-purpose flour
cup milk
round nutmeg
/2 cup shredded Emmentaler cheese (2 oz.)

rim cauliflower. Leave it whole or break into flowerets. Cook in alted water until tender. Drain well, reserving cooking liquid. arrange cauliflower in a heatproof dish. Preheat oven to 400F 205C). In a medium saucepan, melt butter. Stir in flour. Cook 3 minutes, stirring constantly. Do not allow mixture to color. Stir in milk and 1/2 cup reserved cooking liquid. Season with salt and utmeg. Add most of the cheese, stirring over low heat until melted nd sauce has thickened. Pour sauce over cauliflower and sprinkle eserved cheese on top. Bake 10 minutes. Serve immediately. Makes 4 servings.

1-3/4 to 2 lbs. Brussels sprouts
Salt
Water
3 tablespoons butter
1/4 cup all-purpose flour
1 cup milk
Ground nutmeg
1/2 cup shredded Emmentaler cheese (2 oz.)

Trim Brussels sprouts. Make a crisscross incision in base of each Brussels sprout to encourage even cooking. Place Brussels sprouts in a large saucepan of salted water; bring water to a boil. Cook until tender but still crisp. Drain, reserving cooking liquid. Preheat oven to 400F (205C). Place Brussels sprouts in a shallow baking dish. In a medium saucepan, melt butter. Stir in flour. Cook 3 minutes, stirring constantly. Do not allow mixture to color. Stir in milk and a small amount of reserved cooking liquid. Season with salt and nutmeg. Add cheese, stirring over low heat until melted and sauce has thickened. Pour sauce over Brussels sprouts as evenly as possible. Bake 10 minutes or until sprouts are heated through and surface of sauce is lightly colored. Serve immediately. Makes 4 servings.

Ham-Wrapped Endive in Cheese Sauce
Chicorée im Schinkenhemd

Schwetzingen Asparagus
Schwetzinger Stangenspargel

4 Belgian endive
1 tablespoon lemon juice
3 tablespoons butter or margarine
1/4 cup all-purpose flour
1-2/3 cups milk
Salt
Ground nutmeg
1/2 cup shredded Emmentaler cheese (2 oz.)
4 cooked lean ham slices

Cut a cone-shape piece out of base of each endive. This is bitter and should be discarded. Sprinkle endive with lemon juice. Blanch endive in boiling salted water; drain. Preheat oven to 375F (190C). In a medium saucepan, melt butter or margarine. Stir in flour. Cook, stirring constantly, 3 minutes. Do not allow mixture to color. Stir in milk. Season with salt and nutmeg. Add cheese, stirring over low heat until melted and sauce has thickened. Wrap each endive in a ham slice. Place, seam-side down, in a shallow baking dish. Pour cheese sauce over wrapped endive. Bake 10 minutes or until surface of sauce is well browned. Serve immediately. Makes 4 servings.

Note: Belgian endive is very good raw in salads with apples and oranges.

2 to 3 lbs. fresh asparagus
Ground nutmeg, if desired

Trim asparagus, cutting off woody ends and peeling stems; rinse well. If possible, cook asparagus upright in a special asparagus kettle in salted water to which a pinch of sugar has been added. Or, tie asparagus in several equal bunches, 1 bunch per guest, using 2 strands of soft string for each bunch. This will make it easier to lift cooked asparagus out of the boiling water without damaging the very tender tips. Use a fork to hook into strings around each bunch. Cook asparagus 12 to 25 minutes, depending on size and tenderness. Cover a plate with a cloth napkin or towel. Place cooked asparagus on napkin or towel to finish draining. Remove string, if needed. Arrange on a serving dish. Sprinkle with nutmeg, if desired. Makes 4 to 6 servings

Note: Asparagus is one of the Germans' favorite delicacies. The first firm, tender white asparagus spears come on the market in April and the season traditionally ends on June 24th, the Feast of St. John. In Germany, asparagus is almost always eaten with melted butter. It can also be served with little pieces of raw smoked ham, such as Westphalian ham, and new potatoes. Alternative accompaniments are hard-cooked eggs or a delicate sauce, such as Maltese Sauce, page 95.

Mushrooms in Lemon & Cream Sauce
Pilzgemüse

Stuffed Marrow
Schmorgurken gefüllt

3/4 lbs. mushrooms
tablespoons lemon juice
ater
bacon slices, diced
1/2 tablespoons butter or margarine
tablespoons all-purpose flour
2 cup chicken stock
2 cup half and half
lt and white pepper
hopped parsley

im mushrooms; cut in quarters or thin slices. Dilute lemon juice
th a small amount of water. Sprinkle mushrooms with diluted
mon juice to prevent discoloration. Sauté bacon until crisp in a
edium, heavy saucepan. Add mushrooms; sauté gently, turning
veral times. Remove mushrooms to a dish. Add butter or
argarine to saucepan, if needed. Stir in flour until smooth. Stir in
ock and half and half. Cook 3 to 5 minutes, stirring constantly,
ntil slightly thickened. Season with salt and white pepper. Pour
uce over mushrooms. Sprinkle with parsley. Serve immediately.
akes 4 servings.

ote: Wild mushrooms picked in the woods or fields are delicious,
oviding you know which are safe to eat. Chanterelles are
metimes available in good produce shops, but cultivated
ushrooms are also very good prepared in this way. In Bavaria,
ey are usually eaten with dumplings, seldom with meat.

2 to 4 vegetable marrows (2-3/4 lbs.)
1 tablespoon lemon juice
2/3 cup dry breadcrumbs
1 lb. ground meat, browned lightly or, chopped leftover roast meat
1 small onion, finely chopped
1 egg
Salt and pepper
4 bacon slices, diced
1/2 cup chicken stock
Paprika
1 tablespoon tomato paste, if desired
1 tablespoon cornstarch, if desired
1 tablespoon finely chopped fresh parsley or dill

Peel marrows; slit lengthwise and scoop out seeds. Sprinkle surface
of marrow with lemon juice. In a medium bowl, combine
breadcrumbs, meat, onion, egg, salt and pepper. Fill both halves of
each marrow with meat mixture. In a large enamel-lined cast-iron
skillet or heatproof earthenware dish, sauté bacon until fat melts.
Place stuffed marrows in skillet with bacon. Add stock to skillet.
Season with salt, pepper and paprika. Cover and cook over low heat.
When marrows are tender, sauce may be thickened, if desired. To
thicken sauce, combine tomato paste and cornstarch; stir into sauce.
Sprinkle with parsley or dill. Marrows can also be baked. Makes 4
servings.

Variation

Substitute 6 to 8 medium zucchini for vegetable marrow. Do not
peel zucchini. Split zucchini lengthwise. Using a teaspoon or melon
baller, scoop out center of zucchini. Prepare filling; proceed as
above.

Savoy Cabbage
Wirsing

Bremerhaven Curly Kale
Grünkohl Bremer Art

1-1/2 to 2 lbs. Savoy cabbage
6 to 8 bacon slices, diced
1/4 cup plus 2 tablespoons all-purpose flour
2 cups milk or 1/4 cup butter (instead of flour and milk)
Salt
Ground nutmeg

Trim cabbage; cut into quarters. Cook in salted water over low heat 20 minutes; drain. Coarsely chop or shred in a food processor. In a medium skillet, sauté bacon until golden brown. Sprinkle bacon with flour. Stir in milk. Substitute butter for flour and milk, if desired. Cook 2 to 3 minutes. Season with salt and nutmeg. Add chopped cabbage, stirring and turning over low heat until heated through. Makes 4 servings.

Variation

Cabbage can be parboiled, then sautéed in butter and a small amount of water. Cover and cook slowly over low heat 20 minutes. Season with salt and nutmeg. Crisp sautéed bacon can be sprinkled over cabbage before serving.

Note: Savoy cabbage is usually available year round and lends itself to several different preparations. The first method is the most traditional.

2 to 3 lbs. curly kale
1/3 cup lard or goose fat
1 onion, diced
Salt
Water
1/2 lb. bacon, diced
1 lb. pinkelwurst or other pork sausage
1 tablespoon rolled oats

Trim stalks and ribs of kale leaves; wash kale. Blanch kale briefly in boiling water; drain well. Finely chop blanched kale. In a large saucepan, melt lard or goose fat. Add onion; sauté lightly. Add chopped kale, salt, a little water, bacon and sausage. Cover and cook over low heat 1 hour. When kale is tender, thicken cooking liquid by adding rolled oats. Makes 4 to 6 servings.

Note: Each year, on the last Friday in February, the city dignitaries of Bremen are invited to dine on board ship by the captains of the fleet's ships before they sail from Bremerhaven. The traditional dish served on this occasion is curly kale with a special sausage made with fat pork and bran, which is called *Pinkel*. Many years ago, kale was flavored and seasoned with cinnamon, cloves, allspice and sugar.

Red Cabbage
Rotkohl

-3/4 lbs. red cabbage
/4 cup goose fat or lard
 onion, diced
 to 3 tart apples
Red-wine vinegar
 to 3 whole cloves
 small bay leaf
Salt and pepper
ugar
Water
Red wine

Trim cabbage; finely shred. In a medium saucepan, melt fat or lard.
Add onion; sauté lightly. Add cabbage. Peel and slice apples; add to
cabbage. Add vinegar, cloves, bay leaf, salt, pepper and sugar. Add
about 1/2 cup water. Bring mixture to a boil. Reduce heat and
simmer until cabbage is tender, adding water from time to time to
prevent cabbage sticking to bottom of the pan. Near the end of the
cooking time, add wine. Makes 4 servings.

Note: Red cabbage is a typical winter vegetable. It is served with
roast duck, venison and hare and also as the classic accompaniment
to all kinds of roasts. It is excellent with beef roulades and roast
pork.

Braised Sauerkraut
Gedünstetes Sauerkraut

1-3/4 lbs. sauerkraut
1/4 cup lard, cooking fat or vegetable shortening
1 onion, finely chopped
Few juniper berries or 1/2 teaspoon cumin or caraway seeds
Salt
Sugar
1/2 cup chicken stock
White wine, if desired
Piece of smoked pork, 1 pork hock or 1 smoked pork sausage
1 small raw potato, grated or 1 tablespoon cornstarch

Sauerkraut needs to be rinsed only if it has been stored in a barrel.
Rinsing reduces its bitter taste. If canned or other packaged
sauerkraut is used, simply drain it. In a large skillet, melt lard, fat or
shortening. Add onion; sauté lightly. Add sauerkraut, juniper
berries or cumin or caraway seeds, salt, if needed, sugar and stock.
The dish will be greatly enhanced if a little white wine is added.
Sauerkraut is usually cooked with a piece of smoked pork, a pork
hock or a smoked pork sausage on top. Cook about 1 hour over low
heat. Allow less time for canned sauerkraut. Thicken liquid
produced during cooking by adding a grated raw potato or
cornstarch. Makes 4 to 6 servings.

Note: Sauerkraut is popular in all regions of Germany, but is cus-
tomarily a winter dish. In Bavaria, it is also eaten in summer. It is
usually served with roast pork, pork hocks or knuckle of pork, heel
of round or hind shank of veal, smoked pickled pork, Kasseler,
pork sausages, pheasant and partridge. If you wish to prepare your
own basic sauerkraut at home, see page 187.

Rice, Potatoes & Noodles

Germans are known throughout the world as great potato eaters. Only 200 years ago, when potatoes were the staple food in Ireland and popular in Spain, they were virtually unknown in Germany. It was Frederick the Great who ordered peasant farmers of Prussia to grow these strange tubers. Initial resistance gradually gave way to enthusiasm. Today, it is hard to imagine what life in Germany would be like without potatoes. Buns, cakes, rolls and loaves made with whole-grain flour once provided starch in the everyday diet. Today they have been replaced, to a great extent, by potatoes which are served with most meals, usually peeled or boiled. German youngsters, like most other children, favor them creamed.

In Bavaria and Thüringen, industrious housewives make dumplings the size of tennis balls, called *Knodel,* following traditional recipes which have been handed down from generation to generation. If boiled potatoes are left over, they are roasted or turned into a potato salad with white sauce. Potato salad with little Vienna sausages or frankfurters, makes an excellent dish for children's parties or barbecues.

Since the end of the 19th century, an increasing quantity of potatoes has been processed into potato flour for creamed potatoes, dumplings, croquette potatoes, chips and soups. About 25 percent of the crop is now used for manufacturing convenience foods. These cater to the needs of an increasing number of housewives and cooks who have full-time jobs.

In southern Germany, many different types of noodles are consumed, Swabian noodles in particular as well as stuffed pasta, such as ravioli. This southern preference for noodles and rice probably owes much to Italian influence.

Ticino Tomato & Cheese Rice
Tessiner Tomatenreis

1 large onion
2 garlic cloves
1/3 cup vegetable oil
1-1/2 cups risotto rice
1 lb. tomatoes
1/3 cup tomato paste
2 cups light stock
1/4 cup butter
1 cup grated Sbrinz, Romano or Asiago cheese (4 oz.)

Finely chop onion and garlic. Heat oil in a deep skillet over medium heat. Add onion and garlic; sauté lightly. Add rice; stir constantly until each grain is coated with oil. Plunge tomatoes in boiling water for 30 to 45 seconds; peel and chop tomatoes. Add tomatoes to rice. Stir in tomato paste, blending thoroughly. Add stock, a small amount at a time. Stir frequently, adding more stock as needed. Never add too much stock at any one time; the rice should be moistened by the stock rather than submerged. When rice is tender but firm, remove from heat. Stir in butter and cheese. Serve with a green salad for a simple, light but appetizing meal. If a more substantial meal is required, the rice will go well with cutlets, chops and liver. Makes 4 to 6 servings.

Variation

Substitute arborio or short-grain California pearl rice for risotto rice.

Hot Potato Salad in Béchamel Sauce
Bechamelkartoffeln

1-1/2 tablespoons butter
1 onion, diced
1/4 lb. bacon, diced
1/4 cup all-purpose flour
1 cup light stock
1 cup milk
Salt and white pepper
Ground nutmeg
1 teaspoon lemon juice
About 2 lbs. boiled potatoes, peeled

Melt butter in a large heavy saucepan over medium heat. Add onion and bacon; sauté lightly. Sprinkle in flour. Cook, stirring frequently, 5 minutes. Do not allow mixture to color. Gradually add stock and milk, stirring briskly to avoid lumping. Season with salt, white pepper, nutmeg and lemon juice. Slice potatoes about 1/4 inch thick; add to sauce. Cook over low heat, stirring as little and carefully as possible to avoid breaking potatoes. Waxy potatoes will hold their shape better than floury ones. Potato salad is delicious served with sausages and green salad. Makes 6 to 8 servings.

Variation

Chopped chives, parsley, chervil, finely chopped gherkins, or 1/2 cup grated Emmentaler cheese can be added to the sauce for extra flavor.

Note: This recipe originally came from France and was introduced to Berlin in the early 18th century by the Huguenots. It later became popular throughout Germany.

Stuffed Baked Potatoes
Gefüllte Ofenkartoffeln

Farmhouse Breakfast Potato Cake
Bauernfrühstück

8 large baking potatoes
8 small eggs
Salt
Finely chopped chives

Preheat oven to 400F (205C). Scrub potatoes; wrap each in foil. Bake 50 minutes or until tender. Slit foil with 2 intersecting cuts on top of each potato; peel back foil. Scoop out a small quantity of each potato, making a hollow in each large enough for an egg. Break an egg into each scooped-out potato. Sprinkle lightly with salt. Bake 10 to 15 minutes longer to set eggs. Sprinkle with chives. Serve hot. Makes 8 servings.

Note: Baked potatoes are the ideal complement to any grilled meat. This dish can also be served as a light but nourishing vegetarian meal.

5 to 8 boiled potatoes, peeled
1/3 lb. fleischwurst or other smooth, juicy sausage
Leftover roast meat, mortadella or prosciutto
1 small onion
2 gherkins
8 bacon slices, diced
3 tablespoons chopped pimiento, if desired
4 eggs
1/3 cup milk
Salt
Ground nutmeg or cumin
1 tomato, sliced
Finely chopped chives or parsley

Dice potatoes; sausage; meat, mortadella or prosciutto; onion and gherkins. In a large heavy skillet, sauté bacon until golden brown. Add diced potatoes; sauté lightly. Add sausage; leftover meat, mortadella or prosciutto; onion; gherkins and pimiento, if desired. Stir to combine. In a medium bowl, beat together eggs, milk, salt and nutmeg or cumin. Pour egg mixture over potato mixture. Cover and cook over low heat until eggs are set. Invert potato cake onto a warm plate or serving tray. Garnish lightly with tomato slices and chives or parsley. Makes 4 to 6 servings.

Note: This farmhouse potato cake used to be the traditional light meal for farmers. It is quick to prepare, economical, filling and nourishing. The Silesian equivalent is known as *Leineweber*.

Sautéed Potatoes
Bratkartoffeln

5 to 8 raw or cooked potatoes
1/4 cup oil or butter or, 8 bacon slices, diced
1/2 onion, diced
Salt
Cumin, marjoram or chives, if desired

If raw potatoes are used, peel and cut into thin slices. Use oil or butter to fry potatoes in a large skillet over medium heat to ensure even cooking. If cooked potatoes are used, dice or cut potatoes into thick slices. In a large skillet, sauté bacon until golden brown. Add potatoes. Fry 5 minutes before turning to allow potato slices to brown. Add onion when potatoes are about half cooked. Fry without allowing onion to brown too much. After potatoes are browned, season with salt and cumin, marjoram or chives, if desired. Makes 4 to 6 servings.

Note: This recipe provides a useful change for using leftovers and goes well with fried eggs and spinach, green cabbage, or smoked pork loin and salad.

Grated Potato Cake
Rösti

1-3/4 to 2 lbs. potatoes
1/2 cup butter
Salt and white pepper

In a large saucepan, boil potatoes in their skins over low to medium heat. Drain and peel; let stand to cool. Coarsely grate potatoes. Melt 1/4 cup butter in a medium, heavy skillet. Season potatoes with salt and white pepper; sauté in hot butter. Turn potatoes frequently during first 15 minutes of cooking time. Press potatoes firmly into skillet so they form a compact pattie, resembling a flat cake. Add remaining butter, a little at a time. Potato cake should stick together because of the starch in the potatoes. Potatoes used for this recipe should never be prepared ahead of time or rinsed during peeling because starch will be reduced. To prevent potatoes from sticking to bottom of skillet, salt may be added when grated potatoes are already in skillet. Serve directly from skillet or carefully invert onto a warm serving dish. Makes 4 to 6 servings.

Note: Rösti is a Swiss specialty and a good accompaniment to grilled meat or chicken.

Potato Fritters or Pancakes
Kartoffelpuffer

lbs. baking potatoes
onion
eggs
alt and white pepper
tablespoons coarse-ground semolina or farina, if desired
tablespoon finely chopped chives
egetable oil

eel and finely grate raw potatoes and onion. If potatoes produce
oo much liquid, drain off. In a large bowl, combine potatoes,
nion, eggs, salt and white pepper, blending well. If mixture still
eems too moist, add semolina or farina, if desired. Add chives.
over the bottom of a large skillet or griddle with a thin layer of oil.
rop spoonfuls of potato mixture onto hot oil; press into thin
ancakes or fritters. Turn when underside is golden brown and
risp. Brown other side. Serve immediately; they are best when
iping hot and fresh. Serve with salad or with apple compote,
lueberries and sugar. Makes 4 to 6 servings.

Note: These potato fritters are very popular all over Germany.
During celebrations for local festivals, they are made and sold at
utdoor stalls.

Potato Salad
Kartoffelsalat

1-3/4 lbs. boiling potatoes
1/3 cup vegetable oil
1/3 cup vinegar
1/2 cup hot stock
3 tablespoons finely chopped onion
Salt and pepper
Sugar
1 teaspoon prepared mustard
1 tablespoon finely chopped chives
1/4 cup crumbled crisp-cooked bacon, if desired

In a large saucepan, boil unpeeled potatoes until tender but firm.
Drain, peel and thinly slice. Place potato slices in a large bowl. In a
small bowl, combine oil, vinegar, stock, onion, salt, pepper, sugar
and mustard. Pour oil mixture over potatoes; combine, turning
gently. Adjust seasonings to taste. Sprinkle with chives and bacon, if
desired. Serve as a side dish with liver, sausages, hamburgers or
rissoles, fried battered or breaded fish fillets or herring. Makes 4 to
6 servings.

Note: The correct way to prepare this popular salad is the subject of
endless discussions. These usually end in agreement to disagree as
to whether it should be served hot or cold, with or without
mayonnaise.

Raw Potato Dumplings
Rohe Kartoffelklösse

Cooked Potato Dumplings
Gekochte Kartoffelklösse

8 to 10 medium baking potatoes
1 cup milk
1 teaspoon salt
1 tablespoon butter
1/3 cup farina or Cream of Wheat cereal
1/2 teaspoon marjoram, if desired
2 tablespoons margarine
3 slices stale bread, cut in cubes

Cook 3 to 4 potatoes in water until tender. Mash or sieve hot potatoes into a bowl. Cover and refrigerate 12 to 24 hours. Peel remaining 5 or 6 raw potatoes; finely grate or chop into a bowl of cold water. Drain well and wrap in a clean towel. Squeeze to remove excess moisture. In a medium saucepan, combine milk, salt, butter, farina or cereal and marjoram, if desired. Cook over medium heat until mixture boils and thickens. Combine cold cooked potatoes, grated raw potatoes and cooked milk mixture. Melt margarine in a medium skillet. Add bread cubes; sauté until lightly browned. Shape potato mixture into 8 large dumplings, enclosing a few sautéed bread cubes in center of each. Bring a large saucepan of salted water to a boil. Add dumplings, one at a time, to boiling water, making sure they are not overcrowded. Do not cover. Simmer about 15 minutes. Dumplings are done when they float. Carefully remove dumplings using a slotted spoon. Drain well. Serve immediately with roast meat and gravy or sauce. Dumplings are excellent with roast goose or duck. Makes 8 servings.

Note: Floury potatoes with a very high starch content must be used. Otherwise, dumplings fall apart when cooked.

6 to 8 medium baking potatoes
About 1-1/4 cups all-purpose flour
2 eggs
1 teaspoon salt
1/4 teaspoon ground nutmeg
2 tablespoons margarine
3 slices stale bread, cut in cubes

Cook potatoes in water until tender. Cover and refrigerate 12 to 24 hours. Finely chop cooked potatoes or mash thoroughly. In a medium bowl, combine chopped or mashed potatoes, 1 cup flour, eggs, salt and nutmeg to form a firm but light paste. If mixture is too moist, add flour as needed. This will help to keep dumplings from falling apart during cooking. Melt margarine in a large skillet. Add bread cubes; sauté until golden brown. Working with floured hands, form smooth paste into a roll about 2-1/2 inches in diameter. Cut roll in 8 to 10 pieces. Form pieces into dumplings, enclosing a few sautéed bread cubes in center of each. Bring a large saucepan of salted water to a boil. Add dumplings, one at a time, to boiling water, making sure they are not overcrowded. Do not cover. Simmer about 15 minutes. Dumplings are done when they float. Carefully remove dumplings using a slotted spoon. Drain well. Serve immediately with roast meat and gravy or sauce. Dumplings are excellent with roast goose or duck. Makes 8 servings.

Note: In northern Germany these dumplings are usually served with roast beef, roast pork or goulash. If dumplings are left over, slice and sauté in butter or margarine.

Steamed Savory Bread Pudding
Serviettenkloss

Bread Dumplings
Semmelknödel

1 lb. (25 slices) stale white bread
5 eggs, separated
1 to 1-1/2 cups milk
1/4 cup margarine
2 onions, finely diced
3 tablespoons finely chopped parsley
1 teaspoon salt
1/4 teaspoon ground nutmeg
1/2 teaspoon poultry seasoning, if desired

Break bread into small pieces; place in a medium bowl. In a second bowl, beat together egg yolks and 1 cup milk. Pour egg-yolk mixture over bread. Cover and refrigerate 3 to 4 hours. Amount of milk needed will depend on how dry bread is. Add more milk, if necessary. Melt 2 tablespoons margarine in a large skillet. Add onions; sauté until golden brown. Add sautéed onion, parsley, salt, nutmeg and poultry seasoning, if desired, to soaked bread. Combine thoroughly until smooth and mixture forms a firm paste. Beat egg whites until stiff but not dry. Fold beaten egg whites into bread mixture. Form dough into a large, slightly flattened ball. Thinly spread remaining margarine over a large clean cloth napkin. Place bread pudding in center of napkin. Tie napkin, knotting the corners. Thread a skewer or wooden stick under knotted corners. Bring a large saucepan of salted water to a boil. Suspend pudding over boiling water. Be sure pudding does not touch water. Cover pan tightly with foil. Steam pudding 50 to 60 minutes, keeping water boiling briskly. Pudding will be soft and light. Serve with roast or grilled chicken and cucumber salad or with braised meat. Makes 6 to 8 servings.

1/2 lb. (10 slices) stale white bread
1 cup milk, warmed
1 tablespoon vegetable oil
1 medium onion, chopped
3 eggs
1/2 teaspoon salt
1/4 teaspoon white pepper
1/8 teaspoon ground nutmeg
3 tablespoons finely chopped parsley

Break bread into small pieces; place in a medium bowl. Pour warm milk over bread. Heat oil in a medium skillet. Add onion; sauté until golden brown. Add sautéed onion, eggs, salt, white pepper, nutmeg and parsley to bread mixture; blend well. Mixture should be stiff. Add milk or bread to adjust consistency. Working with floured hands, form smooth paste into a roll about 2-1/2 inches in diameter. Cut roll in 8 pieces. Form each piece into a dumpling. Bring a large saucepan of salted water to a boil. Add dumplings, one at a time, to boiling water, making sure they are not overcrowded. Do not cover. Simmer over low heat about 15 minutes. Dumplings are done when they float. Carefully remove dumplings using a slotted spoon. Drain well. Serve immediately with roast meat and gravy or sauce and cooked kale. Dumplings are excellent with roast goose or duck. Makes 8 servings.

Note: These Semmelknödel are most often eaten in southern Germany and Austria and are a very good way to use stale bread. If dumplings are left over, slice, sprinkle with beaten egg and sauté in hot margarine.

Sweet Yeast Dumplings
Hefeklösse

1/4 cup warm water (110F, 45C)
2-1/4 teaspoons active dry yeast
1 teaspoon sugar
1 egg
1/2 cup milk
1/2 teaspoon salt
1/4 teaspoon ground nutmeg
About 3-1/2 cups all-purpose flour
1/4 cup butter, melted, or 3 tablespoons poppy seeds and 3 tablespoons
   sugar, or 1 lb. mixed dried fruit, cooked

Grease a baking sheet; set aside. In a large bowl, dissolve yeast and 1 teaspoon sugar in warm water. Beat in egg, milk, salt and nutmeg. Beat in 2 cups flour. Let stand 10 minutes. Add enough additional flour to make a stiff dough. Turn out dough on a lightly floured surface; knead briefly. Dough should be light and easy to shape, but not sticky. Shape dough into 8 dumplings. Place dumplings on greased baking sheet. Cover and let rise in a warm place, free from drafts, until doubled in bulk, about 30 minutes. Do not let dumplings rise too long or they will not be smooth and round. In a large saucepan, pour water to a depth of 3 inches. Bring water to a boil. Add dumplings, one at a time, to boiling water, making sure they are not overcrowded. Do not cover. Simmer over low heat about 20 minutes. Dumplings are done when they float. Carefully remove dumplings using a slotted spoon. Drain well. Make a hole in each dumpling using 2 spoons. Pour in melted butter, poppy seeds and sugar or cooked dried fruit. Serve immediately. Makes 8 large dumplings.

Variation

Stuff dumplings with apricots, cherries or plums. Cover with a mixture of egg and milk. Bake in a 350F (175C) oven until lightly browned.

Semolina Dumplings
Griessklösse

3 cups water
1/2 cup margarine
1/2 teaspoon salt
1-2/3 cups farina or Cream of Wheat cereal
1/4 cup margarine
2 medium onions, finely chopped

In a medium saucepan, combine water, 1/2 cup margarine and salt. Bring to a boil. Whisk farina or cereal into boiling water. Cook over medium heat, stirring frequently, until mixture forms a firm, compact ball that comes cleanly away from side of pan. Using a tablespoon, scoop out and shape mixture into 8 or more dumplings. Rinse tablespoon frequently in cold water to prevent dough from sticking. Bring a large saucepan of salted water to a boil. Add dumplings, one at a time, to boiling water, making sure they are not overcrowded. Do not cover. Simmer over low heat 20 to 25 minutes. Dumplings are done when they float. Carefully remove dumplings using a slotted spoon. Drain well. Meanwhile, melt 1/4 cup margarine in a large skillet. Add onions; sauté lightly. When dumplings are cooked and well drained, pour sautéed onions over them. Serve immediately. Makes 8 to 12 dumplings.

Note: These dumplings are extremely quick to prepare and can be served with goulash, beef rolls or roulades, roast meat and salad or sauerkraut. A little sugar can be added to the farina or cereal and omit the onions for sweet dumplings that may be served with any cooked fruit or a compote of mixed dried fruit seasoned with cinnamon.

Swabian Noodles with Cheese
Käsespätzle

Ravioli
Maultaschen

Swabian Noodles, page 129
1/4 cup butter
4 medium onions, thinly sliced
2 cups grated Emmentaler cheese (8 oz.)

Prepare Swabian Noodles; cook in boiling water. Remove cooked noodles with a slotted spoon. Place in a warmed serving bowl or tureen; keep warm until serving. Melt butter in a medium skillet. Add onions; sauté until golden brown. To serve, sprinkle hot noodles with cheese. Top with sautéed onions. Serve hot. Makes 4 servings.

Note: These potato noodles go well with salad or sauerkraut. They are a particular specialty of Swabia and Switzerland. Serve noodles piping hot for a simple but tempting dish.

Pasta:
3-3/4 cups all-purpose flour
3 to 4 eggs
Salt
1/3 to 2/3 cup water
Filling:
2/3 cup dry breadcrumbs
Water
1/2 lb. ground meat
Leftover roast meat or prosciutto, cut in strips, if desired
3 tablespoons finely chopped parsley
1 egg
Salt and pepper
Ground nutmeg

To make pasta, in a medium bowl, combine flour, eggs and salt. Gradually add water, working until dough is smooth and firm. Cover and let stand 10 minutes.
To make filling, in a small bowl, soak breadcrumbs in a small amount of water. Squeeze to remove excess water. In a medium bowl, combine ground meat, meat strips, if desired, soaked breadcrumbs, parsley, egg, salt, pepper and nutmeg. On a lightly floured surface, roll pasta dough into a thin sheet. Divide dough in half. Use a pastry cutter to make one half into 4-inch squares. Place a small quantity of filling in center of each square. Brush edges of each square with water. Top with other half of dough sheet; press down with fingers between mounds of filling. Use a fluted pastry cutter to cut finished ravioli. Cook ravioli in boiling salted water about 10 minutes. Serve hot with melted butter, sautéed diced onion and homemade tomato sauce. Makes 4 to 6 servings

One - Dish Meals

Many different regional specialties could loosely and rather inaccurately be called *stews.* In Bavaria, there is a special festival dish called *Pichelsteiner.* It is made with a variety of vegetables and three types of meat, depending on personal preference and availability. This casserole originated in the Bavarian woodlands in the 18th century. On June 16th each year a Pichelsteiner festival takes place in the city of Regen, near the Buchelstein mountains. Another typically regional dish comes from Swabia. It is *Gaisburger Marsch,* the traditional hearty soup which originated in a suburb of Stuttgart from which it takes its name. Potatoes are often the most-important ingredient in northern German stews.

Local opinions differ widely as to the rival merits of various dishes and modes of preparation — whether green-pea soup is better than yellow-split-pea soup and how much vinegar should be added to lentil soup. It is generally agreed that a good smoked sausage or a piece of pork improves almost any soup, stew or casserole.

Leek & Pork Stew
Laucheintopf

Pear, Green-Bean & Bacon Stew
Birnen, Bohnen und Speck

1 lb. lean pork shoulder or butt
1/3 cup vegetable oil
3 onions, thinly sliced
2 cups meat stock
2 lbs. leeks
1 lb. potatoes
Salt and pepper
1 garlic clove, crushed
Finely chopped parsley

Cut pork into 1-inch cubes. Heat oil in a large heavy saucepan. Add pork; brown in hot oil. Add onions; sauté until golden brown. Add stock. Cover and reduce heat. Simmer 20 to 30 minutes. Meanwhile, wash and trim leeks. Cut leeks into rings about 1/2 inch thick. Peel and dice potatoes. Add leeks and potatoes to cooked pork mixture. Season with salt, pepper and garlic. Avoid mixing at this stage. Cover and simmer 30 minutes longer. Adjust seasoning, if necessary. Sprinkle with chopped parsley. Serve as a meal or main course. Makes 4 servings.

2/3 lb. slab bacon or pork belly
1 lb. green beans
1 lb. cooking pears
Water
Summer savory bouquet
Salt and pepper
1 tablespoon finely chopped parsley

Cut bacon or pork belly into large pieces; sauté in a large, heavy cooking pot. Trim beans; cut beans in half. Leave pears whole and unpeeled. Add beans, whole pears and a little water to sautéed bacon. Season with savory, salt and pepper. Cook over medium heat 30 minutes or until beans are tender. Remove savory; discard. Adjust seasoning, as desired. Sprinkle with chopped parsley. Makes 4 servings.

Note: In some regions, this dish is modified to include little dumplings, *Kluten,* made with flour, eggs, water and salt. Other more varied versions include turnips and leeks.

Heaven & Earth
Himmel und Erde

Sauerkraut & Pork Stew
Sauerkrauteintopf

lbs. potatoes
lbs. tart cooking apples
alt and pepper
teaspoon sugar
⁄4 cup lard, cooking fat or goose fat
onions, finely diced
bratwurst or blutwurst

eel and dice potatoes and apples. Cook in separate saucepans in a
ttle water until tender. Season potatoes with salt and pepper.
eason apples with a little sugar. Sieve or mash potatoes. Melt lard
r fat in a medium skillet. Add onions; sauté lightly. Cook sausages
eparately. These can be pork, beef or veal sausages or a blend, or
lood sausages. Place potatoes and apples in a warm dish. Top with
nions and sausages. Makes 4 servings.

1 lb. lean pork shoulder, pork butt or shank cut fresh ham
1/4 cup cooking fat or lard
4 onions, diced
3 tablespoons paprika
3 cups meat stock
Salt
Cumin or caraway seeds
1 lb. sauerkraut
1 lb. potatoes, if desired
1/2 cup dairy sour cream
8 bacon slices, cooked crisp, crumbled

Cut pork into 1- to 1-1/2-inch cubes. Heat fat or lard in a large deep
saucepan. Add pork; brown in hot fat. Add onions; sauté briskly.
Add paprika, stock, salt and cumin or caraway seeds. Cook,
covered, over medium heat 20 minutes. Add sauerkraut. If potatoes
are used, peel and cut into large cubes. Add to pork mixture. Or,
cook potatoes separately and add when pork is tender. Cook over
low heat 45 minutes or until pork is tender. Season to taste. Stir in
sour cream and bacon before serving. Makes 4 servings.

Lamb & Green-Bean Stew
Hammelfleisch mit grünen Bohnen

1 lb. lean lamb shoulder or leg
1-3/4 lbs. green beans
2 onions, chopped
Salt and pepper
Summer savory
3 cups meat stock
6 to 8 potatoes

Remove excess fat from lamb; cut lamb into 1- to 1-1/2-inch cubes. Trim beans; cut beans in halves or thirds. Arrange lamb, beans and onions in alternating layers in a large saucepan. Season with salt, pepper and savory. Pour on stock. Cover and bring to a boil. Reduce heat and cook 45 minutes. Meanwhile, peel and slice potatoes. After first cooking time, add potatoes to meat dish as a top layer. Cover and cook 30 minutes longer. Stir and adjust seasoning, as necessary. Makes 4 servings.

Note: In the suburbs of Berlin, green beans are often replaced by beans cooked in a sweet-sour sauce, called *Schnibbelbohnen.* This is also a popular winter dish in Westphalia.

Silesian Heaven
Schlesisches Himmelreich

2/3 lb. mixed dried fruit
3 cups water
1 lb. slab bacon or pork belly
Salt
Sugar
Piece of lemon peel
Small piece of cinnamon stick
1 tablespoon cornstarch
Sweet Yeast Dumplings, page 120
1 tomato, cut in quarters
Lemon wedges
Parsley

In a medium bowl, soak dried fruit in water overnight. Cut bacon or pork belly in 4 thick slices. In a large skillet, place bacon or pork belly and some water used for soaking dried fruit. Add salt, sugar, lemon peel and cinnamon. Simmer 20 minutes. Add soaked fruit; cook 20 minutes longer. Remove cinnamon stick and lemon peel; discard. In a small bowl, combine cornstarch and a small amount of water. Add to fruit mixture. Cook, stirring constantly, until slightly thickened. Prepare Sweet Yeast Dumplings. Place on top of fruit mixture. Simmer until dumplings are done. When they are tender, use 2 forks to pry them open slightly to allow steam to escape. Garnish with tomato, lemon and parsley. Makes 4 servings.

Curly-Kale Casserole
Grünkohleintopf

Pichelsteiner
Pichelsteiner

lbs. fresh curly kale or 2 (10-oz.) pkgs. frozen chopped kale, thawed
to 10 potatoes
4 cup lard, cooking fat or goose fat
bacon slices, diced
large onion, chopped
qt. chicken stock
alt and white pepper
inch of ground allspice
lb. Kasseler or mettwurst
lilk, if desired

im fresh kale, removing thick stalks and ribs; discard old
imaged leaves. Blanch fresh kale briefly in boiling water; drain
ell and chop. Peel and dice potatoes. Heat lard or fat in a large
illet. Add bacon; sauté lightly. Add onion; sauté until transparent.
dd blanched or thawed kale, potatoes, stock, salt, white pepper
id allspice. Cover and simmer 45 minutes without stirring. Place
rk loin or sausages on top of other ingredients. Cover and cook 20
inutes longer. The casserole can be stirred and potatoes broken up
little, if desired. If the taste of kale is too strong, a little milk can
added, if desired. Serve with mustard and beer. Makes 4 servings.

ote: This casserole is a typical north German dish and usually
eralds the arrival of winter. In many families, it is a regular weekly
sh, sometimes served with roast-goose leftovers.

4 bacon slices, diced
1 large onion, finely chopped
1-1/4 lbs. stewing cubes from beef, pork, veal and lamb or mutton (a
  selection of 2 or 3 of these meats, if possible)
1 qt. meat stock
6 to 10 potatoes
1-3/4 lbs. mixed fresh vegetables
Salt and pepper
Ground nutmeg
3 tablespoons finely chopped parsley

In a large skillet, sauté bacon. Add onion; sauté until pale golden
brown. Add meat cubes; brown lightly on all sides. Add stock.
Cover and simmer 45 minutes. Meanwhile, clean, trim and prepare
potatoes and other vegetables, as necessary. Cut vegetables into
small pieces. Choose a wide range of vegetables for color. This will
make the dish look attractive and appetizing. Add potatoes,
vegetables, salt, pepper and nutmeg. Cover and simmer 30 minutes
longer. The casserole should not be stirred until this point. Adjust
seasoning, if necessary. Sprinkle with chopped parsley. Serve
immediately. Makes 4 servings.

Note: This dish can be made with 1 type of meat, but traditionally 2
or 3 varieties are used. Pichelsteiner is well known in Frankonia and
Bavaria and takes its name from the Buchelstein mountain. The
inhabitants of the city of Regen nearby still congregate each year to
enjoy this traditional regional specialty.

Main-Dish Chicken Soup
Dicke Hühnersuppe

1 small stewing chicken
1 qt. water
Salt
Ground nutmeg
1 leek, sliced
1 celery stalk, sliced
1 carrot, sliced
1 pkg. frozen mixed vegetables or 1 lb. mixed fresh vegetables, diced
1/2 lb. spiral noodles or macaroni
Lemon juice or dry white wine, if desired
3 tablespoons finely chopped parsley

Cut chicken into serving pieces. Place chicken in a large deep saucepan. Cover with water. Add salt, nutmeg, leek, celery and carrot. Cook over medium heat until chicken is tender. Remove from heat; strain, reserving liquid. Remove and discard skin and bones from chicken. Pull or cut flesh into small even pieces. Bring strained stock to a boil. Add water to make 1 quart liquid. Add fresh vegetables and noodles or macaroni. If frozen vegetables are used, boil noodles 5 minutes before adding vegetables. Noodles and vegetables should be ready after a total of 10 minutes cooking time. Add chicken pieces to soup. Season to taste. For extra flavor, a little lemon juice or white wine may be added. Transfer to a warm soup tureen. Sprinkle with chopped parsley. Makes 4 servings.

Gaisburg Broth
Gaisburger Marsch

1-1/4 lbs. beef chuck arm roast
1/2 lb. beef marrow or shank
1 leek, chopped
1 celery stalk, chopped
1 carrot, chopped
1 qt. meat stock or water
4 to 5 potatoes, peeled, diced
Swabian Noodles, page 129
Salt and white pepper
2 tablespoons butter or margarine
1 onion, thinly sliced

In a large pot, place beef roast, beef marrow or shank, leek, celery, carrot and stock or water. Bring to a boil. Skim foam from surface until surface is clear. Reduce heat and simmer 1 hour. Strain stock; return strained liquid to pot. Set beef and vegetables aside. Add potatoes to stock; boil 25 minutes. Prepare Swabian Noodles; drop noodles into stock. While noodles simmer, cut beef in large cubes. Add beef to stock when noodles are nearly tender, 3 to 5 minutes. Season to taste with salt and white pepper. Melt butter or margarine in a skillet. Add onion; sauté until golden brown. Add sautéed onion to each plate when serving. Makes 4 servings.

Lentils with Swabian Noodles
Linsen mit Spätzle

Pea Soup
Erbsensuppe

lb. lentils
lb. smoked salt pork or mettwurst
small onion, diced
carrot, diced
bay leaf
alt and pepper
crushed garlic clove, if desired
Water

Swabian Noodles:
-1/4 cups all-purpose flour
teaspoon salt
eggs
About 1/2 cup water

oak lentils overnight in water; drain. Place lentils in a deep heavy ooking pot. Add pork or sausage, onion, carrot, bay leaf, salt, epper and garlic, if desired. Add enough water to cover. Bring to a oil. Reduce heat and simmer 1 hour.

To make noodles, sift flour and salt into a medium bowl. Add eggs; ombine well. Add water gradually until dough is smooth, light and irm. Let stand 10 minutes. Push dough through the largest holes of grater or metal colander directly into a large pot of boiling salted vater. A firm dough can be pushed through a ricer. After a few ninutes, when noodles are done, drain and refresh in cold water. Add cooked noodles to lentils and meat. Makes 4 servings.

Note: This traditional Swabian delicacy is often enhanced by the ddition of lightly sautéed diced bacon or fried onions.

4 bacon slices, diced
1 onion, finely chopped
1 lb. shelled fresh green peas
2 qts. water
Salt
Celery salt
1 to 1-1/4 lbs. fresh or smoked pork, diced
1 garlic clove, if desired
4 to 8 potatoes
1 leek
1 celery stalk
1 carrot
1 tablespoon finely chopped parsley

In a large heavy cooking pot, sauté bacon until lightly browned. Add onion; sauté lightly. Add peas, water, salt, celery salt, pork and garlic, if desired. While pork and peas are cooking, peel and dice potatoes. Trim and finely chop remaining vegetables; add to pork and peas. Simmer 30 minutes. Potatoes and other vegetables can be broken up slightly with a potato masher, if desired. Season to taste. Sprinkle with chopped parsley. Serve with mustard and a light, cold beer. Makes 4 servings.

Variation

Dried peas can be used instead of fresh peas if they are soaked overnight. Bring drained peas to a boil in salted water. Drain and rinse in cold water before adding to the soup. Cover and cook 1 hour or slightly longer before adding to other ingredients.

Puddings & Desserts

At the end of a traditional German-family meal, a pudding is usually served, especially when children are present. Puddings have changed considerably during the last century. At one time they were substantially made with eggs, butter, sugar and flour or oatmeal and sometimes semolina or leftover cakes and puddings. Additions such as chocolate or nuts gave extra richness. This was cooked in a tightly sealed pudding mold floating in a pan of hot water. Over the years, tastes changed and puddings were no longer as rich and heavy. Vanilla creams, looking like golden-yellow firm custards or blancmanges, were made with milk, sugar, eggs and cornstarch. They were served cold, with raspberry syrup or sauce or a cold vanilla-flavored sauce. Many food manufacturers started making these desserts. The resulting convenience foods proved popular with busy housewives over the last 20 to 30 years.

In recent years, trends have changed again. These custard creams are now being supplanted by desserts made with fruit and soured-milk products. Quark or cottage cheese, which tastes pleasantly like unsweetened cream, is mixed with various fruits and yogurt flavored with blueberries, strawberries and blackberries. It is very popular. Fresh-fruit salad is often served with only a little sugar, providing a low-calorie, low-fat, wholesome dessert. For special occasions, German housewives still take immense pains to prepare smooth, rich, creamy puddings or delicious homemade ice cream. Children's apparently insatiable hunger is satisfied with hot filling puddings that are almost a meal in themselves.

Vanilla Pudding
Vanillepudding

Layered Pudding with Fruit
Schichtpudding mit Früchten

2-1/4 cups milk or half and half
1/3 cup cornstarch
3/4 teaspoon vanilla extract
1/4 cup sugar
2 egg yolks, slightly beaten
2 egg whites, stiffly beaten
Maraschino cherries, drained

In a medium saucepan, combine milk or half and half and cornstarch. Cook over medium heat, stirring constantly, until slightly thickened. Stir in vanilla and sugar until blended. Remove from heat. Stir a small amount of cooked mixture into egg yolks. Add egg-yolk mixture to saucepan. Cook, stirring constantly, 1 minute. Carefully fold in egg whites. Pour into a serving dish or mold. Refrigerate until firmly set. Garnish with maraschino cherries. Makes 4 servings.

Vanilla Pudding, opposite
2 tablespoons unsweetened cocoa powder or instant-coffee powder
3 tablespoons sugar
3 tablespoons half and half
1 small can mandarin-orange segments, drained
1/2 cup whipping cream, whipped

Prepare Vanilla Pudding as directed. Divide 1/2 the pudding into 4 dessert dishes; set remaining pudding aside. Top each serving with a layer of mandarin-orange segments; reserve a few segments for garnish. Stir cocoa or coffee powder, sugar and half and half into reserved pudding. Heat slightly, if necessary, to dissolve cocoa or coffee powder. Spoon mixture evenly over mandarin oranges. Refrigerate until set. Garnish each serving with whipped cream and reserved mandarin-orange segments. Makes 4 servings.

Variation

Substitute other canned fruit such as pitted cherries, peach slices or berries for orange segments.

Bavarian Vanilla & Lemon Cream
Welfenspeise

Vanilla Cream:
2-1/4 cups milk or half and half
1/3 cup cornstarch
3/4 teaspoon vanilla extract
1/4 cup sugar
2 egg whites, stiffly beaten

Lemon Cream:
3 tablespoons cornstarch
1/4 cup cold water
Pinch of salt
3/4 cup hot water
2/3 cup sugar
2 egg yolks, slightly beaten
3 tablespoons lemon juice
1 teaspoon butter
1 teaspoon finely grated lemon peel, if desired

To make vanilla cream, in a medium saucepan, combine milk or half and half and cornstarch. Cook over medium heat, stirring constantly, until slightly thickened. Stir in vanilla and sugar until blended. Remove from heat. Carefully fold in egg whites. Pour mixture into a serving dish. Refrigerate.
To make lemon cream, in a small bowl, combine cornstarch, cold water and salt; set aside. In a medium saucepan, combine hot water and sugar. Bring mixture to a boil. Stir in cornstarch mixture. Cook over medium heat, stirring constantly, until thickened. Stir a small amount of cooked mixture into egg yolks. Add egg-yolk mixture to saucepan. Cook, stirring constantly, 1 to 2 minutes. Add lemon juice, butter and lemon peel, if desired. Cool slightly. Pour cooled lemon mixture over chilled Vanilla Cream. Refrigerate until set. Makes 6 servings.

Apricot Pudding
Aphrodite

1-1/2 lbs. fresh apricots
Juice of 1 lemon
Small piece of lemon peel
1 cup water
1 cup white wine
1/2 cup sugar
1 teaspoon cornstarch
1/2 lb. fresh cherries, pitted
1/2 cup whipping cream, if desired
1 tablespoon sugar
Few drops vanilla extract
Ground nutmeg or cinnamon, if desired

Cook apricots in boiling water until tender; remove peel and pits. Puree apricots in a food processor or blender. In a medium saucepan, combine apricot puree, lemon juice, lemon peel, water, wine and 1/2 cup sugar. Bring mixture to a boil. Dissolve cornstarch in a small amount of water, if desired. Stir into apricot mixture. Stirring constantly, boil gently 2 to 3 minutes or until thickened. Remove lemon peel. Cool pudding slightly. Stir in cherries. Pour into a serving dish or dessert dishes. Refrigerate until chilled. Whip cream until soft peaks form, if desired. Beat in 1 tablespoon sugar and vanilla. Sprinkle with nutmeg or cinnamon, if desired. Serve with pudding. Makes 6 to 8 servings.

Variation

Substitute raspberries or blueberries for cherries.

Strawberries & Cream
Erdbeer mit Sahne

Chocolate Ice Cream
Schokoladeneis

3 pints strawberries
1/4 cup sugar
1/2 cup whipping cream
Few drops vanilla extract

Clean and hull berries; drain well. Place berries in a medium bowl. Sprinkle with 3 tablespoons sugar. Let stand in a cool place or refrigerate to form a sugar syrup. In a medium bowl, whip cream until soft peaks form. Add 1 tablespoon sugar and vanilla; beat until stiff. To serve, spoon berries into 4 dessert dishes. Place a dollop of whipped cream on each serving. Makes 4 servings.

Variation

Chop strawberries. Stir in 1/4 cup orange juice and 1/2 teaspoon grated orange peel. Before serving, stir in about 2 tablespoons Grand Marnier or other orange liqueur. Top with whipped cream.

Note: Germans love strawberries with whipped cream and consume considerable quantities when strawberries are in season.

1-1/4 cups sugar
Pinch of salt
1 tablespoon cornstarch
3 cups whole milk
3 egg yolks, beaten
3 oz. semisweet chocolate, melted
2 cups whipping cream
1 teaspoon vanilla extract or 2 tablespoons rum

In top of a double boiler, combine sugar, salt and cornstarch. Stir in milk. Stir constantly over medium heat until mixture begins to simmer. Stir a little of hot milk mixture into egg yolks. Stir egg-yolk mixture into remaining hot milk mixture. Stir over low heat until slightly thickened, 2 to 3 minutes. Stir in melted chocolate until evenly distributed and mixture is smooth. Stir in whipping cream and vanilla or rum. Cool to room temperature. Pour into an ice-cream canister. Freeze in an ice-cream maker according to manufacturer's directions. Makes about 2 quarts.

Ice Cream with Fruit
Eis mit Früchten

Cottage Cheese with Oranges
Orangenquark

pint ice cream
/2 lb. assorted fruit, such as: pineapple, strawberries, raspberries,
  peaches, kiwi, orange segments, mandarins or bananas
ugar and lemon juice, if desired
/2 cup whipping cream
teaspoon sugar
anilla extract
hopped pistachio nuts or grated chocolate, if desired

emove ice cream from freezer 10 to 15 minutes before serving to
often and bring out flavor. Clean and slice fruits as necessary.
prinkle sugar and lemon juice on fruit, if desired. Let fruit stand a
w minutes before serving. Alternately layer fruit and ice cream in
to 6 dessert dishes. In a small bowl, whip cream until soft peaks
orm. Add 1 teaspoon sugar and vanilla. Beat until stiff. Top each
erving with whipped cream. Garnish with chopped nuts or
hocolate, if desired. Makes 4 to 6 servings.

1-1/4 cups cottage cheese, drained, or ricotta cheese (10 oz.)
1/3 cup sugar
1/2 cup milk or cream
Small piece of orange peel, cut into thin strips or grated
1 tablespoon Grand Marnier or other orange liqueur
2 to 3 oranges
3 tablespoons sugar

In a blender or food processor, combine cheese and 1/3 cup sugar. Process until smooth. Add enough milk or cream to make a smooth creamy mixture. Stir in orange peel and liqueur. Peel oranges, removing any pith. Slice into rounds or small pieces. Reserve a few attractive orange segments to garnish dessert. Sprinkle 3 tablespoons sugar over remaining orange pieces. Add orange pieces to cheese mixture, stirring to combine or, arrange cheese mixture and oranges in layers in dessert dishes. Makes 4 to 6 servings.

Variation

Substitute blackberries, blueberries, strawberries, apricots, peaches or pineapple for oranges. Add a dash of lemon juice to heighten flavor.

Note: Cottage cheese or quark has become tremendously popular for dessert as it is bland and adaptable in flavor and lends itself to last-minute preparations.

Strawberry Cream
Erdbeercreme

Coffee Cream
Mokkacreme

1 (1/4-oz.) pkg. unflavored gelatin
Generous 1/2 cup white wine
1/4 cup sugar
1 pint strawberries
2 egg whites
3/4 cup whipping cream

In a small saucepan, combine gelatin with a small amount of wine. Let stand 5 minutes to soften gelatin. Add remaining wine. Stir over low heat until dissolved. Do not boil. Remove from heat; stir in sugar. Wash and hull strawberries; drain well. Reserve a few whole berries. Puree remaining berries in a food processor or blender. Combine pureed strawberries with gelatin mixture. Refrigerate until slightly set, about 20 minutes. In a small bowl, beat egg whites until stiff but not dry. In another small bowl, beat whipping cream until stiff. Fold beaten egg whites and 2/3 of the whipped cream into strawberry mixture. Spoon into dessert dishes or a large serving dish. Refrigerate until set. To serve, top with remaining whipped cream and whole strawberries. Makes 4 to 6 servings.

1 cup milk
2 to 3 tablespoons instant-coffee powder
1 (1/4-oz.) pkg. unflavored gelatin
2 eggs, separated
1/3 cup sugar
2/3 cup whipping cream
Coffee beans and chocolate curls, if desired

In a small saucepan, combine 1/2 cup milk, coffee powder and gelatin. Let stand 5 minutes to soften gelatin. Stir over low heat until dissolved. Do not boil. Cool slightly. In a medium bowl, combine egg yolks, sugar and remaining 1/2 cup milk. Stir in gelatin mixture. Refrigerate until slightly set, about 20 minutes. In a small bowl, beat egg whites until stiff but not dry. In another small bowl, beat whipping cream until stiff. Fold beaten egg whites and 3/4 the whipped cream into milk mixture. Spoon into dessert dishes or a large serving dish. Refrigerate until set. To serve, garnish with reserved whipped cream, coffee beans and chocolate curls, if desired. Makes 4 to 6 servings.

Variation

Enhance the flavor by adding rum to the gelatin mixture before it starts to set.

Bavarian Cream
Bayerische Creme

Wine & Fruit Jelly
Weingelee mit Früchten

cup half and half
(1/4-oz.) pkg. unflavored gelatin
eggs, separated
/3 cup sugar
/2 teaspoon vanilla extract
/2 cup whipping cream
Maraschino cherries
Whipped cream, if desired

In a small saucepan, combine 1/2 cup half and half and gelatin. Let
stand 5 minutes to soften gelatin. Add remaining half and half; stir
over low heat until gelatin dissolves. Do not boil. In a small bowl,
beat together egg yolks and sugar. Add vanilla. Stir in half and half
mixture. Refrigerate until slightly set, about 20 minutes. In a small
bowl, beat egg whites until stiff but not dry. In another small bowl,
beat 1/2 cup whipping cream until stiff. Fold beaten egg whites and
whipped cream into gelatin mixture. Pour into a serving dish or
mold. Refrigerate until firmly set, 3 to 4 hours. To serve, turn out
into a serving plate. Serve with maraschino cherries or other fruit
and garnish with whipped cream, if desired. Makes 4 servings.

1 whole clove
1 cinnamon stick
Small piece of lemon peel
1/2 cup water
2 (1/4-oz.) pkgs. unflavored gelatin
3 to 4 drops red food coloring, if desired
2 cups sweet white or red wine, or 1 cup wine and 1 cup fruit juice
Juice of 1 lemon
1/3 cup sugar
2 cups drained canned or chopped fresh fruit

In a small saucepan, combine clove, cinnamon, lemon peel and
water. Bring to a boil; set aside to cool. Stir in gelatin and food
coloring, if desired. Let stand 5 minutes to soften gelatin. Heat over
low heat, stirring constantly, until gelatin dissolves. Do not boil.
Pour wine into a large bowl; strain gelatin mixture into bowl of
wine. Stir in lemon juice and sugar. Refrigerate until mixture begins
to thicken, about 20 minutes. Spoon fruit and slightly set gelatin
mixture alternately into dessert dishes. Or, combine fruit and
gelatin mixture. Then put in a large serving dish. Serve as a
refreshing dessert with whipped or unwhipped cream or a vanilla
sauce. Makes 4 servings.

Lemon Cream
Zitronencreme

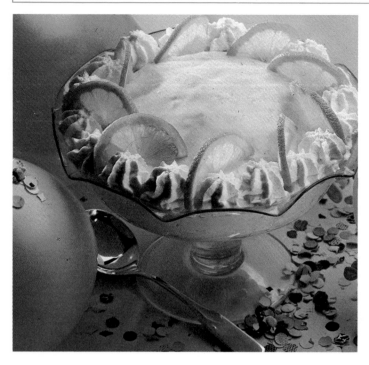

Red Stewed Fruit
Rote Grütze

1 cup sweet white wine
1 (1/4-oz.) pkg. unflavored gelatin
1 teaspoon finely grated lemon peel
3 to 4 tablespoons lemon juice
About 1/4 cup sugar
2 eggs, separated
1 cup whipping cream
Candied lemon slices or finely grated lemon peel

In a small saucepan, combine 1/2 cup wine and gelatin. Let stand 5 minutes to soften gelatin. Heat over low heat, stirring constantly, until gelatin dissolves. Do not boil. In a small bowl, beat together 1 teaspoon lemon peel, lemon juice, remaining wine, sugar and egg yolks. Stir in gelatin mixture. Refrigerate until slightly set, about 20 minutes. In a small bowl, beat egg whites until soft peaks form. In another small bowl, beat whipping cream until soft peaks form. Fold egg whites and half the whipped cream into gelatin mixture. Taste and add sugar if mixture is too tart. Spoon into a large serving dish or dessert dishes. Refrigerate until set, 3 to 4 hours. To serve, garnish with reserved whipped cream and lemon slices or peel. Makes 4 servings.

2 lbs. red fruit, such as: raspberries, red currants, strawberries, cherries, rhubarb
3 cups water
1/4 cup cornstarch
Sugar, as required

Wash and prepare fruit as needed. In a medium saucepan, combine fruit and water. Cook over low heat until tender. Place a piece of cheesecloth in a sieve. Holding sieve over a large saucepan, pour in fruit and cooking liquid. Do not crush fruit. Set fruit aside. Add water to juice to make 1 quart, if needed. Bring juice mixture to a boil over medium heat. Combine cornstarch with a little cold water. Add to hot liquid, stirring constantly. Spoon reserved fruit into a large serving dish or dessert dishes. Pour thickened mixture over fruit. Sprinkle lightly with sugar to prevent a skin forming. Refrigerate. Serve with milk or light cream to pour over fruit pudding, if desired. Makes 4 servings.

Note: This red-fruit pudding must be made with fresh fruit. It is one of the Schleswig-Holstein specialties, famous far and wide. It used to be thickened with cornstarch.

Cottage Cheese & Fruit
Westfälische Quarkspeise

Blushing Maiden
Errötende Jungfrau

large can pitted sweet cherries, drained or 2 cups fresh raspberries or
blueberries
slices dark-rye bread
cup cottage cheese, drained (8 oz.)
/2 cup milk or cream
/3 cup sugar
anilla extract
/2 oz. sweet or semisweet chocolate

poon fruit into dessert dishes. Crumble a little rye bread into each
ass. In a blender or food processor, combine cottage cheese, milk
cream, sugar and vanilla. Process until smooth. Top each dish of
uit with cheese mixture. Grate or flake chocolate; sprinkle on each
rving. Refrigerate until serving time. Makes 4 servings.

ote: Westphalia is the home of a particularly good coarse dark-rye
ead that is baked in cans. It is sliced and often eaten with cheese
d ham. The bread keeps well and retains its moisture and flavor.
rugal and ingenious Westphalian housewives have thought up
ry good uses for the leftovers, such as this scrumptious pudding.

Juice of 1 lemon
3 tablespoons water
1 (1/4-oz.) pkg. unflavored gelatin
1/4 teaspoon finely grated lemon peel
1/3 cup sugar
1 cup buttermilk
Few drops of red food coloring, if desired
1/2 to 1 cup whipping cream
Pistachio nuts, if desired

In a small saucepan, combine lemon juice, water and gelatin. Let
stand 5 minutes to soften. Stir over low heat until gelatin dissolves.
Do not boil. In a medium bowl, beat together lemon peel, sugar and
buttermilk. Whisk in gelatin mixture and food coloring, if desired.
Refrigerate until mixture begins to set, about 20 minutes. In a small
bowl, whip cream until stiff peaks form. Fold 3/4 of the whipped
cream into slightly thickened gelatin mixture. Spoon into a serving
dish or mold. Refrigerate until set. To serve, turn out of mold. Garnish with remaining whipped cream and red fruits, such as
strawberries, cherries or raspberries. Or, garnish with pistachio
nuts, if desired. Makes 6 servings.

Cheese Fritters
Quarkplinsen

Fruit Crepe
Obstpfannkuchen

3 tablespoons butter, room temperature
3 eggs
4 to 6 tablespoons sugar
1/2 teaspoon vanilla extract
Pinch of salt
2 cups cottage cheese, drained, or ricotta cheese (1 lb.)
3/4 cup plus 2 tablespoons all-purpose flour
2/3 cup semolina, farina or Cream of Wheat cereal
2/3 cup currants, if desired
Butter
Sugar and ground cinnamon

In a medium bowl, beat together 3 tablespoons butter, eggs, 4 to 6 tablespoons sugar, vanilla, salt and cottage cheese. Stir in flour; semolina, farina or Cream of Wheat cereal; and currants, if desired. Mixture will be smooth and firm. Melt plenty of butter in a large skillet. Drop large spoonfuls of batter into hot butter to make fritters, about 1/2 inch thick and 4 inches long. Fry until well browned and cooked through. Serve immediately with a sprinkling of sugar and cinnamon. Stewed rhubarb and apples or any other combination of stewed tart fruit is excellent to serve with fritters. Makes 4 to 5 servings.

3 eggs
1 cup milk
1-1/3 cups all-purpose flour
Salt
1 to 1-3/4 lbs. fruit such as: apples, cherries, black currants, blueberries or plums
Butter
Sugar and ground cinnamon, if desired
Kirsch or plum brandy, if desired

In a medium bowl, beat together eggs and milk. Gradually beat in flour and salt. Let stand 15 minutes. Wash, pit, peel and slice fruit as necessary. Melt butter in a large skillet. Spoon in batter to make first crepe. Sprinkle some fruit over half of crepe before it has time to set. Cover skillet and cook gently over low heat. After 1 to 2 minutes or when underside of crepe is lightly browned, fold in half to cover fruit. Transfer carefully to a warm plate. Sprinkle sugar and cinnamon over crepe, if desired. Sprinkle with a few drops of kirsch or brandy, if desired. Repeat until batter and fruit have been used. Makes 4 servings.

Cheese & Fruit Crepe
Pfannkuchen mit Beerenquark

eggs
up milk
1/3 cups all-purpose flour
lt
utter
ups cottage cheese, drained (1 lb.)
3 cup granulated sugar
2 cup milk
1/2 to 2 cups strawberries or raspberries
to 2 tablespoons powdered sugar, if desired

a medium bowl, beat together eggs and milk. Beat in flour and
lt. Let stand 15 minutes. Melt butter in a large skillet. Cook crepes
ntil golden brown, making them fairly thin. Place cooked crepes
n warm plates. In a blender or food processor, combine cottage
eese, 1/3 cup sugar and milk. Process until smooth. Wash and
ull berries. Fold berries into cheese mixture. Spoon cheese
ixture on half of each crepe. Fold over other half to cover.
prinkle lightly with powdered sugar, if desired. Makes 4 to 6
ervings.

Ragged Raisin Crepes
Kaiserschmarren

1/3 cup golden raisins
3 to 5 tablespoons rum
3 eggs
1 cup whole milk
1-3/4 cups all-purpose flour
3 tablespoons sliced almonds
Vegetable oil or butter
Powdered sugar

In a small bowl, combine raisins and rum; let stand a few minutes.
In a medium bowl, beat together eggs and milk. Beat in flour. Let
stand 15 minutes. Stir in rum-soaked raisins and almonds. Heat oil
or butter in a skillet. Spoon batter for 1 crepe into hot fat. Cook
until golden brown. Toss or turn to other side. Using 2 forks, tear
crepe into pieces. Cook slightly longer. Sprinkle with powdered
sugar. Keep warm. Repeat with remaining batter, adding more oil
or butter when necessary. Serve in a large dish or in individual
bowls with fresh or stewed apples, plums or red currants. Makes 4
servings.

Plum & Almond Dumplings
Pflaumen-Mandel-Knödel

Apricot Dumplings
Marillenknödel

1/2 cup sliced almonds
2 cups cold water
1 (1/2-lb.) pkg. potato-dumpling mix or half recipe of Cooked Potato
  Dumplings, page 118
8 purple plums
8 sugar cubes
1/4 cup sugar
Ground cinnamon
3 tablespoons butter, melted

Brown almonds lightly by heating in a pan without any fat, turning so they color evenly. In a medium bowl, combine browned almonds and water. Beat in potato-dumpling mix with a wire whisk; let stand 5 minutes. Or, prepare half recipe of Cooked-Potato-Dumpling dough, adding sliced almonds. Divide dough into 8 portions. Pit plums; place a sugar cube inside each plum. Enclose a sugar-stuffed plum inside each portion of dough, making sure it is well sealed and smoothly rounded. Bring a large kettle of salted water to a boil. Add dumplings. Immediately reduce heat. Simmer 20 minutes. Serve with sugar, cinnamon and melted butter. Makes 4 servings.

2 cups cold water
1 (1/2-lb.) pkg. potato-dumpling mix or half recipe of Cooked Pota
  Dumplings, page 118
8 apricots
8 sugar cubes
2 tablespoons butter
1 cup fresh breadcrumbs
1 tablespoon powdered sugar

In a medium bowl, combine water and dumpling mix using a wi whisk. Let stand 5 minutes. Or, prepare a half recipe Cooked-Potato-Dumpling dough. Divide dough into 8 portions. P apricots; place a sugar cube inside each apricot. Enclose sugar-stuffed apricot inside each portion of dough, making sure it well sealed and smoothly rounded. Bring a large kettle of salte water to a boil. Add dumplings. Immediately reduce heat. Simm 20 minutes. Meanwhile, in a small skillet, melt butter. Ad breadcrumbs; sauté until golden brown. Remove dumplings fro water; drain well. Roll in buttered breadcrumbs. Sprinkle wi powdered sugar. Serve immediately. Makes 4 servings.

Note: Apricot Dumplings can be made with yeast-dumpling doug or potato-dumpling dough. These apricot dumplings are an Austri specialty.

Baked Apples
Bratäpfel

1/2 cup white wine
4 large cooking apples
5 teaspoons marmalade and 5 teaspoons Grand Marnier
5 teaspoons chopped nuts, golden raisins or dried fruit
Sugar and ground cinnamon or 1/3 cup marzipan and 5 teaspoons apricot
    liqueur or apricot brandy
1-1/2 tablespoons butter

Preheat oven to 400F (205C). Butter a soufflé or other
straight-sided baking dish. Pour in wine. Wash apples. Use an apple
corer or small sharply pointed knife to remove cores. Place apples in
wine. Fill apples with marmalade and Grand Marnier, and nuts,
raisins or dried fruit. Sprinkle sugar and cinnamon or marzipan and
liqueur or brandy over filled apples. Dot with butter. Bake 20 to 40
minutes, depending on size and variety of apples. Serve
immediately with whipping cream or half and half, if desired. Makes
4 servings.

Note: This is a particularly good fall and winter dessert.

Stuffed Crepes
Palatschinken

1-1/4 cups all-purpose flour
1 cup milk
2 eggs
4-1/2 teaspoons butter, melted
Salt
Butter
1/2 cup cottage cheese, drained or ricotta cheese (4 oz.)
2 eggs, separated
1/3 cup sugar
1/4 cup golden raisins
Finely grated lemon peel
1/2 cup milk
Vanilla extract

Preheat oven to 400F (205C). In a medium bowl, beat together
flour and 1 cup milk. Beat in 2 eggs, 4-1/2 teaspoons butter and salt.
Let stand 20 minutes. Melt a small amount of butter in a small
skillet. Make thin crepes. Add butter to skillet, as needed. Keep
crepes warm. In a blender or food processor, combine cottage
cheese or ricotta cheese, egg yolks and half the sugar. Process until
smooth. In a small bowl, beat egg whites until stiff but not dry. Fold
egg whites, raisins and lemon peel into cheese mixture. Place some
filling on each crepe; roll up. Place in a rectangular baking dish with
high sides, large enough to hold 1 layer of crepes. In a small bowl,
combine 1/2 cup milk, remaining sugar and vanilla. Pour mixture
over crepes. Bake 20 minutes or until hot through. Serve
immediately. Makes 4 servings.

Rhubarb Crumble
Rhabarberauflauf mit Streuseln

Bread & Butter Pudding with Cherries
Kirschenmichel

2 lbs. rhubarb
Grated lemon peel
1-1/3 cups sugar
1-3/4 cups all-purpose flour
2/3 cup sugar
1/3 to 1/2 cup butter
Pinch of ground cinnamon

Preheat over to 400F (205C). Butter a soufflé dish; set aside. Trim rhubarb; cut in 2-inch pieces. Arrange rhubarb pieces in layers in buttered dish alternately with lemon peel and 1-1/3 cups sugar. In a medium bowl, combine flour, 2/3 cup sugar, butter and cinnamon. Using a fork or pastry cutter, work mixture together until coarse crumbs form. Sprinkle mixture over rhubarb. Bake 45 to 50 minutes. Serve hot with custard or vanilla sauce, half and half or whipped cream. Makes 4 to 6 servings.

Variation

Substitute gooseberries, plums or apples for rhubarb.

1-3/4 to 2 lbs. tart cherries
1/2 lb. (10 slices) stale white bread
Butter
4 eggs
1 cup milk
3/4 cup granulated sugar
1 teaspoon vanilla extract
Rum, if desired
Powdered sugar

Preheat oven to 400F (205C). Butter a soufflé dish; set aside. Wash and pit cherries. If canned cherries are used, drain well and pit. Slice bread; spread each slice with butter. Arrange bread and cherries alternately in dish, finishing with a bread layer. Dish should be nearly filled. In a medium bowl, beat together eggs, milk, granulated sugar and vanilla. Pour mixture over bread. Sprinkle rum over pudding for added flavor, if desired. Bake about 50 minutes or until top layer forms a golden crust. Sprinkle powdered sugar over top. Serve warm with custard. Makes 4 servings.

Note: This pudding is extremely quick to prepare and is an excellent way to use stale bread.

Fruit Soufflé
Apfelauflauf mit Früchten

Fruit-Filled Melon
Gefüllte Melone

3/4 to 1 lb. (about 2 cups) prepared fruit, such as: apples, apricots, blueberries, red currants, cherries, gooseberries or plums
1/3 to 1/2 cup sugar
3 oz. Neufchâtel cheese
1/4 cup butter, room temperature
2 eggs
1/4 cup sugar
2 tablespoons cornstarch
1-1/4 teaspoons baking powder
1 teaspoon vanilla extract
1 teaspoon finely grated lemon peel
3 tablespoons fresh breadcrumbs
3 tablespoons sugar
3 tablespoons sliced almonds
1/2 teaspoon ground cinnamon
2 tablespoons butter

Preheat oven to 400F (205C). Generously grease a soufflé dish or 8-inch-square baking pan; set aside. Wash and drain fruit. Peel, core and slice apples. Chop other fruit, if necessary. Sprinkle fruit with 1/3 to 1/2 cup sugar, according to tartness of fruit. In a medium bowl, beat together cheese, 1/4 cup butter, eggs, 1/4 cup sugar, cornstarch, baking powder, vanilla and lemon peel. Fold fruit gently into cheese mixture. Turn into greased dish or pan; smooth surface. In a small bowl, combine breadcrumbs, 3 tablespoons sugar, almonds and cinnamon; sprinkle over fruit. Dot with 2 tablespoons butter. Bake 50 to 60 minutes. Serve hot. Makes 4 to 6 servings.

1 honeydew or canteloupe melon
2 lbs. mixed fresh fruit, such as: strawberries, cherries, apricots, peaches, bananas, kiwi or dates
Juice of 2 lemons
Sugar
1/4 cup Grand Marnier or kirsch
Whipped cream, if desired

Chill all fruit. Slice immediately before serving. Scoop out and discard seeds from melon. Use a melon baller to remove most of the flesh or, remove with a spoon and slice into small pieces. Wash and prepare other fruits as necessary. Cut into fairly large pieces. In a medium bowl, combine fruit pieces except melon, lemon juice, sugar and liqueur. Let stand 5 to 10 minutes in refrigerator, if desired. Add melon balls or pieces to other fruit before filling melon with fruit salad. Serve with whipped cream, if desired. Makes 4 servings.

Cakes & Pastries

Germans are world-famous as pastry cooks. German housewives usually bake a cake for the weekend, especially when children are around. Each family has its own favorite recipe, often a highly guarded secret. The type of cake may vary according to the season. During summer, flans are made with fresh fruit, such as strawberries, cherries, raspberries, gooseberries and red or black currants. Autumn is the season for flavorsome apple or honey cakes.

Next come sweet yeast breads or cakes that keep well. Marble Cake is often baked for children and always popular. Each new slice reveals a fresh swirling pattern of chocolate and vanilla. Sandtorte or Pound Cake and Nut Cakes are irresistible. In the north, a great many *Zuckerkuchen,* sugar cakes and buns, and *Streuselkuchen,* crumbly flans, are eaten. When fresh baked and warm from the oven, these are so good that one piece never seems to be enough. In the southeast, *Guglhupf* is quite typical. It is a sweet bread containing raisins or currants and almonds. Equally popular are *Hefenapfkuchen,* yeast buns, which are usually dunked in coffee.

Sweet Fritters
Ausgezogene Knieküchle

Spiral Fruit Buns
Schneckennudeln

1/4 cup warm water (110F, 45C)
1 (1/4-oz.) pkg. active dry yeast (1 tablespoon)
1 teaspoon granulated sugar
1 cup milk
6 tablespoons vegetable oil
1/2 cup granulated sugar
2 eggs
1 teaspoon finely grated lemon peel
4 to 4-1/2 cups all-purpose flour
Vegetable oil for deep-frying
Powdered sugar or a mixture of granulated sugar and cinnamon

In a large bowl, dissolve yeast and 1 teaspoon sugar in water. Let stand until foamy, 5 to 10 minutes. Beat in milk, 6 tablespoons oil, 1/2 cup sugar, eggs and lemon peel. Beat in 2 cups flour. Let stand 10 minutes. Add enough remaining flour to make a soft dough. Turn out dough onto a lightly floured surface. Clean and grease bowl. Knead dough lightly, 1 to 2 minutes. Place dough in greased bowl, turning to coat all sides. Cover and let rise in warm place, free from drafts, until doubled in bulk, 30 to 45 minutes. Punch down dough. Knead dough well on a lightly floured surface. Cover and let stand 10 minutes. Form dough into a roll; slice roll into 18 pieces. Form each slice into a soft ball using the palm of your hand against a pastry board. Pour oil in a deep saucepan or deep-fat fryer. Heat oil to 350F (180C) or until a 1-inch cube of bread turns golden brown in 65 seconds. With your thumbs in the center of a dough ball, flatten it and pull out dough slightly so center is dimpled and sides are thicker, as shown above. Repeat with all dough pieces. Fry fritters, a few at a time, in hot oil until golden brown. Place fried fritters on paper towels to drain. Sprinkle lightly with powdered sugar or a mixture of granulated sugar and cinnamon. Makes 18 fritters.

Dough:
2-1/2 cups all-purpose flour
1 tablespoon baking powder
8 oz. Neufchâtel cheese, room temperature
1/4 cup vegetable oil
1/2 cup milk
1/2 cup plus 1 tablespoon sugar
1 teaspoon vanilla extract
1/3 cup cream or milk

Filling:
1/3 cup sugar
1/3 cup seedless golden raisins
1/3 cup chopped almonds or walnuts
1/3 cup candied citron

To make dough, preheat oven to 400F (205C). Grease 2 baking sheets; set aside. Sift together flour and baking powder into a large bowl. Stir in cheese, oil, 1/2 cup milk, 1/2 cup plus 1 tablespoon sugar and vanilla until firm and smooth. Transfer dough to a well floured surface. Roll dough into a 12'' x 10'' rectangle. Brush lightly with 1/3 cup cream or milk.

To make filling, in a small bowl, combine 1/3 cup sugar, raisins, nuts and citron. Sprinkle mixture over dough. Using your fingers, press lightly so sugar mixture sticks to dough. Starting on a long side, firmly roll dough jelly-roll style. Using a very sharp knife, cut roll into 1/2-inch-thick slices; place on greased baking sheets. Bake 20 minutes or until golden brown. Makes about 24 buns.

Sweet Raisin Bread
Guglhupf

Poppy Seed Roll
Mohnstriezel

sliced almonds
/2 cup seedless golden or dark raisins or currants
tablespoons kirsch
/4 cup warm water (110F, 45C)
-1/2 (1/4-oz.) pkgs. active dry yeast (4-1/2 teaspoons)
teaspoon granulated sugar
/2 cup butter, room temperature
/2 cup granulated sugar
eggs
cup milk
to 4-1/2 cups all-purpose or bread flour
cup coarsely chopped blanched almonds
/2 cup chopped candied orange peel
/2 cup chopped candied lemon peel
owdered sugar, if desired

utter a fluted 10-cup ring mold. Sprinkle with sliced almonds; set
side. In a small bowl, soak raisins or currants in kirsch. In a large
owl, dissolve yeast and 1 teaspoon sugar in water. Let stand until
oamy, 5 to 10 minutes. Beat in butter, 1/2 cup sugar, eggs and
ilk. Beat in 2 cups flour. Let stand 10 minutes. Add enough re-
aining flour to make a soft dough. When dough starts to leave side
f bowl, stir in chopped almonds, candied peels and soaked raisins.
urn dough into buttered mold. Let rise in a warm place, free from
rafts, until nearly doubled in bulk. Preheat oven to 350F (175C).
ake 50 minutes. Remove from pan and place on a cooling rack;
ool slightly. Dust lightly with powdered sugar, if desired. Makes 1
10-inch) loaf.

Note: Gugelhopf or Guglhupf is a Bavarian specialty that originally
ame from neighboring Alsace. It is often eaten for breakfast,
ipped in hot, creamy coffee.

Filling:
2-1/4 cups milk
1/2 lb. freshly ground poppy seeds
5 tablespoons cornstarch
1 tablespoon butter
1/2 cup granulated sugar
1 egg yolk, slightly beaten
2 to 3 tablespoons chopped candied lemon peel
1/4 cup chopped blanched almonds

Dough:
1/4 cup warm water (110F, 45C)
1 (1/4-oz.) pkg. active dry yeast (1 tablespoon)
1 teaspoon granulated sugar
1/2 cup margarine, room temperature
1/4 cup granulated sugar
2 eggs
1/2 cup milk
1 teaspoon finely grated lemon peel
Pinch of salt
4 to 4-1/2 cups all-purpose or bread flour

Glaze:
1 cup powdered sugar
1 egg white
3 to 5 tablespoons arrak or rum

To make filling, heat 2 cups milk in a saucepan. Add poppy seeds;
let stand 10 minutes. Dissolve cornstarch in 1/4 cup milk. Add cornstarch mixture, butter and sugar to poppy-seed mixture. Cook
slowly until thickened; cool. Add egg yolk, peel and nuts.
To make dough, grease a baking sheet. In a large bowl, dissolve
yeast and 1 teaspoon sugar in water. Let stand until foamy. Beat in
margarine, 1/4 cup sugar, eggs, milk, peel and salt. Beat in 2 cups
flour. Let stand 10 minutes. Add enough flour to make a soft
dough. Roll out dough to a 15'' x 12'' rectangle 1/2 inch thick.
Spread filling over dough. Mark lengthwise center of dough. Roll
each side to center. Place on baking sheet. Cover and let rise 25
minutes. Preheat oven to 375F (190C). Bake 1 hour or until golden.
To make glaze, combine powdered sugar, egg white and arrak or
rum. Brush glaze over top of warm roll. Makes 1 large roll.

Butter Cake
Butterkuchen

Crumble Flan
Streuselkuchen

Dough:
1/4 cup warm water (110F, 45C)
1 (1/4-oz.) pkg. active dry yeast (1 tablespoon)
1 teaspoon sugar
1 cup milk
1 egg
1/2 cup vegetable oil
1/2 cup sugar
4 to 4-1/2 cups all-purpose or bread flour
1/2 cup cream or milk

Topping:
2/3 cup sugar
1 teaspoon ground cinnamon
3/4 cup finely chopped hazelnuts or almonds
1/4 to 1/3 cup butter

To make dough, lightly flour a 15'' x 10'' jelly-roll pan; set aside. In a large bowl, dissolve yeast and 1 teaspoon sugar in water. Let stand until foamy, 5 to 10 minutes. Beat in 1 cup milk, egg, oil and 1/2 cup sugar. Beat in 2 cups flour. Let stand 10 minutes. Add enough remaining flour to make a soft dough. Turn out dough onto a lightly floured surface. Clean and grease bowl. Knead dough 8 to 10 times or until smooth and elastic. Place dough in greased bowl, turning to coat all sides. Cover and let rise in a warm place, free from drafts, about 20 minutes. Roll out dough to the size of floured pan or, roll dough directly onto pan. Make indentations in dough surface with your finger tips. Brush dough lightly with 1/2 cup cream or milk.
To make topping, in a small bowl, combine 2/3 cup sugar and cinnamon; sprinkle over rolled dough. Sprinkle nuts over dough. Dot dough with butter. Cover and let stand in a warm place, free from drafts, 30 minutes. Preheat oven to 400F (205C). Bake 20 to 25 minutes or until golden brown. Cool slightly. Cut into squares. Makes about 20 servings.

Butter-Cake dough, opposite
1/2 cup cream or milk
2 cups all-purpose flour
2/3 cup butter
3/4 cup sugar
1/2 teaspoon ground cinnamon
Pinch of salt

Prepare Butter-Cake dough, as directed. Brush rolled dough with cream or milk. Using a fork or pastry blender, combine flour, butter, sugar, cinnamon and salt until mixture is crumbly. Sprinkle flour mixture over rolled dough. Cover and let stand in a warm place, free from drafts, 30 minutes. Preheat oven to 400F (205C). Bake 20 to 25 minutes or until golden brown. Cool slightly. Cut into squares. Makes about 20 servings.

Variation

After brushing dough with cream or milk, arrange 1-3/4 to 2 pounds sliced apricots, plums or apples on top. Then top with crumb mixture. Proceed as directed above.

Plum Flan
Zwetschgenkuchen

Cream Puffs
Windbeutel

Butter-Cake dough, opposite, or Spiral-Fruit-Buns dough, page 148
3 to 4 lbs. plums
1/2 cup fresh breadcrumbs
1/2 cup chopped almonds
1/2 cup sugar
1/2 teaspoon ground cinnamon

Prepare dough as directed. Roll out dough in a greased 15'' x 10'' jelly-roll pan. If Butter-Cake recipe is used, let stand 20 minutes in a warm place, free from drafts. Meanwhile, clean and pit plums. Preheat oven to 400F (205C). Sprinkle rolled dough with breadcrumbs. Arrange pitted plums, close to each other, over entire dough surface. Sprinkle with almonds, sugar and cinnamon. Bake 30 minutes. Cool slightly. Cut into squares. Makes about 20 servings.

Variation

A crumble topping, such as for Crumble Flan, opposite, can be sprinkled over plums before cooking. Or, sprinkle lightly with toasted breadcrumbs, sugar and cinnamon.

Note: Spiral-Fruit-Bun dough has the advantage of remaining fresh several days. This fruit flan freezes very well.

Dough:
1/2 cup plus 1 tablespoon water
1/4 cup butter
1-1/4 cups bread flour
5 eggs

Filling:
2 cups whipping cream
1/4 cup powdered sugar
1 teaspoon vanilla extract
Powdered sugar

To make dough, preheat oven to 400F (205C). Lightly flour a baking sheet; set aside. In a medium saucepan, bring water to a boil; add butter. Reduce heat. Add flour, all at once, beating vigorously. Continue cooking over low heat, stirring constantly. Mixture will be very thick. Cook until dough pulls away cleanly from side of pan and forms a ball. Do not overcook or dough will not puff when baked. Remove from heat. Add 1 egg; quickly work egg into mixture using a wooden spoon. Continue adding 1 egg at a time, working each in totally before adding another. Using a tablespoon, drop small portions of dough onto floured baking sheet. Or, use a pastry bag fitted with a large fluted pastry tube to pipe an equal amount of pastry onto floured baking sheet. Bake 25 to 30 minutes. Do not open oven door during first 20 minutes of baking. Cool buns on a rack. Use a knife or scissors to cut off tops. Remove any damp strands of dough from inside. Let stand until cool.
To make filling, whip cream in a medium bowl until stiff peaks form. Fold in granulated sugar and vanilla. Spoon or pipe cream mixture into bottom of each bun. Replace bun tops. Dust lightly with powdered sugar. Makes 18 to 24 cream puffs.

Berlin Chocolate Ring
Berliner Napfkuchen

1 cup butter, room temperature
1 cup sugar
4 eggs
4-1/4 cups cake flour
4 teaspoons baking powder
3/4 cup milk
1 teaspoon vanilla extract
1 teaspoon finely grated lemon peel
3/4 cup currants
7 oz. bitter or semisweet chocolate, melted
1/2 cup pistachios or pine nuts

Preheat oven to 375F (190C). Grease an 8-cup fluted ring mold; set aside. In a large bowl, beat together butter and sugar. Beat in eggs until light and fluffy. Sift together flour and baking powder. Gradually add flour mixture and milk, alternately, to butter mixture. Stir in vanilla, lemon peel and currants. Batter should hold its shape when mixed but should be moist enough to drop slowly off a wooden spoon. Pour batter into greased mold. Bake 1 hour or until a wooden pick inserted in center comes out clean. Cool 5 to 10 minutes in pan. Then turn out of pan on a cooling rack. Spoon melted chocolate over warm cake, coating completely. Sprinkle nuts over cake. Cool completely. Makes 1 cake.

Marble Cake
Feiner Marmorkuchen

1 to 2 tablespoons fine breadcrumbs
1 cup butter or margarine, room temperature
1-1/3 cups granulated sugar
6 eggs
1 teaspoon vanilla extract
3 cups cake flour
2-1/2 teaspoons baking powder
5 tablespoons milk
3 tablespoons unsweetened cocoa powder
3 tablespoons granulated sugar
3 tablespoons rum
1/2 cup grated almonds
1/3 cup rum
1/2 cup powdered sugar
1/3 cup unsweetened cocoa powder

Preheat oven to 375F (190C). Grease an 8-cup fluted ring mold. Sprinkle lightly with breadcrumbs; set aside. Beat together butter or margarine and 1-1/3 cups sugar. Beat in eggs and vanilla until light and fluffy. Sift together flour and baking powder. Gradually add flour mixture and milk, alternately, to butter mixture. Remove 1/3 of the batter to a small bowl. Stir 3 tablespoons cocoa, 3 tablespoons sugar, 3 tablespoons rum and almonds into 1/3 of batter. Pour half the uncolored batter into greased mold. Pour chocolate batter over uncolored batter. Top with remaining uncolored batter. Draw a spatula through batter to form a swirl pattern. Bake about 1 hour or until a wooden pick inserted in center comes out clean. Cool 5 to 10 minutes in pan. Then turn out of pan on a cooling rack. Sprinkle cake with 1/3 cup rum. Dust with powdered sugar and 1/3 cup cocoa. Makes 1 cake.

Pound Cake
Sandtorte

cup butter or margarine, room temperature
cup granulated sugar
eggs
cups cake flour
teaspoon finely grated lemon peel
owdered sugar

reheat oven to 375F (190C). Butter a long, narrow loaf pan, about
0'' x 3''. Line with waxed paper. In a large bowl, beat together
utter or margarine and granulated sugar. Beat in eggs until light
nd fluffy. Sift flour into butter mixture; stir to combine. Stir in
emon peel. Pour batter into lined pan; smooth the surface. Bake
bout 1 hour or until a wooden pick inserted in center comes out
lean. Cool 5 to 10 minutes in pan. Then turn out of pan on a cooling
ack. Dust with powdered sugar. Makes 1 cake.

Variation

'or a more sandy texture, substitute 3/4 cup cornstarch and 1-1/4
ups all-purpose flour for cake flour.

Note: Pound cake keeps well and remains moist because of the high
at content.

Cheesecake
Quarktorte

Pastry:
2 cups all-purpose flour
1/2 cup butter, room temperature
1/3 cup sugar
1 egg
1 teaspoon vanilla extract

Filling:
1 lb. ricotta cheese
10 oz. Neufchâtel cheese
1/2 cup vegetable oil
1-1/4 cups sugar
3 eggs, separated
1/2 cup cornstarch
1 teaspoon finely grated lemon peel
2/3 cup currants or golden raisins, if desired

To make pastry, grease a 10-inch springform pan; set aside. In a
large bowl, beat together flour, butter, 1/3 cup sugar, 1 egg and
vanilla. Form pastry into a ball; wrap and refrigerate until chilled
through. Roll out chilled pastry on a lightly floured surface. Line
bottom and side of greased pan. Lightly prick pastry with a fork.
Preheat oven to 350F (180C).
To make filling, in a blender or food processor, combine cheeses,
oil, 1-1/4 cups sugar, egg yolks, cornstarch and lemon peel. Process
thoroughly. In a medium bowl, beat egg whites until stiff peaks
form. Fold beaten egg whites into cheese mixture. Fold in currants
or raisins, if desired. Spoon filling into pastry-lined pan; smooth
surface. Bake 1 hour. Turn oven heat off, but do not open oven
door. Let stand in warm oven to cool. When cool, remove pan side.
Slice and serve. Makes 1 (10-inch) cake.

Strawberry Torte
Erdbeertorte

Cherry Tart
Kirschtörtchen

Pastry:
2-1/4 cups all-purpose flour
1/2 cup plus 1 tablespoon butter, chilled
1/3 cup sugar
1 egg

Filling:
1/2 cup red-currant jelly
5 cups fresh strawberries
1 pkg. commercial glazing mix or, 1 cup sweetened fruit juice and 2 tablespoons cornstarch
1 cup whipping cream, whipped

To make pastry, in a large bowl, cut butter into flour until well distributed. Stir in sugar. Make a well in center of flour mixture. Break egg into well. Stir to combine egg and dry mixture. Pastry should be smooth and firm like a pie dough. If too dry, add a few drops of water. Wrap and refrigerate until chilled through, about 30 minutes. Preheat oven to 400F (205C). Grease a 10-inch springform pan. Roll out pastry on a lightly floured surface. Fit pastry to bottom of greased springform pan. Use your fingers to create a slightly raised edge around pastry. Bake 20 to 25 minutes. Using a knife, loosen pastry from edge of pan. Remove pan side. Cool pastry.

To make filling, spread surface of cooled pastry with jelly. Arrange strawberries close together over entire surface. Prepare glazing mix following package directions. Or, in a small saucepan, combine fruit juice and cornstarch. Cook over medium heat, stirring constantly, until thickened and clear. Cool slightly. Pour warm glaze evenly over strawberries. To serve, garnish with whipped cream. Makes 1 (10-inch) torte.

Variation

For variety, substitute other fruit such as: raspberries, blueberries, pineapple chunks, orange sections or kiwi slices. For a colorful torte, use a medley of fruit.

Cake:
3 eggs
1/2 cup plus 1 tablespoon sugar
1/2 teaspoon vanilla extract
1-1/4 cups cake flour

Filling:
1 (1-lb.) can cherry-pie filling
1 cup whipping cream
4 teaspoons sugar

To make cake, preheat oven to 400F (205C). Heavily grease bottom and side of a 10-inch fluted flan pan or cake pan. Line pan with waxed paper, if desired; set aside. In a medium bowl, use a whisk or electric mixer to beat together eggs and 1/2 cup plus 1 tablespoon sugar until light and frothy. Beat in vanilla. Sift flour into egg mixture; gently fold in flour. Pour mixture into prepared pan smooth surface. Bake 20 minutes. Cool slightly. Use a knife to loosen cake from pan. Place cake, upside down, on a serving plate.

To make filling, spread pie filling over cake. In a medium bowl, whip cream until stiff peaks form. Fold in sugar. Garnish tart with whipped cream. Refrigerate until ready to serve. Makes 1 (10-inch) tart.

Variation

Other thickened fruit mixtures can be substituted for cherry filling. Fresh fruit can also be used with a sweetened glaze, such as glaze from Strawberry Torte, opposite. Tart can also be made in 4 to 8 individual tart pans, depending on size.

Spicy Cherry Cake
Würziger Kirschkuchen

/3 cup butter or margarine, room temperature
/4 cup granulated sugar
eggs
oz. unsweetened chocolate, grated
/3 cup grated walnuts or blanched almonds
cup fine breadcrumbs
-1/2 tablespoons all-purpose flour
-1/4 teaspoons baking powder
-1/4 teaspoons ground cinnamon
/4 teaspoon ground nutmeg
/4 teaspoon ground allspice
teaspoon finely grated orange peel
teaspoon finely grated lemon peel
lb. tart cherries, pitted
/4 cup granulated sugar
tablespoon powdered sugar

Preheat oven to 375F (190C). Butter a 10-inch springform pan or pan pan with removable bottom; set aside. Beat together butter or margarine and 3/4 cup sugar. Beat in eggs until light and fluffy. Add chocolate, nuts, breadcrumbs, flour, baking powder, cinnamon, nutmeg, allspice, orange peel and lemon peel. Stir until well blended. Spoon into buttered pan; smooth surface. Cover with cherries. Sprinkle cherries with 1/4 cup sugar. Bake 45 minutes. Cool in pan 5 to 10 minutes. Carefully remove cake from pan. Cool on a rack. Dust cake with powdered sugar. Makes 1 (10-inch) cake.

Variation

Substitute apricot halves, mandarin-orange segments, pineapple chunks or peach slices for cherries. All fruit should be well-drained to avoid a soggy cake.

Note: This cake has a very subtle and delicious flavor. Grated nuts should always be used. Ground nuts release too much oil.

Orange Cake
Orangenkuchen

1 to 2 tablespoons fine breadcrumbs
1 cup butter or margarine, room temperature
1 cup granulated sugar
4 eggs
2-1/2 cups all-purpose flour
2-1/2 teaspoons baking powder
Finely grated peel of 1 lemon
Finely grated peel of 1 orange
3/4 cup powdered sugar
3 tablespoons Grand Marnier or other orange liqueur
Juice of 2 oranges
1 tablespoons coarsely grated orange peel

Preheat oven to 350F (175C). Grease a 10-inch springform or round cake pan. Lightly sprinkle pan with breadcrumbs; set aside. In a large bowl, beat together butter or margarine and granulated sugar. Beat in eggs until light and fluffy. Add flour, baking powder, lemon peel and peel of 1 orange. Pour mixture into greased pan. Bake 1 hour or until a wooden pick inserted in center comes out clean. While still hot, prick surface with a fork. In a small bowl, combine powdered sugar, liqueur, orange juice and 1 tablespoon orange peel. Sprinkle mixture over hot baked cake. When cake has completely cooled, remove from pan. Makes 1 (10-inch) cake.

Note: This popular cake is easy and quick to make. It has a delicate, fresh flavor and is moist and light. If there is any leftover, it will keep well for several days.

Apple Cake
Badischer Apfelkuchen

Chocolate Fudge & Cookie Cake
Kekstorte

Pastry:
2-1/4 cups all-purpose flour
1/2 cup plus 1 tablespoon butter or margarine, chilled
1/3 cup sugar
1 egg
2 teaspoons finely grated lemon peel

Filling:
2 lbs. golden delicious apples (6 to 7 apples)
3 eggs
1/2 cup whipping cream
1/2 cup sugar
1 teaspoon vanilla extract

To make pastry, preheat oven to 400F (205C). Grease a 12-inch springform pan; set aside. In a large bowl, cut butter or margarine into flour until well distributed. Add 1/3 cup sugar, 1 egg and lemon peel. Use your hands to press pastry together in a ball. Roll out pastry on a lightly floured surface. Line bottom and side of greased pan.
To make filling, peel, quarter and core apples. Cut into rounded side of each apple quarter, making several lengthwise parallel deep incisions so that each quarter fans, as shown above. Place prepared apple quarters, sliced-side up, on top of pastry. Bake 35 minutes. In a medium bowl, beat together 3 eggs, cream, 1/2 cup sugar and vanilla; pour mixture over hot cake. Bake cake 20 to 25 minutes longer or until custard is set. Makes 1 (12-inch) cake.

1 cup butter
2 eggs
1-1/4 cups powdered sugar
1/3 cup unsweetened cocoa powder
1 tablespoon instant-coffee powder
2 tablespoons arrak, Grand Marnier or brandy
1 teaspoon finely grated lemon peel
1/2 lb. rectangular shortbread or rich tea cookies
Chopped pistachios, almonds, candied cherries or chocolate candies

Foil line a 10-inch-long narrow rectangular, straight-sided cake or bread pan; set aside. Melt butter over medium heat; cool slightly. In a large bowl, combine eggs, powdered sugar, cocoa, coffee powder, liqueur and lemon peel. Gradually add melted butter, stirring constantly. Make a generous layer of chocolate mixture on bottom and sides of pan. Alternate layers of cookies and chocolate mixture in pan, ending with a chocolate layer. Cover with foil; refrigerate 24 hours. Cookies will absorb moisture and flavor from chocolate mixture and soften slightly. Unmold cake. Garnish with nuts, candied cherries or chocolate candies. To serve, cut in thin slices. Refrigerate any leftovers. Makes 1 (10-inch) cake.

Frosted Fruit Cake
Früchtebrot

Dresden Christmas Sweet Bread
Dresdner Christstollen

Cake:
eggs
1/2 cup granulated sugar
1 cup hazelnuts
1 cup almonds
1 cup candied citron
1 cup dried figs
1 cup dried pitted dates
1 cup currants or golden raisins
1 cup all-purpose flour
1 tablespoon baking powder
1 teaspoon ground cinnamon
1/2 teaspoon ground cloves

Frosting:
1-3/4 cups powdered sugar
4-1/2 teaspoons rum or cherry brandy
3 tablespoons water
Candied cherries or whole almonds for garnish

To make cake, preheat oven to 350F (175C). Grease a 9" x 5" loaf pan; set aside. In a large bowl, beat together eggs and granulated sugar until light, frothy and thick. Coarsely chop hazelnuts, almonds, citron, figs, dates and currants or raisins. Sift together flour, baking powder, cinnamon and cloves. Add flour mixture to egg mixture alternately with chopped fruit and nuts, blending with a wooden spoon. Spoon mixture into greased pan. Bake about 70 minutes or until a wooden pick inserted in center comes out clean. Remove from pan; place on a cooling rack.
To make frosting, in a small bowl, beat together powdered sugar, rum or brandy and water. Coat cooled cake generously with frosting. Garnish with candied cherries or whole almonds. Makes 1 large fruitcake.

Variation

Fruitcake can also be baked in miniature loaf pans, coffee or vegetable cans, or any other appropriate pan size. Grease baking pans well. Cake makes about 4 cups batter.

1 lb. golden raisins
3 tablespoons rum
1/4 cup warm water (110F, 45C)
3 (1/4-oz.) pkgs. active dry yeast (3 tablespoons)
1 teaspoon granulated sugar
2 cups milk
1 cup granulated sugar
2 cups unsalted butter, room temperature (1 lb.)
1/2 teaspoon ground cardamom
1/2 teaspoon ground nutmeg
1 teaspoon finely grated lemon peel
2 teaspoons salt (omit if using salted butter)
8-1/2 to 9 cups all-purpose or bread flour
1 cup chopped candied orange peel
1 cup chopped candied citron
1 cup chopped blanched almonds
1/2 cup coarse brown sugar
1 cup powdered sugar
1/2 cup butter, melted

In a medium bowl, combine raisins and rum. Cover and let stand 12 to 24 hours. Grease 2 baking sheets. In a large bowl, dissolve yeast and 1 teaspoon sugar in water. Let stand until foamy, 5 to 10 minutes. Beat in milk, 1 cup granulated sugar, 2 cups butter, cardamom, nutmeg, lemon peel and salt, if using. Beat in 4 cups flour. Let stand 10 minutes. Add enough remaining flour to make a soft dough. Turn out dough onto a lightly floured surface. Clean and grease bowl. Knead dough 8 to 10 minutes or until smooth and elastic. Place dough in greased bowl, turning to coat all sides. Cover and let rise in a warm place, free from drafts, until doubled in bulk. Punch down dough. Knead in soaked raisins, orange peel, citron and almonds. Divide dough in half. Roll each half to an oval, 10 to 12 inches long and 3/4 inch thick. Fold each nearly in half. Place on greased baking sheets. Cover and let rise until doubled in bulk. Preheat oven to 350F (175C). Bake 70 to 90 minutes or until golden brown. Meanwhile, in a small bowl, combine brown sugar and powdered sugar. While bread is hot, brush with melted butter. Sprinkle with sugar mixture. When completely cooled, wrap tightly and store until ready to serve. Makes 2 large loaves.

Sachertorte
Sachertorte

Black Forest Gâteau
Schwarzwälder Kirschtorte

7 oz. unsweetened chocolate
1 cup butter, room temperature
1 cup sugar
8 eggs, separated
1-1/2 cups all-purpose flour
1 cup apricot jam, sieved
7 oz. unsweetened or semisweet chocolate

Preheat oven to 325F (165C). Grease a 10-inch springform or round cake pan; set aside. In a double boiler, melt 7 oz. unsweetened chocolate over hot water, stirring until smooth; cool. In a medium bowl, beat together butter and sugar until light and fluffy. Beat in egg yolks, one at a time. Beat 15 to 20 minutes. Gradually beat in melted chocolate. In another medium bowl, beat egg whites until stiff but not dry. Stir about 1/4 the beaten egg whites into chocolate mixture. Alternately fold in remaining beaten egg whites and flour. Spoon batter into greased pan. Bake 80 to 90 minutes or until a wooden pick inserted in center comes out clean. Cake will pull away from side of pan slightly. Cool 5 to 10 minutes in pan. Remove from pan; cool completely on a rack. When cooled, cut cake horizontally into 2 layers. Spread top surface of lower half with apricot jam. Place upper half, cut-side down, over jam-spread layer. In a double boiler, melt remaining 7 oz. chocolate over hot water, stirring until smooth. Spread melted chocolate over entire cake. Makes 1 (10-inch) cake.

Note: This cake should be made 24 hours before it is to be eaten because it improves with age. If a larger cake is required, simply use 1-1/2 times the quantities given. Sachertorte was created over a century ago for Prince Metternich by his cook, Franz Sacher. Since then, it has become famous all over the world. The "original" recipe is a jealously guarded secret of the hotel and restaurant of the Sacher family in Vienna.

2 recipes Chocolate Cake, opposite
1 (1-lb.) can tart cherries
1/3 to 1/2 cup granulated sugar
2 tablespoons cornstarch
6 tablespoons kirsch
1 qt. whipping cream
1/4 cup powdered sugar
1 teaspoon vanilla extract
15 to 20 maraschino cherries
2 oz. semisweet chocolate, cut in curls or 1/4 cup chocolate candy sprinkles

Prepare 2 recipes Chocolate Cake. Cut each cake horizontally into 2 layers. Drain cherries, reserving juice. In a small saucepan, combine 1/2 cup cherry juice, granulated sugar and cornstarch. Adjust sugar depending on sweetness desired. Cook over low heat, stirring constantly, until thickened and clear. Remove from heat. Add kirsch and drained cherries; cool mixture. In a large bowl, whip together cream, powdered sugar and vanilla until stiff peaks form. To assemble cake, place 1 cake layer on a serving plate. Top with a 1/2-inch-thick layer of whipped-cream mixture. Place another cake layer on the cream. Spread second layer with cherry mixture. Place a third cake layer on cherries. Spread with a layer of whipped-cream mixture. Place final cake layer on top. Completely cover cake with whipped-cream mixture. Garnish cake with whipped cream, maraschino cherries and chocolate curls or chocolate sprinkles. Makes 1 large cake.

Variation

Substitute 1 (1-pound) can cherry-pie filling for tart cherries, granulated sugar and cornstarch. Stir kirsch into pie filling. If you wish to make this cake in advance, use the topping from Chocolate Cake, opposite, as it will hold up better.

Chocolate Cake
Schokoladen-Biskuittorte

Hazelnut Torte
Nusstorte

Cake:
eggs, separated
/2 cup plus 1 tablespoon sugar
 teaspoon vanilla extract
-1/2 teaspoons rum
/3 cup unsweetened cocoa powder
/4 cup all-purpose flour

Frosting:
 cups whipping cream
 tablespoons sugar
 teaspoon vanilla extract
-1/2 teaspoons unflavored gelatin
 tablespoons cold water
 tablespoons half and half
Chocolate curls for garnish

To make cake, preheat oven to 400F (205C). Grease the bottom of
 10-inch springform or round cake pan; set aside. In a large bowl,
beat egg whites until stiff but not dry. Gradually add 1/2 cup plus 1
tablespoon sugar, 1 teaspoon vanilla and rum. Beat in egg yolks, one
at a time. Sift together cocoa and flour; fold into egg mixture. Pour
batter into greased pan. Bake 15 to 25 minutes or until a wooden
pick inserted in center comes out clean. Cool 5 to 10 minutes in pan.
Then remove from pan and cool on a rack. Cut cake horizontally
into 2 layers.
To make frosting, in a medium bowl, whip cream until stiff peaks
form. Fold in 7 tablespoons sugar and 1 teaspoon vanilla. In a small
saucepan, combine gelatin and cold water. Let stand 5 minutes to
soften. Heat gelatin mixture over low heat to dissolve. Add half and
half; heat to combine but do not boil. Let stand to cool. Fold gelatin
mixture into whipped cream. Place 1 cake layer on a serving plate.
Top with a 1/2-inch-thick layer of cream mixture. Top with
remaining cake layer. Generously cover top and sides of cake with
cream mixture. Garnish with cream mixture and chocolate curls.
Makes a 2-layer (10-inch) cake.

Note: Make a double recipe for a 4-layer cake.

Cake:
1 to 2 tablespoons fine breadcrumbs
8 eggs, separated
1-1/4 cups granulated sugar
1-1/4 teaspoons finely grated orange peel
1-1/4 teaspoons finely grated lemon peel
1-1/2 cups coarsely grated hazelnuts
1 teaspoon ground cinnamon
1/4 teaspoon ground cloves
1/8 teaspoon ground allspice
1/8 teaspoon ground nutmeg
3/4 cup all-purpose flour

Icing:
2 cups powdered sugar
1/3 cup rum or arrak
1 tablespoon instant-coffee powder
1/4 cup chopped hazelnuts, if desired

To make cake, preheat oven to 325F (165C). Grease the bottom of
a 10-inch springform or round cake pan. Sprinkle lightly with
breadcrumbs; set aside. In a large bowl, beat egg whites until stiff
but not dry. Gradually beat in 1-1/4 cups sugar and egg yolks, one at
a time. Add orange peel and lemon peel. In a second bowl, combine
1-1/2 cups hazelnuts, cinnamon, cloves, allspice, nutmeg and flour.
Fold nut mixture into egg mixture. Pour batter into greased pan;
smooth surface. Bake 50 minutes or until a wooden pick inserted in
center comes out clean. Turn oven heat off, but do not open oven
door. Let stand in warm oven until cool. When cool, remove from
pan.
To make icing, in a medium bowl, combine powdered sugar and
rum or arrak. Stir until smooth. Spread icing over top and sides of
cake, reserving a small quantity of icing. Using reserved icing, stir in
coffee powder. Pipe or drizzle coffee-flavored icing onto cake in a
spiral pattern. Draw a knife lightly across cake surface from center
to outer edge to create desired design. Rinse knife in hot water after
each stroke. Press 1/4 cup chopped hazelnuts onto side of cake, if
desired. Makes 1 (10-inch) cake.

Breads

In Germany, bread shapes vary considerably. Included are little crusty rolls; large round loaves; long, thin loaves like French bread; rectangular loaves and small oval loaves. The bread itself, however, varies little. Bread rolls are baked in the early morning hours, then eaten at breakfast that same morning. These rolls are generally made with white flour. In days gone by, bakers' apprentices delivered fresh, crusty bread to people's homes, leaving it in bags hanging from front-door knobs.

In Germany, large white loaves have never been as popular as in other countries. Black or dark-brown bread is the favorite. It is soft and yeasty. Or, it is made with sourdough and flavored with caraway, fennel or coriander. Bread is generally not eaten with hot dishes. It is sliced, spread with lard, butter or margarine and then topped with sausage, ham or cheese. Visitors to Germany are always intrigued by black bread. Grains of rye, barley and wheat used for this bread are coarsely ground. In the Münster district, bread is made with a rye-sourdough mixture which gives a slightly tangy taste. Rye bread or *pumpernickel* dates back at least 500 years. It keeps well for several months if wrapped in foil. For that reason, it can be easily exported all over the world. It must be baked at a low temperature 24 hours. It is often eaten with Westphalian ham.

Rhineland Easter Manikins
Rheinische Weckmänner—Ostermännchen

Cheese Crescents
Quarkblätterteigkipfel

1/4 cup warm water (110F, 45C)
1 (1/4-oz.) pkg. active dry yeast (1 tablespoon)
3 tablespoons sugar
1 cup milk
1 egg
5 tablespoons vegetable oil
1/2 teaspoon salt
Finely grated peel of 1 lemon
4 to 4-1/4 cups all-purpose or bread flour
6 hard-cooked eggs
2 to 3 tablespoons milk
Currants and almonds

Grease a baking sheet; set aside. In a large bowl, dissolve yeast and 1 teaspoon sugar in water. Let stand until foamy, 5 to 10 minutes. Beat in 1 cup milk, egg, oil, salt, lemon peel and remaining sugar. Beat in 2 cups flour. Let stand 10 minutes. Add enough remaining flour to make a soft dough. Turn out dough onto a lightly floured surface. Clean and grease bowl. Knead dough 8 to 10 minutes or until smooth and elastic. Place dough in greased bowl, turning to coat all sides. Cover and let rise in a warm place, free from drafts, until doubled in bulk, about 45 minutes. Punch down dough. Divide dough into 6 pieces. Working with 1 piece, pinch off about 1/3. Shape half of this piece into a ball for the head. Shape other half into a rope for arms. Shape larger piece into a 4-inch-long roll for body. Place body portion on greased baking sheet. Press hard-cooked egg into body; enclose with arms, tucking ends under shoulder portion of body. Attach head. With scissors or a sharp knife, cut a 2-inch slash in body to form legs; slightly separate legs. Repeat with remaining dough and eggs. Insert currants and almonds for facial features. Cover and let rise until doubled in bulk, about 30 minutes. Brush lightly with milk. Preheat oven to 425F (220C). Bake 20 minutes. Remove from baking sheet; cool on racks. Makes 6 bread men.

2 cups all-purpose flour
1 cup butter or margarine
1 cup Neufchâtel cheese

Sift flour into a large bowl. Cut butter or margarine and cheese into flour. Or, place ingredients in a food processor. Process until in coarse pieces. Using your hands, knead mixture until well blended. Refrigerate, uncovered, 20 to 30 minutes. Preheat oven to 425F (220C). Roll out chilled dough on a lightly floured surface into a 16-inch diameter circle about 1/4 inch thick. Using a knife, mark dough like spokes of a wheel. Cut dough into triangles with a short base of 4 inches and the 2 long sides measuring 8 inches. Roll up each triangle beginning with short base. Pull ends of each roll out and forward, bending them slightly to form a crescent. Rinse a baking sheet with cold water. Place rolls on cold baking sheet. Bake 20 minutes or until golden brown. Remove from baking sheet; cool on a rack. Serve at breakfast with butter, jam or honey. Or, serve with cheese and a glass of wine. Makes about 12 crescents.

Poppy & Caraway-Seed Rolls
Monhnbrötchen und Kümmelstangen

Salted Pretzel Rolls
Salzbrezeln

1/4 cup warm water (110F, 45C)
1 (1/4-oz.) pkg. active dry yeast (1 tablespoon)
1/2 teaspoon sugar
1 cup milk or buttermilk
1 egg
1/3 cup vegetable oil
1 teaspoon salt
4-1/4 to 4-1/2 cups all-purpose flour
3 tablespoons milk blended with 1 egg yolk for glaze
2 to 3 tablespoons poppy seeds
2 to 3 tablespoons caraway seeds

Grease a baking sheet; set aside. In a large bowl, dissolve yeast and sugar in water. Let stand until foamy, 5 to 10 minutes. Beat in milk or buttermilk, egg, oil and salt. Beat in 2 cups flour. Let stand 10 minutes. Add enough remaining flour to make a soft dough. Turn out dough onto a lightly floured surface. Knead dough 8 to 10 minutes or until smooth and elastic. Divide dough in half. Roll 1 piece into a long, fat sausage-shape piece; cut into 6 pieces. Roll each piece into a ball. Place on greased baking sheet. Brush each with milk glaze; sprinkle with poppy seeds. Make a crisscross slash in top of each roll. Roll out remaining dough into a 1/2-inch thick circle. Cut in 6 triangles. Shape as Cheese Crescents, opposite. Place on greased baking sheet. Brush each with milk glaze; sprinkle with caraway seeds. Cover and let rise in a warm place, free from drafts, until doubled in bulk, about 30 minutes. Preheat oven to 425F (220C). Bake 15 to 20 minutes or until golden brown. Remove from baking sheet; cool on a rack. Makes 12 rolls.

1/2 cup warm water (110F, 45C)
1-1/8 teaspoons active dry yeast
1 teaspoon sugar
3/4 cup milk
1 teaspoon salt
4-1/2 teaspoons vegetable oil
4-1/4 cups all-purpose flour
2 teaspoons salt
1 teaspoon baking soda
Coarse salt crystals

Grease a baking sheet; set aside. In a large bowl, dissolve yeast and sugar in water. Let stand until foamy, 5 to 10 minutes. Beat in milk, 1 teaspoon salt and oil. Beat in 2 cups flour. Let stand 10 minutes. Add enough remaining flour to make a soft dough. Turn out dough onto a lightly floured surface. Clean and grease bowl. Knead dough 8 to 10 minutes or until smooth and elastic. Place dough in greased bowl, turning to coat all sides. Cover and let rise in a warm place, free from drafts, until doubled in bulk, about 30 minutes. Punch down dough. Divide dough in half. Roll each half into a long roll; cut each into 12 pieces. Roll each piece into a 14-inch rope. Twist and loop into pretzel shape, as shown above. Cover and let rise 10 minutes. Preheat oven to 425F (220C). Bring a large saucepan of water to a boil. Add 2 teaspoons salt and baking soda. Drop pretzels into boiling water. Do not crowd pretzels in water. As soon as pretzels rise to the surface, use tongs or a slotted spoon to remove from water. Place on a thick towel or several layers of paper towels to drain. Transfer drained pretzels to greased baking sheet. Make a few shallow incisions at an angle on the surface of each pretzel. Sprinkle coarse salt over pretzels. Bake 30 minutes or until lightly browned. Remove from baking sheet; cool on a rack. Makes 24 pretzels.

Note: Pretzels are delicious when eaten warm with wine or chilled beer.

Spiced Buns
Gewürzfladen

Wheat & Rye Bread
Mischbrot

1/4 cup warm water (110F, 45C)
1 (1/4-oz.) pkg. active dry yeast (1 tablespoon)
1/2 teaspoon sugar
1 cup milk
2 eggs
1 teaspoon salt
1 teaspoon anise seeds, crushed
1 teaspoon caraway seeds or ground coriander
4 to 4-1/4 cups all-purpose or bread flour
1 cup rye flour
1/4 cup milk
3 to 4 tablespoons coarse salt, caraway seeds or poppy seeds

Grease a baking sheet; set aside. In a large bowl, dissolve yeast and sugar in water. Let stand until foamy, 5 to 10 minutes. Beat in 1 cup milk, eggs, salt, anise seeds and 1 teaspoon caraway seeds or ground coriander. Beat in 2 cups all-purpose or bread flour. Let stand 10 minutes. Add rye flour and enough remaining all-purpose or bread flour to make a soft dough. Turn out dough onto a lightly floured surface. Clean and grease bowl. Knead dough 8 to 10 minutes or until smooth and elastic. Place dough in greased bowl, turning to coat all sides. Cover and let rise in a warm place, free from drafts, until doubled in bulk, about 45 minutes. Punch down dough. Divide dough in 16 portions. Roll each piece into a ball, then flatten with your hand. Place on greased baking sheet. Brush rolls lightly with 1/4 cup milk; sprinkle coarse salt, caraway seeds or poppy seeds over rolls. Cover and let rise until nearly doubled in bulk, 20 to 30 minutes. Preheat oven to 425F (220C). Bake 20 minutes. Remove from baking sheet. Serve hot. Makes 16 rolls.

1/4 cup warm water (110F, 45C)
2-1/4 teaspoons active dry yeast
1/2 teaspoon sugar
2 cups milk or buttermilk
2 teaspoons salt
1 teaspoon ground anise
1 teaspoon caraway seeds, fennel seeds or ground cardamom
4-1/2 to 5 cups all-purpose or bread flour
2-1/2 cups rye flour

Grease a baking sheet; set aside. In a large bowl, dissolve yeast and sugar in water. Let stand until foamy, 5 to 10 minutes. Beat in milk or buttermilk, salt, ground anise and caraway seeds, fennel seeds or cardamom. Beat in 2 cups all-purpose or bread flour. Let stand 10 minutes. Add rye flour and enough remaining all-purpose or bread flour to make a soft dough. This is a sticky dough. Turn out dough onto a lightly floured surface. Clean and grease bowl. Knead dough 8 to 10 minutes or until smooth and elastic. Place dough in greased bowl, turning to coat all sides. Cover and let rise in a warm place, free from drafts, until doubled in bulk, about 1 hour. Punch down dough. Shape into 1 large round loaf or 2 small round loaves. Place on greased baking sheet. Cover and let rise until doubled in bulk, 30 to 40 minutes. Preheat oven to 400F (205C). Lightly score surface of unbaked loaf. Place bread in hot oven. Immediately reduce oven to 350F (175C). Bake 70 to 80 minutes for large loaf or 50 to 60 minutes for small loaves. Remove from baking sheet; cool on a rack. Makes 1 large loaf or 2 small loaves.

Variation

For a more dense bread, omit first rising. After kneading dough, shape into loaves. Proceed as directed.

Wholemeal Bread
Weizenschrotbrot

1/4 cup warm water (110F, 45C)
1 (1/4-oz.) pkg. active dry yeast (1 tablespoon)
1/2 teaspoon sugar
1 cup milk or buttermilk
1/2 cup vegetable oil
1 teaspoon salt
1/2 teaspoon ground anise
1/2 teaspoon ground fennel
1-3/4 to 2 cups all-purpose or bread flour
1-3/4 cups whole-wheat flour
1-1/2 cups unprocessed wheat bran

Grease a 9" x 5" x 3" loaf pan; set aside. In a large bowl, dissolve yeast and sugar in water. Let stand until foamy, 5 to 10 minutes. Beat in milk or buttermilk, oil, salt, anise and fennel. Beat in 1 cup all-purpose or bread flour. Let stand 10 minutes. In a small bowl, combine whole-wheat flour and bran. Add to dough along with enough remaining all-purpose or bread flour to make a soft dough. Turn out dough onto a lightly floured surface. Knead dough 8 to 10 minutes or until smooth and elastic. Shape dough into loaf; place in greased pan. Cover and let rise in a warm place, free from drafts, until doubled in bulk, 30 to 40 minutes. Preheat oven to 375F (190C). Pour boiling water to a 1/2-inch depth in a pie pan or other shallow pan; place in bottom of oven. Bake bread 70 minutes or until a wooden pick inserted in center comes out clean. Remove from pan; cool on a rack. Makes 1 large loaf.

Note: Oil helps keep this bread moist and fresh several days.

White Bread
Weissbrot

1/4 cup warm water (110F, 45C)
1 (1/4-oz.) pkg. active dry yeast (1 tablespoon)
1/2 teaspoon sugar
1 cup milk or buttermilk
1/4 cup vegetable oil
1 teaspoon salt
4 to 4-1/2 cups all-purpose flour
1 tablespoon water or milk for glaze
Poppy seeds

Grease a 9" x 5" x 3" loaf pan or a baking sheet; set aside. In a large bowl, dissolve yeast and sugar in water. Let stand until foamy, 5 to 10 minutes. Beat in milk or buttermilk, oil and salt. Beat in 2 cups flour. Let stand 10 minutes. Add enough remaining flour to make a soft dough. Turn out dough onto a lightly floured surface. Knead dough 8 to 10 minutes or until smooth and elastic. Shape dough into a rectangular or round loaf. Place in greased pan or on baking sheet. Brush lightly with water or milk; sprinkle with poppy seeds. Cover and let rise in a warm place, free from drafts, until doubled in bulk, about 40 minutes. Preheat oven to 400F (205C). Bake 40 to 45 minutes or until a wooden pick inserted in center comes out clean. Remove from pan; cool on a rack. Makes 1 loaf.

Note: This bread does not keep a long time.

Holiday Sweets

The Feast of St. Nicholas, on December 6th, is a very important day for all German children. On that day, they look forward to a visit from the Saint and his servant, Ruprecht. Each child has to learn a poem to be recited from memory, with some trepidation, to the Saint. He then takes out his golden book and reads a list of the child's good and bad deeds during the past year. If the child has been naughty, St. Nicholas orders Ruprecht to give him a smack on his bottom with a cane. More often than not, however, the little boy or girl is rewarded with apples, oranges, mandarins, nuts, marzipan figures, quince jelly, chocolate bars and all sorts of delicious little sweet things. Strangely enough, they all bear a striking resemblance to those cookies and cakes he or she helped mother make only a few days before!

Of course, St. Nicholas cannot find time to visit every child personally, so some find a shoe filled with candy left outside the front door or a Witch's House made of candy and spice bread waiting for them on the window sill. This house recalls the fairy tale of Hansel and Gretel, in which two children lose themselves in the woods. While in the woods, they come upon an enchanting little house made of sugar candy and cakes. The brother and sister are so hungry that they start to nibble away at the house. Out darts the wicked witch and drags the children into a stable where she keeps them as prisoners. But this rather frightening tale is forgotten in the child's delight at the sight of this gift from St. Nicholas.

Butter Cookies
Butterplätzchen

2 cups all-purpose flour
1-1/4 cups powdered sugar
3/4 cup butter, room temperature
2-1/3 cups flaked coconut
1/2 teaspoon vanilla extract
1 egg plus 1 egg yolk
1 egg yolk blended with 1 tablespoon water for glaze
Walnuts, almonds and candied citron, orange peel and cherries

In a large bowl, combine flour, powdered sugar, butter, coconut, vanilla, egg and egg yolk. Blend thoroughly. Cover and refrigerate 1 to 2 hours. Preheat oven to 400F (205C). Grease baking sheets; set aside. Divide dough into thirds. On a lightly floured surface, roll out each third to 1/8 to 1/4 inch thick. Using cookie cutters, cut dough in assorted shapes. Place cutout cookies on greased baking sheets. Brush with egg-yolk glaze; garnish with nuts and candied fruit, pressing firmly into dough. Bake 8 to 12 minutes. Remove cookies from baking sheets; place on cooling racks. When cooled, store in a tightly sealed container. Makes about 80 cookies.

Variation

Omit coconut and 1 egg yolk, if desired.

Hussars' Shakos
Husarenhütchen

1-1/2 cups all-purpose flour
1-1/4 teaspoons baking powder
1/2 cup sugar
1 teaspoon vanilla extract
2 egg yolks
1/2 cup butter
1 cup ground hazelnuts
Jelly or candied-cherry halves
Powdered sugar, if desired

Sift flour and baking powder into a large bowl; make a well in center. Place sugar, vanilla and egg yolks in well. Dot flour with butter; sprinkle with hazelnuts. Using a knife or pastry blender, cut butter and other ingredients into flour. Rinse your hands in cold water; dry thoroughly. With cold hands, knead mixture quickly until smooth and evenly blended. Cover and refrigerate 1 to 2 hours. Preheat oven to 425F (220C). Grease baking sheets; set aside. Again, rinse your hands in cold water but do not dry your hands. Using your damp hands, form small rounds of dough about the size of walnuts. Make a small indentation in top of each cookie using the tip of a wooden spoon. Place cookies on greased baking sheets. Fill indentations with jelly or a candied-cherry half. Bake 12 minutes or until lightly browned. Remove cookies from baking sheets; place on cooling racks. Dust lightly with powdered sugar, if desired. Makes about 30 cookies.

Sugar Cookies
Zuckerplätzchen

2-1/2 cups all-purpose flour
1 egg
3/4 cup butter
1/2 cup sugar
1/4 cup sugar
1/2 teaspoon vanilla extract

Sift flour into a large bowl; make a well in center. Break egg into well. Dot butter over flour; sprinkle with 1/2 cup sugar. Using a knife or pastry blender, cut butter and other ingredients into flour. Rinse your hands in cold water; dry thoroughly. With cold hands, knead mixture quickly until smooth and evenly blended. Cover and refrigerate 20 minutes. Preheat oven to 350F (175C). Grease baking sheets; set aside. In a small bowl, combine 1/4 cup sugar and vanilla; set aside. Divide dough in half. On a lightly floured surface, roll out each half to 1/2 to 3/4 inch thick. Cut dough into strips, 2 inches wide and 5 inches long. Cut each strip lengthwise along 1/3 of its length at each end, leaving center 1/3 uncut. Twist ends around to nearly meet each other on either side, forming 2 crescents joined in the middle. Place on greased baking sheets. Bake 10 to 12 minutes or until light golden brown. Remove cookies from baking sheets; place on cooling racks. Immediately sprinkle with sugar mixture. When cooled, store in a tightly sealed container. Makes about 36 cookies.

Variation

Cookies can also be glazed with your favorite icing.

Vanilla Shortbread Crescents
Vanillekipferl

1 cup finely grated almonds
1-1/4 cups all-purpose flour
1/2 cup plus 2 tablespoons butter, room temperature
1/4 cup granulated sugar
2 tablespoons granulated sugar
1/2 teaspoon vanilla extract
1 tablespoon powdered sugar

In a large bowl, combine almonds, flour, butter and 1/4 cup granulated sugar. Knead until mixture is well blended. Roll dough into a sausage shape. Cover and refrigerate 1 hour. Preheat oven to 350F (175C). Grease baking sheets; set aside. In a small bowl, combine 2 tablespoons granulated sugar, vanilla and powdered sugar; set aside. On a lightly floured surface, roll out dough to about 1/2 inch thick. Cut out crescent or half-moon shapes with a pastry cutter or rim of a drinking glass. Place on greased baking sheets. Bake 15 minutes. Remove cookies from baking sheets; place on cooling racks. Immediately sprinkle with sugar mixture. Makes about 48 cookies.

Cinnamon Star Cookies
Zimtsterne

Anise Cookies
Anisplätzchen

3 egg whites
1 cup granulated sugar
1 teaspoon ground cinnamon
2 to 3 cups unblanched almonds, ground
1 tablespoon rosewater
Powdered sugar

Preheat oven to 400F (205C). Grease baking sheets; set aside. In a large bowl, beat egg whites until stiff peaks form. While continuing to beat, gradually add granulated sugar. Remove 5 tablespoons egg-white mixture; set aside. Fold cinnamon, 2 cups almonds and rosewater into remaining meringue mixture. Continue adding almonds until mixture keeps its shape and is firm enough to handle. Lightly sprinkle powdered sugar over a work surface. Roll out dough to 1/2 to 3/4 inch thick. Using a star-shape cookie cutter, cut dough. Place on greased baking sheets. Spread cookies with a thin coating of reserved meringue mixture. Bake 15 to 20 minutes or until lightly colored. Remove cookies from baking sheets; place on cooling racks. Makes about 24 cookies.

Note: Be careful not to use too much ground almonds or more than a light coating of powdered sugar on the work surface or to bake cookies at too high a temperature. Any of these factors can make cookies hard, rather than crisp and melting. If cookies become hard, store in a tightly sealed container with a lemon or apple wedge.

2 eggs, separated
1/4 cup sugar
1-1/4 cups all-purpose flour
1/2 teaspoon anise extract or 1 teaspoon anise seeds, crushed

Grease and flour baking sheets; set aside. In a medium bowl, beat egg whites until stiff peaks form. While continuing to beat, gradually add sugar. In another medium bowl, combine egg yolks, flour and anise extract or seeds. Combine meringue mixture and egg-yolk mixture. Drop mixture by teaspoonfuls onto prepared baking sheets. Cover and set baking sheets in a cool place 10 to 12 hours. Preheat oven to 325F (165C). Bake 10 minutes. Remove cookies from baking sheets; place on cooling racks. Makes about 24 cookies.

Note: Anise Cookies are typically Swabian Christmas fare. They have a most interesting texture.

Macaroons
Makronen

Chocolate Macaroons
Schokoladenmakronen

3 egg whites
1-1/4 teaspoons lemon juice
3/4 cup sugar
2 to 2-1/3 cups shredded coconut or chopped hazelnuts, walnuts or
  almonds
Whole hazelnuts

Preheat oven to 325F (165C). Line baking sheets with foil or waxed paper; set aside. In a large bowl, beat egg whites and lemon juice until stiff peaks form. While continuing to beat, gradually add sugar. Fold in coconut or chopped nuts until mixture is evenly blended. Drop mixture by teaspoonfuls onto lined baking sheets. Top each cookie with a hazelnut. Bake 30 minutes. If cookies start to brown, slightly reduce oven temperature. Cookies should not brown. Remove cookies from baking sheets; place on cooling racks. When cooled, store in a tightly sealed container. If cookies are to be stored longer than 1 to 2 days, add a lemon or apple wedge to storage container. This will keep cookies from becoming hard. Makes about 30 cookies.

4 egg whites
1/2 cup sugar
2 cups grated almonds
5 oz. unsweetened or semisweet chocolate, finely grated
3 tablespoons kirsch or water
1/4 teaspoon ground cinnamon
Dash of ground allspice
Dash of ground nutmeg
Dash of ground cardamom

Preheat oven to 300F (150C). Line baking sheets with foil or waxed paper; set aside. In a large bowl, beat egg whites until stiff peaks form. While continuing to beat, gradually add sugar. Fold in almonds, chocolate, kirsch or water, cinnamon, allspice, nutmeg and cardamom. Drop mixture by teaspoonfuls onto lined baking sheets. Bake 20 to 25 minutes. Remove cookies from baking sheets; place on cooling racks. When cooled, store in a tightly sealed container. Makes about 36 cookies.

Variation

Top baked cookies with melted chocolate, finely shredded orange or lemon peel or grated fresh gingerroot, if desired.

Nuremberg Spice Cookies
Nürnberger Lebkuchen

Honey Cookies
Braune Kuchen

Cookies:
1-1/4 cups coarsely grated almonds
1-1/4 cups coarsely grated hazelnuts
1 cup sugar
3 tablespoons honey
1/2 cup finely chopped candied citron
1/2 cup finely chopped candied orange peel
1 teaspoon ground cinnamon
1/4 teaspoon ground cloves
1/4 teaspoon ground nutmeg
1/4 teaspoon ground cardamom
6 egg whites
1/4 to 1/2 cup all-purpose flour

Frosting:
1-1/2 cups powdered sugar
4-1/2 teaspoons water
4-1/2 teaspoons kirsch or 1 teaspoon vanilla extract and 1 tablespoon water
Whole nuts and candied fruit
5 oz. unsweetened or semisweet chocolate, melted, if desired

To make cookies, line baking sheets with foil. Lightly grease foil; set baking sheets aside. In a large double boiler, combine almonds, hazelnuts, sugar, honey, citron, orange peel, cinnamon, cloves, nutmeg, cardamom and egg whites. Heat over hot water, stirring constantly, until hot, 20 to 30 minutes. Do not allow mixture to boil. Remove from heat. Add enough flour to make a firm, manageable dough. Drop mixture by heaping teaspoonfuls onto prepared baking sheets. Smooth tops of cookies with a knife dipped in hot water. Cover and let stand in a cool place 10 to 12 hours. Preheat oven to 350F (175C). Bake 15 minutes. Remove cookies from baking sheets; place on cooling racks.
To make frosting, in a small bowl, combine powdered sugar, water and kirsch or vanilla and water. Stir until of spreading consistency. Frost cooled cookies; garnish with whole nuts and candied fruit. For chocolate frosting, blend in melted chocolate. Frost and garnish as desired. Store cookies in a tightly sealed container. If cookies become hard, place an apple wedge in storage container. Makes about 40 cookies.

1-1/2 cups honey
1/2 cup margarine
1 cup firmly packed brown sugar
5-3/4 cups all-purpose flour
5 teaspoons powdered sugar
1 egg
3/4 cup chopped almonds
3 tablespoons unsweetened cocoa powder
1 teaspoon ground cloves
1 teaspoon ground cinnamon
1/4 teaspoon ground nutmeg
1/4 teaspoon ground allspice
1/4 teaspoon ground cardamom
1 egg white, slightly beaten
Chopped candied fruit, chopped almonds and colored candy sprinkles

Preheat oven to 325F (165C). Grease baking sheets; set aside. In a small saucepan, heat honey, margarine and brown sugar over medium heat, stirring constantly, until blended. Remove from heat; cool. In a large bowl, combine flour, powdered sugar, egg, almonds, cocoa, cloves, cinnamon, nutmeg, allspice and cardamom. Stir in honey mixture until smooth and well blended. Divide dough in thirds. On a lightly floured surface, roll each third into a thin sheet. Using cookie cutters, cut dough in assorted shapes. Place on greased baking sheets. Bake 10 minutes. Remove cookies from baking sheets; place on cooling racks. Brush warm cookies with egg white. Decorate with candied fruit, almonds or candy sprinkles. Makes about 80 cookies.

Chocolate-Walnut Cookies
Walnussplätzchen

Speculaas
Spekulatius

Cookies:
1 cup butter, room temperature
1 cup powdered sugar
1 egg yolk
2-1/2 cups all-purpose flour
1/2 cup finely chopped walnuts
1/2 teaspoon vanilla extract
1/2 teaspoon grated lemon peel
1/2 teaspoon ground cinnamon
1/2 teaspoon ground ginger

Filling & Frosting:
Powdered sugar
8 oz. marzipan
1 cup apricot jam, sieved
8 oz. semisweet chocolate
Whole walnuts

To make cookies, in a large bowl, beat together butter and 1 cup powdered sugar. Beat in egg yolk, flour, chopped walnuts, vanilla, lemon peel, cinnamon and ginger. Cover and refrigerate 30 minutes. Preheat oven to 400F (205C). Grease baking sheets. On a lightly floured surface, roll out chilled dough until 1/4 inch thick. Using cookies cutters, cut dough in assorted shapes. Place on greased baking sheets. Bake about 12 minutes. Remove cookies from baking sheets; place on cooling racks.

To make filling & frosting, lightly sprinkle work surface with powdered sugar. Roll marzipan into a thin layer on work surface. Cut into same shapes as cookies. Spread underside of 2 cooled cookies with a thin layer of apricot jam. Place a layer of marzipan between cookies to form a sandwich with the marzipan as filling. Repeat until all cookies and marzipan are used. In a double boiler, melt chocolate over hot water. Cover cookie sandwiches generously with chocolate. Press a walnut half onto top of each cookie while chocolate is soft. Let stand until chocolate is firm. Makes about 36 cookies.

4-1/4 cups all-purpose flour
1 cup firmly packed dark-brown sugar
1/2 cup butter, room temperature
3/4 cup finely grated almonds
2 eggs
4-1/2 teaspoons milk
1/2 teaspoon salt
1 teaspoon ground cinnamon
1/2 teaspoon ground cloves
1/4 teaspoon ground nutmeg
1/4 teaspoon ground allspice
1/2 cup sliced almonds

In a large bowl, beat together flour, brown sugar, butter, grated almonds, eggs, milk, salt, cinnamon, cloves, nutmeg and allspice. Cover and refrigerate 1 hour. Preheat oven to 325F (165C). Grease baking sheets. Press dough firmly onto a floured Speculaas mold. Trim off any dough that extends over the level of the mold. Carefully turn out onto a greased baking sheet. Repeat with remaining dough. Or, on a lightly floured surface, roll out dough. Cut into squares or other desired shape. Place on greased baking sheets. Sprinkle sliced almonds over cookies. Bake 15 to 20 minutes or until lightly browned. Remove cookies from baking sheets; place on cooling racks. When cooled, store in a tightly sealed container. Makes about 60 cookies.

Note: Speculaas molds are available in a variety of shapes and sizes. They can be purchased in gourmet shops and bakeware departments.

Aachen Spice Cookies
Aachener Printen

Spice Bread
Pfefferkuchenpuppen

1-1/3 cups molasses
3 tablespoons water
1/2 cup sugar
1 teaspoon baking soda
5-1/4 cups all-purpose flour
1/2 cup finely chopped candied lemon peel
2-1/2 teaspoons ground cinnamon
1/4 teaspoon ground cloves
1/4 teaspoon ground coriander
1/4 teaspoon ground nutmeg
1/4 teaspoon ground cardamom

In a small saucepan, combine molasses and water. Heat over medium heat, stirring constantly, until blended; cool slightly. Stir sugar into cooled molasses mixture. In a large bowl, combine baking soda, flour, lemon peel, cinnamon, cloves, coriander, nutmeg and cardamom. Gradually stir molasses mixture into flour mixture. Blend quickly and thoroughly until smooth. Divide dough into thirds. On a lightly floured surface, roll out dough into a thin sheet. Cut into 3'' x 1'' rectangles using a ruler and pastry wheel. Rinse a baking sheet in cold water. Do not dry. Place cutout cookies on damp baking sheet. Bake 8 to 10 minutes. Remove cookies from baking sheets; place on cooling racks. When cooled, store in a tightly sealed container. Makes about 100 cookies.

Variation

Frost cookies with melted unsweetened or semisweet chocolate. Sprinkle with toasted chopped almonds or coarse sugar.

Cookies:
2/3 cup honey
1/2 cup firmly packed dark-brown sugar
1/2 cup butter
4-1/4 cups all-purpose flour
1-1/4 teaspoons baking powder
3 tablespoons unsweetened cocoa powder
1/2 teaspoon ground cinnamon
1/2 teaspoon ground nutmeg
1/2 teaspoon ground allspice
1/2 teaspoon ground cardamom
1/2 teaspoon black pepper
1/2 teaspoon ground coriander
1 egg
Frosting, page 172

Decorating Icing:
1-3/4 cups powdered sugar
1 egg white
4-1/2 teaspoons lemon juice
Small candies

To make cookies, preheat oven to 400F (205C). Grease bakir sheets; set aside. In a small saucepan, combine honey, brown suga and butter. Heat over medium heat, stirring constantly, unt blended; cool slightly. In a large bowl, combine flour, bakir powder, cocoa, cinnamon, nutmeg, allspice, cardamom, pepper ar coriander. Gradually blend in egg and honey mixture. Knead doug until smooth. Divide dough into thirds. On a lightly floured surfac roll out dough until 1/8 to 1/4 inch thick. Using cookie cutters, c dough in assorted shapes. Place on greased baking sheets. Bake 8 10 minutes. Open oven door, but leave cookies in oven to coc Remove from oven when completely cooled. Prepare chocolate vanilla Frosting. Frost cookies.
To make icing, in a small bowl, combine powdered sugar, egg whi and lemon juice. Spoon icing into a small pastry bag or decoratir tube. Using a fine tip, pipe designs on frosted cookies. Decora with small candies. Makes about 100 cookies.

The Witch's House
Hexenhaus

Quince-Jelly Candies
Quittenbrot

recipes Spice Bread, opposite
egg whites
1/2 cups powdered sugar
ssorted candies and marshmallows

repare Spice-Bread dough. Let stand 2 to 4 hours. Preheat oven to 00F (205C). Grease baking sheets; set aside. Make a cardboard attern for the house, drawing and cutting out suitably sized ctions for walls and roof. Divide dough into thirds. On a lightly oured surface, roll out and cut dough using pattern pieces as a uide. Use 1/3 dough for roof, 1/3 dough for walls and 1/3 for base. ny dough scraps can be shaped into a chimney, wood-pile, fence r other features. Transfer dough pieces to greased baking sheets. ake as directed in Spice-Bread recipe. Remove from baking sheets; lace on cooling racks. Cool completely before assembling. In a rge bowl, beat egg whites until light and frothy. Slowly beat in owdered sugar. Continue beating until mixture will stand in peaks. ssemble walls and base of house using icing as cement. Top with oof sections. Decorate house with remaining icing, candies and narshmallows, as desired. Makes 1 house.

4-1/2 lbs. quince
1 piece orange peel
1 piece lemon peel
1 cinnamon stick
Cold water
About 4-1/2 cups sugar
3 tablespoons kirsch, if desired
1/2 cup finely diced candied citron or orange peel, if desired

Clean quince; cut into quarters. In a large saucepan, combine quince, orange peel, lemon peel and cinnamon. Add cold water to cover. Bring to a boil. Reduce heat and cook 45 minutes. Cover and let stand overnight. Preheat oven to 225F (105C). Remove peel and cinnamon; discard. Remove quince; drain well. Press quince through a sieve. Measure quince puree. Use 1 cup sugar to each cup quince puree. In a large saucepan, combine quince and sugar. Cook, stirring constantly, until mixture comes away from sides of pan. Remove from heat. Add kirsch and citron or orange peel, if desired. Spread mixture in a shallow baking pan or jelly-roll pan. Smooth surface with a knife. Place in warm oven to dry slowly, 3 to 12 hours. When dry, cut into small pieces. Coat with sugar. Makes 50 to 60 (1-inch) pieces.

Drinks

The first mention of beer, in the form of a reference to its beautiful golden color, came to us from the Mesopotamian civilization. It is thought that as long as 5,000 years ago, a drink was brewed that resembled beer. In Germany, brewing goes back over 1,000 years. Today, a third of the world's beer still comes from Bavaria. The total annual production of beer in Germany reaches a staggering 2,408 million gallons. To produce this quantity, a great deal of barley is grown. Hops are cultivated mainly in the Holleddu region of Bavaria and also near the Bodensee. Apart from this, a considerable amount is imported from Czechoslovakia. The average annual per-capita beer consumption in Germany is 36 gallons, which represents a bottle a day. The figure for Bavaria is well above average at 60 gallons annual individual consumption. When one considers that this figure includes babies, children and invalids, it is quite impressive. German breweries produce several unique types of beer.

The annual consumption of wine per person reaches only 5-1/2 gallons. German wines are of very high quality. They have a favorable climate and soil and take meticulous care of the vines. The exacting standards of the German wine industry make German wines among the finest in the world.

Fresh Fruit Milk Shake
Fruchtmilch

Peaches in Wine
Kullerpfirsich

1 banana, 3 to 5 apricots, 1 fresh peach or 1/2 cup fresh strawberries, blueberries, raspberries or blackberries
Juice of 1/2 lemon or orange
1-1/2 to 3 tablespoons sugar
1 cup milk
Whipped cream
1 teaspoon flaked or grated chocolate, if desired

Clean and prepare fruit, as necessary. Puree fruit in a food processor or blender. Add lemon or orange juice and sugar. Add milk; process briefly before pouring into 2 glasses. Top each serving with whipped cream and chocolate, if desired. Serve immediately. Makes 2 servings.

Variation

Vanilla or lemon ice cream added with the milk and processed briefly makes this refreshing summer drink even more delicious.

4 ripe peaches, peeled
1 bottle sparkling white wine, chilled
Sugar, if desired

Pierce each peach several times with a fork, pushing prongs in deeply until they touch the pit. Place 1 peach in each of 4 deep, rounded glass goblets. Fill goblets with sparkling wine. After a few moments, the peaches will begin to rotate. To accentuate this effect, sprinkle a little sugar onto each peach, if desired. Place small fruit plates with fruit knives and forks on the table. When guests have finished their drinks, they can eat the peaches. This is a delicious and extremely original drink to serve on a warm summer evening. The peaches must be ripe, without any bruising or blemishes. Makes 4 servings.

Summer Wine Cup
Sommerbowle

Red-Wine Cup
Rotweinbowle

1/2 pint fresh strawberries
1/2 pint fresh sweet cherries
2 ripe peaches
1 to 2 oranges
1/3 cup sugar
1/2 cup water
1 teaspoon instant-tea powder
Juice of 1/2 lemon
6 tablespoons Grand Marnier or other orange liqueur
1 bottle white wine, chilled
1 bottle sparkling white wine, chilled

Wash and hull strawberries; cut large berries into halves. Rinse and pit cherries. Peel and slice peaches. Peel oranges, removing any pith; cut flesh into small pieces. Place fruit pieces in a large glass bowl. Sprinkle with sugar. In a small bowl, combine water, tea, lemon juice and liqueur. Pour water mixture over fruit. Cover and let stand 1 hour. Pour in chilled wines. Use a ladle to fill individual goblets. Makes 12 to 14 servings.

Variation

A variety of fruits can be chosen for this recipe. For a lighter, more thirst-quenching drink, add a little sparkling mineral water or club soda.

1 banana
Juice of 1 lemon
1/2 lb. white grapes
1/2 lb. black or dark-purple grapes
1 orange
2 to 3 tablespoons brandy or cognac
1-1/2 qts. light red wine, chilled
1 small bottle sparkling white wine, if desired, chilled

Peel and thinly slice banana. Place in a large pitcher. Sprinkle immediately with lemon juice to prevent discoloring. Wash and drain grapes. Peel orange, removing any pith. Using a serrated knife, cut orange in half, then into thin slices. Add grapes and orange slices to pitcher. Sprinkle with brandy or cognac. Cover and let stand 10 minutes. Add red wine and white wine, if desired. Makes 10 to 12 servings.

Variation

Rosé can be substituted for red wine. If a weaker drink is required, add a little sparkling mineral water or club soda.

Eggnog
Eiergrog

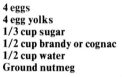

4 eggs
4 egg yolks
1/3 cup sugar
1/2 cup brandy or cognac
1/2 cup water
Ground nutmeg

Using an electric mixer, in a medium bowl beat eggs and yolks together until light and frothy. Gradually add sugar, continuing to beat well. Warm the brandy or cognac and water in a small saucepan. Do not allow to boil because it will lose its alcoholic content. Pour a thin stream of this hot liquid into beaten egg mixture, continuing to beat well. Add nutmeg to taste. Serve hot in heatproof glasses or mugs. Makes 2 to 3 servings.

Note: Eggnog is a very old delicacy and makes a good dessert or a fortifying bedtime drink.

Rum Punch
Teegrog

Jamaican dark rum
Sugar
1 lemon slice
Strong, freshly made tea

Use a large heatproof glass for this hot drink. Pour some rum into a glass. Add a little sugar and a lemon slice. Fill glass with boiling hot tea. Makes 1 serving.

Note: There are no set quantities for rum punch. Each person makes it according to his or her own taste and preference. There is an old saying about rum punch: "To make a good punch you must have rum. You can use sugar but the water isn't really necessary."

Mulled Wine
Glühwein

Rum & Red-Wine Punch
Feuerzangenbowle

1 lemon
4 cinnamon sticks
4 whole cloves
4 to 8 sugar cubes
3-1/4 cups full-bodied red wine

Wash lemon; peel, removing as much pith as possible. Slice lemon. Use lemon slices or peel. If peel is to be used, pare away any pith. In a small saucepan, combine lemon slices or peel, cinnamon, cloves sugar cubes and wine. Heat over low heat. The wine must not boil or it will lose its alcoholic content and its taste will be affected. If it is heated slowly, the wine will absorb the flavor and aroma of the lemon and spices. Strain hot wine into heatproof glasses or mugs. Makes 3 to 4 servings.

Variation

Smaller quantities can be made whenever a warm drink is needed on a cold winter day. The version made with white wine and a small quantity of golden raisins or *sultanas,* is called "Bischof."

2 bottles light red wine
Juice of 2 oranges, strained
Juice of 1 lemon, strained
1/2 lb. loaf sugar
1/2 bottle Jamaican rum, heated

Heat wine but do not allow to boil; pour into a warmed, heatproof pitcher or pot. Stir in orange and lemon juice. Sprinkle 1 tablespoon hot rum over loaf sugar. Place on a small grid securely positioned over rim of pitcher or pot. Position pitcher or pot over canned fuel to keep the wine warm but not boiling. Using a long match, ignite hot-rum-soaked sugar. Continue to feed flame with tablespoonfuls of warm rum, keeping bottle well away from flame so it will not ignite and explode. The burning spirit will gradually melt the sugar. Resulting rum syrup will drip into hot wine. Ladle straight from pitcher or pot into heatproof glasses or mugs. Makes 10 to 12 servings.

Preserves & Pickles

For centuries, homemakers everywhere have felt the need to lay in stores for the winter and against periods of scarcity. Although fresh food is almost always available nowadays, many people enjoy filling their cupboards with all sorts of preserves and pickles.

Homemade jams and jellies remain very popular in Germany. Their flavor and purity appeal to German homemakers. Homemade jam is always served at a traditional German breakfast. In this section, you'll find cherry, blackberry and plum jam. *Rumtopf* is a traditional way of preserving fruit in a mixture of sugar and rum. As fresh fruits come into season, add them with an equal amount of sugar and enough rum to cover the mixture. Use the fruit and sauce as a topping for ice cream or plain cake. Baste roasted poultry with the juice and serve the drained fruit as a condiment with pork, ham or game.

Large quantities of sweet and sour pickles made from summer squash or pumpkins and cucumbers usually accompany roasts. Or use them to add the finishing touch to feasts of sliced sausages and cured meats. Recipes in this section use the latest, up-to-date methods and promise crisp, fresh-tasting pickles. The world over, Sauerkraut is known as a German specialty, although history tells us it may have come from China. Most German families eat steaming hot plates of sauerkraut with pork or sausages at least once a week. We have given you the option of freezing or canning this tangy condiment.

Cherry Jam
Sauerkirschkonfitüre

Blackberry Jam
Brombeerkonfitüre

4 cups chopped, pitted red tart cherries
1 (1-3/4-oz.) pkg. dry pectin
Small piece of lemon peel
5 cups sugar

Wash 5 or 6 (8-oz.) or 3 pint jars in hot soapy water; rinse. Keep hot until needed. Prepare lids as manufacturer directs. In a 6- to 8-quart pot, stir together cherries, pectin and lemon peel. Measure sugar; set aside. Stirring constantly, bring fruit mixture to a full rolling boil over high heat. Add sugar all at once. Continue heating until jam comes to a rolling boil that cannot be stirred down. Stirring constantly, boil *exactly* 1 minute. Remove from heat. Remove lemon peel. Stir and skim. Ladle into hot jars to within 1/4 inch of top, filling and closing 1 jar at a time. Wipe rims of jars with a clean damp cloth. Attach lids. Place filled jars on a rack in a large pot of boiling water. Water should cover jars by 1 to 2 inches and have room to boil. Cover pot. Bring water back to a boil. At sea level, boil 10 minutes. For every 1000 feet altitude, add 1 minute to boiling time. Store up to 1 year. Makes 5 to 6 (8-oz.) or 3 pint jars.

Variation

For a gourmet jam, stir in 2 to 3 tablespoons kirsch before ladling into jars.

4 cups crushed blackberries
3 cups sugar
2 to 4 tablespoons lemon juice
1 to 2 teaspoons cognac, if desired

Wash 3 to 4 (8-oz.) jars in hot soapy water; rinse. Keep hot until needed. Prepare lids as manufacturer directs. Place a small plate in refrigerator to chill. In a large pot, stir together blackberries, sugar and lemon juice. Let stand 20 minutes until juices form. Stirring constantly, cook over low heat until sugar dissolves. Stirring constantly, bring fruit mixture to a boil over medium-high heat. Boil until jam begins to thicken, about 20 minutes. Remove pot from heat. Place a spoonful of hot fruit mixture on chilled plate. Place in freezer 1 minute. After 1 minute, there should be no watery ring around mound of jam. Draw your finger through mixture. It should retain its shape and not flow into trough. Stir cognac into jam in pot, if desired; skim. Ladle into hot jars to within 1/4 inch of top, filling and closing 1 jar at a time. Wipe rims of jars with a clean damp cloth. Attach lids. Place filled jars on a rack in a large pot of boiling water. Water should cover jars by 1 to 2 inches and have room to boil. Cover pot. Bring water back to a boil. At sea level, boil 10 minutes. For every 1000 feet altitude, add 1 minute to boiling time. Store up to 1 year. Makes 3 to 4 (8-oz.) jars.

Plum Jam
Pflaumenmus "Powidl"

Rumtopf
Rumtopf

5 cups chopped, pitted purple plums
4 cups sugar
2 cinnamon sticks
1 tablespoon rum

Wash 5 to 6 (8-oz.) jars in hot soapy water; rinse. Keep hot until needed. Prepare lids as manufacturer directs. Place a small plate in refrigerator to chill. In a large pot, stir together plums and sugar. Add cinnamon sticks. Let stand 20 minute until juices form. Stirring constantly, cook over low heat until sugar dissolves. Stirring constantly, bring fruit mixture to a boil over medium-high heat. Boil until jam begins to thicken, about 15 minutes. Remove pot from heat. Remove and discard cinnamon sticks. Place a spoonful of hot fruit mixture on chilled plate. Place in freezer 1 minute. After 1 minute, there should be no watery ring around mound of jam. Draw your finger through mixture. It should retain its shape and not flow into trough. Stir rum into jam in pot; skim. Ladle into hot jars to within 1/4 inch of top, filling and closing 1 jar at a time. Wipe rims of jars with a clean damp cloth. Attach lids. Place filled jars on a rack in a large pot of boiling water. Water should cover jars by 1 to 2 inches and have room to boil. Cover pot. Bring water back to a boil. At sea level, boil 10 minutes. For every 1000 feet altitude, add 1 minute to boiling time. Store up to 1 year. Makes 3 to 4 (8-oz.) jars.

Note: Plum jam, sometimes called *Powidl* in Germany, is often eaten at breakfast spread on fresh bread. It is also used as a filling for dumplings.

Fruit, one kind or a mixture
Superfine or granulated sugar
White rum
90 proof white gin or vodka, if desired

Clean, trim and pit fruit as necessary. Slice or dice fruit, as desired. Suggested fruit includes strawberries, kiwi, apricots, peaches, cherries, cooked pears and bananas. Place fruit in a large, clean earthenware or glass bowl. Add an equal amount of sugar, cup for cup. Add rum to a generous 1/2 inch above fruit. Add a small amount of gin or vodka, if desired. Stir until sugar dissolves. Cover and let stand in a cool place 4 weeks before using. Stir occasionally. As fruit is used, add other fruit, sugar, rum to cover and gin or vodka, if desired. Rum must be added or added fruit will ferment as solution grows weaker. Rumtopf fruits are delicious with cottage cheese, cream caramel or vanilla mold, rice pudding, Pound Cake, page 153, or simply with whipped cream.

Pickled Squash
Eingelegter Kurbis

Pickled Gherkins
Gewürzgurken

3 cups white-wine vinegar
1 cup water
3 cups sugar
8 whole cloves
1 cinnamon stick
6 to 8 cups diced, peeled squash

Wash 3 or 4 pint jars in hot soapy water; rinse. Keep hot until needed. Prepare lids as manufacturer directs. In a saucepan, bring vinegar, water, sugar, cloves and cinnamon to a boil. Simmer about 10 minutes; strain reserving liquid. Pack squash in hot jars. Pour reserved liquid over squash, filling 1 jar at a time. Leave 1/4 inch headspace. Cover squash completely. Wipe rims of jars with a clean damp cloth. Attach self-sealing lids. Place filled jars on a rack in a large pot of boiling water. Water should cover jars by 1 to 2 inches and have room to boil. Cover pot. Bring water back to a boil. At sea level, boil 25 minutes. For every 1000 feet altitude, add 1 minute to boiling time. Store up to 1 year. Serve these squash cubes with meat soups, stews and game. They also go very well with substantial suppers of fresh bread, sliced sausages and cheese. Makes 3 to 4 pint jars.

2 qts. small pickling cucumbers, 1 to 2 inches long (about 2 lbs.)
1 qt. water
3 cups pickling onions (about 1 lb.)
1/4 cup pickling salt
1 qt. hot water
1 qt. white-wine vinegar
1 cup water
3 tablespoons sugar
24 black peppercorns
6 tablespoons minced fresh tarragon or 2 tablespoons dried leaf tarragon
2 teaspoons minced fresh dill
1/2 cup finely chopped sweet red and green peppers

Gently scrub cucumbers with a brush to remove spines. Remove blossom fragments; set aside. In a large saucepan, bring 1 quart water to a boil. Add onions; blanch 30 seconds. Drain; cover with cold water. Peel onions. In a large saucepan, combine washed cucumbers and peeled onions; set aside. Stir pickling salt into 1 quart hot water until dissolved. Pour over cucumbers and onions. Cover; let stand 2 days at room temperature. Drain; discard brine. Rinse cucumbers in cold water. Wash 6 (1/2-pint) or 3 pint jars in hot soapy water; rinse. Keep hot until needed. Prepare lids as manufacturer directs. Combine vinegar, 1 cup water and sugar. Bring to a boil; keep hot. Divide peppercorns, tarragon, dill and sweet peppers among jars. Pack cucumbers and onions into 1 jar at a time, leaving 1/4 inch headspace. Add hot vinegar mixture to cover. Use a table-knife blade to remove air spaces. Wipe rim of jar with a clean damp cloth. Attach lid. Place filled jars on a rack in a large pot of boiling water. Water should cover jars by 1 to 2 inches and have room to boil. Cover pot. Bring water back to a boil. At sea level, boil 10 minutes. For every 1000 feet altitude, add 1 minute to boiling time. Store up to 1 year. Makes 6 (1/2-pint) or 3 pint jars.

Homemade Sauerkraut
Sauerkraut Bereitung

!0 lbs. firm, green cabbage
About 1-1/4 cups pickling salt
About 3 qts. water
1/2 cup juniper berries, if desired

Remove and discard outer cabbage leaves; wash cabbage. Thinly shred 1/4 of the cabbage. Place in a large bowl. Sprinkle with 3-1/2 tablespoons salt. Stir to distribute. Pour into a 5-gallon crock or nonmetal container. Repeat, shredding and mixing 1/4 cabbage at a time with 3-1/2 tablespoons salt. Sprinkle each layer with juniper berries, if desired. Level top. Place a clean heavy cloth over top. Tuck edges down into container. Let stand at room temperature overnight to wilt and make its own liquid. Make a brine of 1/4 cup salt dissolved in 2 quarts water. If necessary, pour brine over cabbage to cover. On top of cabbage, place a heavy china or glass plate that fits inside container as exactly as possible. Finally, place a clean, heavy stone or weight on plate. Keep container in an extremely clean place at about 35F (15C). A cellar is an ideal place. Let cabbage ferment 3 weeks. The cloth must be changed each day and replaced with a clean one. Moisture will seep into cloth together with a grey-like scum cabbage produces as it ferments. After 3 weeks, begin checking sauerkraut. When liquid no longer bubbles, fermentation is complete. Mix remaining 2 tablespoons salt with 1 quart water. Cover; set aside. Heat sauerkraut in a large pot over medium heat until 185F (85C) or simmering. Do not boil.

To freeze sauerkraut, cool sauerkraut and brine. Spoon sauerkraut into freezer containers, leaving 1 inch headspace. Add brine to cover. Attach lids. Store in freezer up to 6 months.

To can sauerkraut, wash 10 quart jars in hot soapy water; rinse. Prepare lids as manufacturer directs. Pack sauerkraut into 1 hot jar at a time, leaving 1/2 inch headspace. Add hot brine to cover. Attach self-sealing lid. Place filled jars on a rack in a large pot of boiling water. Water should cover jars by 1 to 2 inches and have room for water to boil. Cover pot. Bring water back to a boil. At sea level, boil 20 minutes. For every 1000 feet altitude, add 1 minute to boiling time. Store up to 1 year. Makes 10 quarts.

Index

German Recipe Titles

8.435308163990